P9-CKW-065

Library Resource Center
Renton Technical College
Renton, WA 98056

DISCARDED

THE VILLAGE BAKER

Library Resource Center
Renton Technical College
Renton, WA 98056

Library Resource Center
Renton Technical College
3000 NE 4th St.
Renton, WA 98056-4195

DISCARD

The Village Baker

*Classic Regional Breads
from Europe and America*

Joe Ortiz

Foreword by Marion Cunningham

Ten Speed Press
Berkeley, California

641
.815
ORTIZ
1992

Copyright © 1993 by Joseph Ortiz. All rights reserved. No part of this book may be reproduced in any form, except for brief reviews, without the written permission of the publisher.

🔟

TEN SPEED PRESS
P.O. Box 7123
Berkeley, California 94707

First Printing, 1993

Cover and text design by Nancy Austin
Front cover photo by Joe Ortiz: a communal oven in the Alps of southern France.
Back cover illustration by Ann Miya: the bakery on rue Paul-Bert in Aix-en-Provence.
Photographs by Joe Ortiz
Illustrations copyright © 1993 by Ann Miya

Library of Congress Cataloging-in-Publication Data

Ortiz, Joe, 1946–
    The village baker : Classic regional breads from Europe and America / by Joe Ortiz.
        p.   cm.
    ISBN 0-89815-489-8
    1. Bread.   2. Cookery, European.   I. Title.
TX769.078   1993
641.9'—dc20   93-23212
                                                                        CIP

Printed in the United States of America

1 2 3 4 5 - 97 96 95 94 93

TO MY WIFE, GAYLE

*Without whose dreams, inspiration, and support
there would have been no bread or book
because
there might never have been a bakery in the first place.*

CONTENTS

Library Resource Center
Renton Technical College
Renton, WA 98056

PART 1: BREADMAKING— THE VILLAGE BAKER'S CRAFT

DURING THESE LAST TWELVE YEARS, bread consciousness has risen like leavened dough all over the country. Only a dozen years ago most American bread was white, bland, and soft. But as the trend in food focused more on freshness, simpler preparations, and healthier diets, rustic, wholesome loaves became vital to the table. Such good bread can turn a drab meal into a pleasant, satisfying one, or, with butter, make a good meal in itself.

Years ago, many people told me about Gayle's Bakery in Capitola, California, run by Gayle and Joe Ortiz. They loved Gayle's fine pastries and Joe's fulfilling breads. This bakery was famous throughout Northern California, so I finally drove seventy miles to experience what all the excitement was about. It was even better than I expected.

Joe is passionate about learning more and more about European breads, and over the years he and Gayle have traveled to Europe twelve times. They have visited cities and villages in France, Germany, and Italy, seeking out the best town bread bakers. From them, Joe has learned many variations on the basic method of making a starter, sometimes using a *levain*, building the dough, forming and baking loaves. He has also traveled around the United States and sought out our own master bread bakers. He is insatiable in his adventurous quest for all possible new ways and ideas about making bread—starting with flour and water and ending with exciting tastes and textures.

The Village Baker has been a long time in coming, and many of us have prodded Joe about getting it done, but his philosophy about bread baking is the same for writing: "You should not hurry the natural process either of making a loaf of bread or of writing a book." Filled with clear directions, well-tested recipes, and wonderful adventures in bread baking, this book has been well worth the wait. Enjoy!

—MARION CUNNINGHAM

Library Resource Center
Renton Technical College
Renton, WA 98056

CRUSTY, FLAVORFUL BREAD—with a chewy, voluptuous texture, the aroma of nuts, and a caramelized crust—has been appearing with increasing frequency in American homes and on restaurant tables because of the recent rise of neighborhood bakers. Whether we find them in small towns or simply in districts of a large city, these dedicated men and women artisans can still be considered "village bakers" because, like their European counterparts, they work in small shops baking bread for their communities. Despite their use of mixers, molders, and commercial ovens, their main task is to make bread by hand. The small scale and intense nature of their work, whether they are making two hundred loaves a day or two thousand, allow them an intimate control in a craft that twenty years ago was a dying art.

When I first started making bread fifteen years ago, I could not find a single book from which to learn the craft of professional baking. I found that I had to go to France to get my first real lessons about how to make bread. In fact, many of the new village bakers in America have gone to Europe to learn their craft. I, too, like most of them, have a greater yearning to smell the earthy sourdough aroma clinging to the walls of an ancient European bakery and to taste a local baker's bread than to visit a museum or cathedral. All of us, in our own way, have searched out dusty basement bakeries in France, Italy, and Germany in order to unearth the secrets of a local artisan whose bread is so astonishingly better than the factory bread we know so well.

Bread production in Europe is becoming more and more industrialized all the time, but many local village bakers are still using ancient, natural practices. These old techniques are what most fascinate us as village bakers in America: The ancient methods of using sourdough, the benefits of long, slow fermentations, and the use of less-refined, nutritionally superior flours are just a few of the things we have learned in our attempts to create an inspired loaf of bread.

Some home bakers would be happy with a few new, practical recipes to add to their repertoire; others want to know how to bake. After teaching numerous classes in bread baking and speaking with hundreds of home bakers, I can see that many people view commercial baking as a mystical, esoteric craft. They long to discover the so-called secrets of village baking; they want to know why bread behaves the way it does and how to create different qualities of taste and texture in a homemade loaf.

This book is written for both kinds of bread enthusiast. For those who just want to bake a few loaves of bread, it contains recipes that stand alone. For those who want to learn more about the craft of bread baking, it contains full yet concise explanations of professional baking from the village baker's point of view. For every commercial recipe I have developed, I have created one home recipe, where possible duplicating a recipe rather than oversimplifying it for the home baker. Surprisingly, many of the recipes *are* simple (many of the yeast and sponge recipes can even be adapted for use with bread machines); several others are for the more ambitious home baker.

The professional recipes may be used, not only by a person baking for a large group—a family, a restaurant, a catered event, a school, or a small bakery—but also by home bakers, who can compare the bulk and the single-loaf recipes and easily see that there are only subtle differences between the two, differences merely of degree rather than of special machinery or secret technique.

At home we might not be able to achieve the subtleties of a refined crust because some commercial bakers have deck ovens equipped with steam injection, but the home baker, by being aware of the process of fermentation and all of the subtle techniques a commercial baker uses, can achieve some of the same flavors and texture of crumb. It is this reason, along with the belief that it is the degree of care each baker is willing to take, that leads me to state that we can make as good a loaf at home as anything possible in a village bakery.

ACKNOWLEDGMENTS

TO FRIENDS AND BAKERS: Marion Cunningham, Flo Braker, Joanne Fusco, Lindsey Shere, Steve Sullivan, Carol Field, Louisa Beers, Dennis Maggiora, Claudio Cantore, Thérèse Monrad-Shere, Bob Wacks, David Morris

TO FAMILY AND FRIENDS: Christie Carlson, Scott Bader, Ann Cowan, Ginger and Charles Mostov, Richard and Dida Merrill, Jodi, Rick and Clary Alward, Jack and Fern Tomlinson, George Germon, Johanne Killeen, Lisa Ekus, Charles Shere, Steve McGuirk, Lisa McAndrews, Denise Cano, Sue Wilson and clan, Irwin Joseph, Joe Wampler, Ken Conklin, Dean Metcalf, Ann Miya, Laura Ortiz, John Tullius

TO BAKERS IN EUROPE: M. Robert, M. Bernard, Jean-Claude Poilpré, Maurice Duquerroy, M. Haettel, Kurt König, Signore Danova, M. Costa and his family

TO BAKERS FORMERLY AT GAYLE'S: Glen Hess, Jeff Loeffler, Joseph Platin, Peter Beckman, Peter Conn

TO RECIPE TESTERS AND MANUSCRIPT HELPERS: William S. Lynch, Jr., John McAndrews, Jay Leite, Frances Raboff, Jamilah Vittor, Sandy Brown, Dan and Connie Rogers

TO GAYLE'S STAFF: Lisa Hindley, Kristen Chavez, Roy Brown, Sergio Mesa, Katy Elliot, Chris Rominger, Tomas Hernandez, Rebecca Thielbar; and the whole crew of ninety other great folks

TO MY EDITOR, Frances Bowles, for making sense out of a jumbled manuscript and a scattered mind

And to all those people who, in my fifteen years of baking, have taught me more than they will ever realize, my thanks.

The Village Baker

MARCEL PAGNOL'S CLASSIC MOVIE *La Femme du Boulanger* (The Baker's Wife) tells the story of a village baker whose wife runs off with another man. So saddened is he by his loss that the *boulanger* cannot bake, creating a dilemma for the townspeople. They must either find the baker's wife or endure life without their daily bread.

At the height of his anguish the *boulanger* says to the town:

> If you return to me my Aurélie and rid me of this loss, then you will once again have a true baker. I will knead each batch half an hour longer, and I will mix rosemary in the branches I use to heat the oven. And, while the bread bakes, I will not sleep, as we bakers are accustomed to doing, but I will open the oven door every five minutes so that the loaves will never leave my sight. I will make for you a bread so good that it will never again be used as an accompaniment for other foods; it would be a nourishment in itself, a food for gourmands. One would never again say, "I have eaten a *tartine* of cheese on some bread." One would say instead, "I have savored a *tartine* of bread underneath some cheese." And each day, above and beyond my batch of bread, I will mix five kilos for the poor. And in each loaf that I make for you, there would be great friendliness and a grand thank you.

Some experts on bread might question the baker's promises—to mix the bread longer, to open the oven door every five minutes, to make bread that tastes better than the food it's meant to accompany—but no one could doubt the baker's honest intentions.

As he tells us, the village baker must guard his loaves, putting honesty and a thank you in each and every one. He must bake to the villagers' preferences, giving them a bread that is an accompaniment as well as nourishment even when eaten alone. And he must give something back to the community—if only by showing up each day to do his job.

Most people have a feeling of trust for their village baker because they know him. They see him in his bakery every day; they can feel confident that his workplace is clean, his methods sound, and his ingredients pure. Like the villagers in the movie, most customers of village bakers feel that their bread contains more than just nourishment: It has an extra ingredient—the energy and dedication of the person who made it. A loaf of bread made by a local baker is not only sustenance for the body, it is also fuel for the spirit.

The spirit of village bread baking began over five thousand years ago when families and small tribes huddled together around the campfire to eat mush. Made from water and crushed grains, the first porridge or gruel had to be eaten immediately. One day, the porridge was accidentally left over the fire and it cooked into a rock-hard cake or *galette*. Dense and unappealing as it may have been, that primitive bread would last a few more days, heralding the first historic preservation of grains. It also made it easier to carry along on the hunt and into battle.

Still later, that same mush, left out in a warm, moist atmosphere, fermented. The result was a bubbly mixture—the original sourdough culture and the first yeast. When this fermented mush was mixed with fresh grain and then baked on a stone over the campfire, it became lighter and more edible: the first leavened bread as we know it.

The evolution of mush is important in the development of the village bakery because it shows us that the mistake that made gruel into bread was also the first real recipe for bread, even though it was just a set of crude proportions based simply on experience. It shows that baking is a natural process that can be guided by someone in order to yield a predictable loaf. Long before there were village bakers, people learned that the craft of bread baking was as organic as that of making wine or cheese. Almost everyone knew the simple, natural time patterns that made up the method. Gradually—over perhaps the first few thousand years—making bread became another task around the house, like maintaining the hearth fire, building the compost mound, or tending the garden. As an ongoing process, it took on a life of its own. Bread had to be watched, guarded, responded to.

Bread was made in a primitive way—as a recipe of proportions and a method of observation—for thousands of years before the first true village bakers started using that original recipe to make bread for their communities. During that time bread moved westward from the Middle East, being carried along on wars and migrations, until it reached Greece, where its flavor improved and it began to look like modern bread.

The first signs of village baking may have appeared around 800 B.C. when the Romans began to make and eat bread. They also established a privileged organization of bread bakers that was restricted to certain families. Around the time of Christ, village bakers started to appear in big cities. Raymond Calvel, Professeur honoraire de boulangerie de l'école française de meunerie, the baking school attached to the French mill, the Grand Moulin, in Paris, notes that thirty years before Christ there were over three hundred bakeries in Rome. Breads dating from around 79 A.D. were discovered in the ruins of Pompeii, where village bakers' shops have been uncovered. As Julius Caesar spread the Roman Empire westward, some authorities believe that he must have taken ideas about bread baking with him. And even though some so-called village bakers were working in the larger cities of Greece and Rome, it appears that, as late as the fifth century, when the Romans retreated from Gaul, many Europeans were still making their bread at home.

Communal ovens were the next major step in the development of the village bakery. The construction of the *four banal,* or communal oven, made it easier for all the citizens' bread to be baked, very often on a weekly basis. The individual families mixed, shaped, and set their own breads to rise. When the loaves were ready to be baked, each housewife marked her bread to distinguish it from her neighbor's. In some regions the baker's signature or symbol—a cross, a circle, the family's initial—was cut into each loaf.

The art of bread baking progressed slowly during the Dark Ages. Bread production would remain a family task in small villages and in the countryside for many hundreds of years, but commercial village bakers started to appear in the cities of France as early as the sixth century.

By the end of the twelfth century, the king and the aristocracy relinquished the right to build ovens, a right they had assumed when the first communal bakers could not afford the construction costs. A few hundred years later citizens were allowed to build their own ovens. Even in a metropolis such as Paris, baking continued to be done in communal ovens until the end of the fifteenth century. Some were still to be found in Paris and they flourished in the countryside until the beginning of the twentieth century. Where they were used, the ancient methods of making bread were still practiced.

What was it about these methods that led the craft from the ancient to the modern era and continues to be important to all bakers? At the heart of the baker's craft is the original recipe for the simple procedure of building a ferment or sourdough starter into a bread dough. Once a baker knew the basic proportions of ingredients and the simple time patterns (those time patterns that we see today formalized in written recipes), he could vary the amounts of ingredients and the treatment of the leavening—the sourdough, sponge, or straight yeast—to create a unique loaf.

French village bakers show us that, by combining methods and using both natural and yeasted starters, crust, flavor, and texture are infinitely variable; German bakers use many variations of sourdough, what they call *Sauerteig,* to achieve breads with tangy flavors and dense textures; Austrian bakers, in methods named *Viennese* because of the city of origin, use sponges made with yeast and doughs enriched with eggs, butter, milk, and sugar; Italian village bakers increase the proportion of water in some bread doughs, vary the amount of salt (sometimes leaving it out completely), and use a fast dough process with a yeast-based starter, a *biga.* Beyond these variations of the recipe, the first village bakers have much to teach modern bakers about ingredients, the regional quality of breads, and about fermentation, hand techniques, and equipment.

French, German, and Italian bakers make distinct breads by using regional ingredients. The French use numerous millings of wheat and rye flour, *farine gruau,* their finest wheat flour, fava bean flour as an improver, *farine méteil,* a flour made of half wheat and half rye, and *farine bise,* a second milling, much like our whole wheat flour, that has not had all of the nutrients sifted out. The French occasionally add raisins, nuts, olives, and herbs. German village bakers achieve their dense textures and hearty flavors by using many grades of coarse rye and wheat flours. They provide sturdy, healthful substance to their breads by adding seeds, herbs, spices, and even cooked legumes to the dough. Italian village bakers use their own regional flours to add local color to bread texture and flavor. Durum flour (a hard winter wheat used to make pasta), semolina (a granular hard-wheat flour, also used in pasta making), and *doppio zero* (double zero or 00, a fine milling of wheat flour) all give that earthy flavor that goes so well with regional Italian food. Olive oil and olives are abundant and are often found in loaves or on a flat bread called *focaccia.*

Regional ingredients lead to regional differences and the many varieties in taste, aroma, and texture. For example, some of the flavors and textures that are uniquely Provençal are captured in the breads of that region because the local honey is often used as a catalyst in the sourdough starters, the *levains.* The addition of a bit of honey to a pasty mixture of flour and water not only boosts the activity of the fermentation, feeding it with natural sugars, but also adds an enzymatic quality to the dough that helps it pull a regional strain of sourdough culture out of the air. Because the honey was made by bees that feed on lavender and typical Provençal herbs, it adds a local flavor to the finished loaf.

In Lionel Poilâne's book, *Guide de l'amateur de pain,* he lists and explains eighty different French regional breads, each variation having as much to do with climate, local eating habits, and local preferences for different shapes as it does with ingredients. Many of the shapes found in different regions may be attributed to the way in which bread is used with local foods. Dense large loaves, often made to last for up to a week, are used fresh on the table alongside stews, game, and dishes with sauce. Later in the week the stale bread is put in soup. Many *couronnes,* or crown-shaped loaves, have been developed because the peasants liked large loaves but preferred them to have more crust. Shapes also affect texture and consistency, as apprentice bakers were taught in the years between the two world wars when French bakers called *compagnons* were required—as part of their advancement from apprentice to journeyman baker—to create a unique shape of bread. This, according to some authorities, is one thing that accounts for the many shapes to be found in France.

The fermentation is another subject we can learn from ancient village bakers. *La manière de raccommoder les levains* is the phrase French bakers use to describe the way to control or repair starters. *Raccommoder* means "to repair" or, literally, "to sew" or "to mend." The tricks professionals use to control starters that have become too active can be used at home or in the village bakery to control the fermentation of every batch of dough.

Modern mixers and modern ovens are the main things that make home baking different from commercial baking. However, some modern village bakers are emulating hand mixing by using slower speeds and shorter mixing times, modifications that allow the dough to ferment more naturally, rather than depending on the intense action of the mixer to inflate the dough with air. Modern bakers are also learning that a better loaf can be baked in old brick ovens than in modern convection ovens.

What is known in France as *la fabrication artisanale* is the artisan's craft of using hand techniques, closely watched methods, and personal judgment, a mode of work that today's best village bakers learned from the first home bakers. Despite their use of mixers, molders, and commercial ovens, modern village bakers have retained the artisan's approach of treating each loaf with special care, and this is still the best way to make a loaf of bread. Once it was the other way around; now excellent handmade bread from village bakers has given us an example of what we can achieve at home. What the home baker can learn are the secrets of the professional baker as artisan: How a recipe can be regarded as a set of variable proportions and therefore how it can be changed to yield a unique regional or family bread; how handwork techniques can help make better bread; how to use wetter doughs to get more interesting textures; how to control starters and therefore how to control the entire bread baking process; and, finally, how observation and judgment can help us turn a scientific craft into a highly personalized method.

The best village bakers take recipes as guidelines but they must trust their own sense of when a dough is ready to go on to the next stage. A home baker who learns to make such a leap of faith can advance from being merely a recipe follower to being a baker, responding to the activity of the bread instead of following a rigid timetable. By being aware of the atmosphere in the kitchen, the climate outside, and the activity of the dough, home bakers—like village bakers—can use technique, observation, and sensitivity to create a distinctive and personalized loaf of bread.

Breadmaking—
The Village Baker's Craft

Much of the first part of the book is written from the French village baker's point of view. The French—because of people such as Poilâne, Calvel, and Parmentier—have a highly codified *métier* and they make use of all aspects of fermentation and hand techniques in their daily production. Furthermore, they have defined the craft in the same way as they have perfected the art of wine making. Where appropriate, I have included equivalent terms, usages, or variations that are practiced by Italian, German, or American village bakers.

CHAPTER I

Ingredients

As BASIC INGREDIENTS, there are none more simple, universal, and readily accessible than flour, water, salt, and packaged yeast—although they may often be of the most common quality. Home bakers who are willing to seek out specialized ingredients, such as organic flour and sea salt, can add flavor and healthful qualities to their bread. But special ingredients are not necessary. The common ingredients found in most supermarkets will yield exceptional results and a simple, honest loaf.

∗∗∗∗∗∗∗∗∗∗∗∗∗∗∗ *The Four Basic Ingredients* ∗∗∗∗∗∗∗∗∗∗∗∗∗∗∗

The French art of bread baking proves that a superior loaf can be made without any of the so-called natural improvers, such as malt extract, sugar, honey, milk, shortening, butter, or eggs, that are used in America. All of these ingredients do have a place in bread making, but not in the recipes for true French bread. Using only four basic ingredients: flour, water, yeast, and salt (and small amounts of ascorbic acid and possibly rye flour, both permissible under French law), the French baker produces scores of variations of bread, distinct not only in appearance, shape, and color, but also in crust, texture, and flavor.

Grains from different growing regions possess their own distinctive flavor. Variations in milling techniques create different types of breads. Varying proportions of the four basic ingredients yield different results. (Italian bakers in Piedmont, for example, use more water, giving their bread a moist texture and an uneven crumb.) Adjustments—because of personal style and the preferences of their customers—made even by bakers who work with similar ingredients under similar conditions result in breads that are remarkably distinct.

Flour

Throughout the world wheat flour is the primary ingredient for bread because it contains a form of protein called gluten. When combined with water and developed into a dough, wheat flour provides an elastic quality called "extensibility," a characteristic that allows the dough to expand, just as the surface of a balloon expands when it is blown up, and provide the proper tension to entrap the gases created by the yeast.

In America the standard level of gluten in bread flour is between 11 percent and 13 percent. All-purpose flour is softer and is between 8 percent and 10 percent gluten. Pastry flour (often called cake and pastry flour in America) has less gluten but it is of a superior quality; this softer flour can be mixed with bread flour and used for hard rolls, Parker House rolls, muffins, *pane duro*, puff pastry, and some tart doughs, in which a tighter texture is desired in the crumb.

American all-purpose flour can be successfully used at home for bread. Some bakers go out of their way to find the sort of high-gluten bread flour that is used in commercial bakeries. But using stronger flour in home baking is hardly worth the trouble because hand mixing is rarely vigorous enough to show a difference in the crumb.

As for organic bread flour, my preference is for the flour milled by Guisto's (241 East Harris Avenue, South San Francisco, California 94080), a company that sells a good quality flour, organic and unbleached. Nonetheless, the different types of white flour give only slightly different results; use whatever you have—bleached or unbleached, all-purpose or bread flour, organic or not.

In France, and generally in Europe, bread flour has much less gluten, necessitating longer mixing and the use of certain legally permissible, natural improvers.

A grain of wheat is composed of the envelope, the germ, and the flour-making part, which is called the *amande farineuse* in French. The envelope (12 percent to 15 percent of the grain) is usually cracked and sifted away in the form of bran. The germ (3 percent), as the living part of the grain and that which allows the

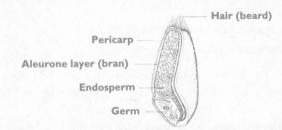

Hair (beard)
Pericarp
Aleurone layer (bran)
Endosperm
Germ

plant to regenerate itself, is nearly always eliminated during milling. Full of vitamins and minerals, the germ also contains fats and oils that might cause the flour to go rancid more quickly. The flour-making part of the grain (82 percent to 84 percent) contains gluten and starch.

Starch makes up between 68 percent and 72 percent of flour and is essential in the fermentation of bread because some of it is transformed into the sugars that are so important for the action of the yeast to feed on. Gluten makes up

Library Resource Center
Renton Technical College
Renton, WA 98056

8 percent to 12 percent of flour and gives the plastic properties to the resulting dough. Qualities of cohesion, elasticity, and plasticity are determined by the quality and the quantity of gluten. Ash, .5 percent to .6 percent of flour, is the mineral content, and it is calculated by burning a measured amount of flour, the resulting ash being weighed to determine the ash content.

The higher the ash content, the *taux de cendre,* in bread flour, the grayer the crumb. The tendency in France and in America has been to reduce the ash content through bleaching in order to make the bread look whiter, cleaner, and more appealing. Reducing the ash also reduces the nutritive quality of the loaf, so the use of unbleached flour is to be recommended.

Bakers who use *farine bise,* the second milling of flour, obtain a loaf with a gray cast. This flour, which is much like a light-colored whole wheat flour, hasn't gone through the final four or five millings that make most modern bread flours immaculately white and empty of anything that's good for us. Because it's not overrefined, the flour retains more of the germ, more of the entire wheat grain, and has a higher ash content, resulting in a more nutritive loaf. A bread made out of *farine bise,* which is weaker in gluten but higher in nutrients, not only has a smoky-colored crumb, but also a more irregular and chewy texture.

FARINE BISE MIXTURE

To simulate a slightly darker flour, you can prepare a mixture that may be added to any white bread formula. It will help to give a darker color to the crumb and a more healthful loaf. All of the flours can be found in organic form at health food stores.

Durum flour, a hard wheat flour used for making pasta, can be purchased in many specialty food shops.

> 2 cups rye flour
>
> 2 cups whole wheat flour
>
> 2 cups durum flour

Mix all the flours together and store in a labeled container. If the flours are organic they will tend to go rancid if left out too long. The mixture can, however, be kept in the refrigerator for several months.

The flour mixture can be used in any white flour bread recipe. For example, in a 6-cup recipe, substitute ½ cup *farine bise* mixture for ½ cup white flour. For a darker loaf, it can be used as a substitute for as much as 3 cups of white flour.

Many regional French, Italian, and German breads are made with various grains that give them a local distinction. A home baker can create a distinctive family bread with a unique mixture of grains. Here is just one example.

I cup rolled wheat

I cup rolled oats

I cup cracked wheat

I cup wheat berries

I cup cracked rye berries

I cup cornmeal

Mix all the ingredients together and store in a labeled container.

The day before using, place 1 cup of grain mixture in a bowl or container and cover with 1 cup of boiling water and set aside to soak overnight.

Use the mixture as it is, being aware that the quantity of water in the recipe may have to be reduced to make up for the wet grains. (Or roast the mixture in a 350°F oven on a cookie sheet for between 10 and 12 minutes, until it has dried out. Allow it to cool before using.)

This grain mixture may be used as a substitute for white flour in the proportion of 1 cup of mixture to every 5 cups of white flour in any bread recipe.

Water

Lionel Poilâne, the celebrated Parisian baker, and his mentor, professor Raymond Calvel of the *Grand Moulin de Paris,* both call water the primordial ingredient. Poilâne, we assume, is quoting his older, more learned teacher, but it is hard to tell whether Calvel was inspired by Parmentier's book, *Le parfait boulanger,* the Bible, Shakespeare, or some impassioned French poet. Water is an essential ingredient—more essential than either salt or yeast. Water is the catalyst that helps the dough ferment because it gives life to the sleeping flour.

Yeast

There are two basic kinds of yeast, commercial yeast, which is made in factories and yields predictable results, and natural yeast (sourdough or *levain*), which is in the air in thousands of forms and is only predictably controlled under the most guarded of conditions. Commercial yeast allows us to make breads in a straightforward, three- or four-step process; it allows home bakers to create simple breads quickly; it allows village bakers to mix many, unrelated batches of bread in the course of a day's production; and it gives loaves with the simple flavor and light texture that suit modern tastes.

Natural yeast, by contrast, is a primitive, spontaneous ingredient that grows out of a mixture of flour and water. It is more difficult and time consuming to use, but the resulting bread is not only more complex in texture and flavor, but also will keep longer.

The two types of yeast widely available, cake or compressed, and active dry yeast are interchangeable. One package of active dry yeast measures out to be one scant tablespoon or two and a half teaspoons; a half-ounce cake of compressed yeast is generally regarded as the equivalent of a quarter-ounce (seven-gram) package of dry yeast. (The texture of bread made with the minimum of yeast is so superior that it is worth experimenting with proportions: one quarter of a teaspoon of yeast will adequately leaven four cups of flour, and possibly more, if the dough is allowed to rise for long enough.) Dry yeast is also available in bulk, usually from health-food stores, where it is sold without preservatives and much more cheaply. Packaged yeast will be viable until the date stamped on the package; properly stored, in an airtight container in the refrigerator, bulk active dry yeast will keep for months—if it has been properly stored in the market as well.

I use packaged dry yeast in my home recipes because it is easier for home bakers to keep on hand and, by proofing it in warm water before using, the home baker can be assured that it is alive.

Salt

Salt enhances the flavor of most foods. In bread it brings out the natural flavor of the wheat and it has a chemical function: It controls fermentation. By tightening the gluten so that it can hold on to itself in an elastic network, salt enables the dough to entrap the carbonic gases that cause bread to rise. Salt will also retard the action of the yeast. Salt has a marked effect on the crumb and the color of the crust. Salt also helps the retention of moisture: Salt-free breads go stale more quickly than do breads made with salt.

The first breads in which salt was an ingredient were made from sea water, and sea salt is still preferable to that processed from inland underground deposits that have acquired residual trace minerals as a result of centuries-long stratification of layers of earth sediments and sea water. Two percent salt is the basic addition in most French bread recipes. This means that if a recipe calls for 100 pounds of flour (flour being the basis of the percentage calculation), there should be two pounds of salt. For the home baker that percentage is roughly one tablespoon of salt to six cups of flour.

Bread can be made without salt, as is shown by bakers in Tuscany who, during the sixteenth century, were forced to forgo salt in their breads because of an oppressive salt tax. They became so accustomed to the flavor that they continue, to this day, to make their breads without salt.

Improvers are additional ingredients included in French bread and considered not harmful to the human body. Legally permissible improvers are those ingredients permitted under French law; other improvers, such as butter, eggs, and milk, are ingredients that American bakers have traditionally used to extend the shelf life of their French-style breads.

Natural Improvers in France

In any bread he calls French bread, the French village baker can add only the following ingredients: fava bean flour, vitamin C, rye flour, and *levit*.

FAVA BEAN FLOUR

Anyone who has walked the streets of Paris at dawn has had the unforgettable pleasure of smelling the distinct aroma of French bread wafting from every basement *boulangerie*. This unique aroma is a cherished by-product of the fava bean flour, *farine de fève*, an additive that Monsieur Costa, a baker in Aix-en-Provence says also helps improve the flavor. Fava beans are plentiful in most of France as they are planted in fallow fields to replenish the nitrogen in the soil. Milled into a fine flour and added to most grades of wheat flour produced in French mills at the rate of 2 percent or less, they also help to add flavor, boost the rising process, and whiten the crumb of breads made with less refined flours that have a high ash content and therefore a gray coloration.

VITAMIN C

The same magical powder that we Americans ingest in massive doses in hope of avoiding the common cold is used by French bakers to give their dough a property they call *tolérance*. ("How much rising time can a dough tolerate before it collapses?") A wet dough that undergoes a fermentation of between four and six hours is likely to collapse if it is not put into the oven at the precise moment it is ready. Vitamin C, *acide ascorbique*, gives tenacity to a limp, weak bread dough—providing the strength to permit the full development of the loaf.

Ascorbic acid is added in the most minute quantities, to a maximum of fifty milligrams per quintal of flour (one quintal is 100 kilos), or as a friend who is an oceanographer-turned-baker put it, two hundred parts per million. In everyday baking terms, this works out to about ⅛ teaspoon in 100 pounds of flour.

INGREDIENTS

13

RYE FLOUR

Although most bakers in France would not think of using rye flour in either their *pain ordinaire* or *pain de campagne,* under French law, it is permitted as an improver at a maximum rate of 2 percent of the flour. In such quantities the rye flour will not noticeably change the hydration (moisture content) of the dough nor the flavor of the loaf. Some people can detect its presence. My wife, Gayle, for example, surprised Lionel Poilâne one day when he had invited us into his office on the rue du Cherche-Midi for a chat. After praising his apple tart, she asked him if he had used rye flour in the dough. Surprised at her observation, he admitted that he did indeed use rye flour for the slight tang of flavor it added to the crust.

Small quantities of rye flour in bread will improve the texture and aroma of the crumb, give a richer color to the crust, and add a silkiness to the dough, making it easier to work. Its greatest benefit, however, is in increasing the shelf life of the final product.

LEVIT

A type of yeast food invented by French millers, *levit* is composed of wheat flour, salt, dry yeast, ascorbic acid, and amalyse. (Yeast normally feeds on the natural sugars found in flour; amalyse, a natural enzyme, aids in the fermentation process by providing extra food for the yeast.) *Levit* improves the strength and rising abilities of weak flours, those containing a low percentage of gluten.

FAVA BEAN IMPROVER

The American home baker can make a similar, nutritious improver that may be added to any bread dough to make a superior, lighter loaf.

The rye flour provides a distinctive taste and aroma to your bread. The whole wheat gives a nutty flavor and a darker color to the crumb. Dried fava beans may be purchased at local feed stores. Buy about a pound of the favas and grind them in a food processor until they are almost completely pulverized. Sift out the larger particles before measuring out the quantity you need. Powdered vitamin C, which helps to give more volume to the loaf, may be purchased in small quantities at most drug stores. The addition of salt and yeast to the improver assures that these ingredients are not deficient in your final bread recipe.

> 2 cups organic rye flour
>
> 2 cups organic whole wheat flour
>
> I cup fava bean flour
>
> I teaspoon vitamin C powder
>
> I scant tablespoon salt
>
> I teaspoon dry yeast

Mix all the ingredients together and store in an airtight container in the refrigerator.

Add 1 cup of the mixture to any 6-cup bread recipe. You will need to add more water—between ¼ and ⅓ cup—to the dough so that it is not too dry.

Best used in rye or whole wheat breads, caraway powder is a flavoring agent similar to that used by German bakers to add distinctive tastes to different breads. Other spices and dried herbs may be used: cumin, fennel seeds, coriander seeds, cardamom, oregano, parsley, and basil.

¼ cup chopped onion

¼ cup caraway seeds

I tablespoon ground black pepper

I tablespoon sea salt

Preheat the oven to 300°F.

Place the onion on a baking sheet and bake it for 20 minutes. Set aside.

Grind the caraway seeds in a food processor fitted with the metal blade or in a mortar with a pestle. Sift the resulting powder to make sure that there are no large chunks of seed left.

Combine all the ingredients and store in an airtight container. Add the prepared powder to the dry ingredients in any bread recipe, using 1 or 2 teaspoons for every 3 cups of flour.

Natural Improvers in America

In America, as there is no legal prohibition against additives for products given the name of French bread, many improvers are used, the most common natural improvers being milk, eggs, sugar, malt extract, and shortening. These ingredients enrich the bread, in some cases make it more nutritious, in others, more flavorful, and more appealing to the eye. Mainly, however, they increase the shelf life and so are used almost exclusively in large-scale factories for supermarket French breads. But those same qualities can be obtained by varying the methods and techniques of any bread recipe. By using the sourdough and sponge methods of bread baking, bakers can alter the rhythm of the fermentation—and its results—while still using only the four basic ingredients.

MILK

When used as an additive to French bread, milk gives a richer flavor, a deeper color to the crust, and a softer body to the crumb. The protein in milk adds to the nutritive quality of the finished loaf and keeps it fresh longer. Milk also helps to provide some of the flavor of a lactic fermentation that happens naturally in a sourdough process.

EGGS

Because they contain glycerin, lecithin, and protein, eggs constitute an excellent preservative for bread. The use of eggs comes to us, by way of the French, from the Viennese. It was they who developed and perfected the use of enriched bread doughs. They used eggs in their *brioche,* milk in their *pain au lait,* and butter in their *croissant.* Nowadays any method in which enriched doughs are used is termed *viennoise.*

SUGAR

Sweeteners of any type (honey included) furnish food for the commercial yeast. Whereas salt holds back or controls the activity of the yeast (and therefore the activity of the fermentation), any sweetener added to the bread dough makes the yeast more active than it would be if it were simply allowed to feed on the natural sugars present in the flour.

Not only is the cost of bread dough increased by the added cost of any sweetener, but also the extra sweetener consumes the yeast. Because the fermentation speeds up, the dough must be watched more carefully. Enriched breads, because of the heavy weight of the added ingredients, need much more yeast than do straight French breads and the costs of the sweetener and the extra yeast must be accounted for. There is much to be said for the argument that a common bread for the people should forgo such additives: the flavor will be simpler, the price more reasonable. Moreover, the baker can offer his customer enough other products that use the extra, deluxe ingredients. *Brioche, croissants, pain au lait,* and *pain de mie* are all specialty products that go beyond the scope of the French bread that is eaten every day.

MALT EXTRACT

Aside from augmenting the activity of a sluggish *levain* (and in some *croissant* recipes), malt extract is not used frequently in France, because it is not legally permitted in recipes for straight French bread (*pain ordinaire*); it is permitted in *croissants, brioche,* and other enriched doughs, but is not always used in them. In America it is used occasionally in French-style breads. Malt extract is more concentrated than sugar and has a more distinctive and appealing flavor.

Italian village bakers use malt extra in their dough for, among other baked goods, *pizza, focaccia,* and *michette.*

FAT

In America shortening, butter, margarine, or lard are all used in French-style factory bread to some extent to make the dough machine more easily (that is, to allow the dough to be more easily worked, without being torn, in a mechanical molder), but usually to prolong freshness. Most American village bakers who have their clients' health in mind decline to use any extra enriching improvers in straight French breads. Italians use shortening in breadsticks, in certain types of rolls, and in a flat bread called *schiacciata.*

CHAPTER 2

Leavening

LOAVES ARE TRANSFORMED from dough into bread by the same process whether the baker uses a homegrown starter or a foil package of dried yeast. The difference between the two agents is apparent in every other aspect of the bread—taste, texture, keeping qualities, and so on—but both work in the same way, to induce fermentation.

Fermentation

The activity of the dough is described as *la fermentation,* a term that is also used to describe the action of bacterial growth, whether it be of commercial yeast or sourdough starter. The bacteria, in consuming the sugars in the flour, create carbonic gas as a by-product. This gas, when entrapped within a well-developed bread dough, causes the dough to rise and, when baked, to become lighter and therefore more flavorful and more digestible than bread made from an unleavened dough. When kneaded properly, strands of gluten in wheat flour form a network that binds the dough together in such a fashion that the carbonic gas becomes entrapped in thousands of microscopic pockets. This is the process that gives bread its cellular structure and its lightness.

Fermentation is the heart of bread baking. Once it is set in motion, it has a life of its own. Like other living things, the bacteria are affected by outside influences. And it is the results of these influences that impose a three-part task.

First, the bread baker must be aware, before the mixing begins, of the outside influences on the fermentation so that he or she can predict the results. Second, the baker must observe the fermentation as it unfolds, being aware of its rhythms. And, last, after judging the level of activity of the fermentation, the baker must accommodate the dough by making minor adjustments in handling and rising times in leading it to its natural end.

Unfortunately we have been spoiled by the step-by-step recipe system in making breads. We have forgotten what the home bakers of old knew by heart: that if a baker observes the activity of a bread dough, he can respond to its movement and take it more readily to its logical and artful conclusion as bread.

A bread baker must accommodate or correct a bread process as it unfolds. Observing a speedy fermentation, for example, he should either slow it down or stand prepared to bake the loaves early.

French bakers use some very descriptive words for the levels of activity of the fermentation: "the push," "the force," "tenacity," "extensibility," and "tolerance." Each time a fermentation is set in motion when a dough is mixed by the baker, it takes on a level of activity: It may be active, or sluggish or any intensity in between. The push *(la pousse)* is synonymous with the fermentation itself. It describes visually and metaphysically the fermentation's movement during the baking process. The force *(la force)* designates one of the aspects of the physical properties of the dough. To some extent the force will improve the dough's elasticity (its ability to stretch). But too much force provokes tenacity *(la ténacité),* an excessively plastic quality that makes the dough undesirably tight and unworkable. Tolerance *(la tolérance)* is the dough's ability to support a minor fault (slight overmixing or undermixing, too much water) or excess fermentation, either at *le pointage* (the first proofing or rising) or at *l'apprêt* (the final rising), without impairing the quality of the bread.

All of these descriptive terms help measure the dough's behavior. The baker must be aware of the precise level of activity so as to be able to manipulate the dough and control the fermentation. The baker should look at the factors separately and then as a whole, in order to discover the overall mood of the fermentation. Having learned to judge the level of activity in fermentation, the baker is able to shape the outcome of a particular loaf.

Controlling the Fermentation

The baker's task is to work the controls of the fermentation the way a puppeteer works the strings of a puppet. Parmentier, in his book, *Le parfait boulanger,* published in 1778, describes *la manière de raccommoder les levains,* the manner of correcting and controlling or accommodating starters—a series of techniques the baker has at his command to steer the activity of the fermentation. These "accommodations" have as much to do with controlling yeasted direct-method doughs as they do with sourdough.

A *levain,* starter, or yeasted dough must be controlled because each has an optimum level of activity and a baker can take advantage of that level to create the perfect loaf for the method. Starters that are too sour create texture and flavor irregularities in the final bread. In the straight-dough method, a fermentation that is too active will have to be baked off sooner or it will lose color and volume. A bread that is not active enough will never attain the proper volume and the crumb will not develop adequately.

The basic factors that may be controlled are: the temperature of ingredients, dough, and room, the hydration of the dough, the humidity of the bakery (or kitchen), the amount of salt used, the method of leavening chosen, and the mixing and handling of the dough in its several stages of development.

Two communal ovens in
the south of France

The basic rule governing the control of the fermentation is: *When both the dough and the environment are wet and warm, the dough tends to be more active. When the dough is firm and cool it tends to be more inactive or sluggish.* This rule applies to yeasted doughs and to sourdoughs in all stages of development.

DOUGH TEMPERATURE

Recipes for most American breads call for a dough temperature of 80°F; virtually all French breads are mixed at 75°F. The lower temperature allows for a slower, cooler fermentation that helps to develop flavor in the final rising and sets up the dough for a wild explosion of activity—when the loaf hits the oven— at the spot were the baker has made a cut with the razor.

The temperature of the room in which you are baking is less easily manipulated than is the temperature of the dough itself. French bakers take the temperatures of their room and ingredients as fixed and adjust the water temperature in order to arrive at a precise dough temperature, generally 75°F. If all the other conditions were also ideal, that is, if 75°F were the average of the combined totals of the temperatures of the room, water, and dough, what they call *la température de base* would be 225°F. To arrive at the proper water temperature proceed as follows: If the air temperature is, in fact, 80°F, the flour is likely to be that temperature as well. (To make sure, bakers can put a probe type thermometer right into the bulk flour itself.) Multiplying 80°F by two will give you 160°F. But, before assuming that your water temperature will, therefore, be 225°F minus 160°F, you must account for the heat created in mixing the dough, heat that will raise the temperature of the dough and put all your careful calculations out of kilter. (Kneading by hand will do little to change the temperature of the dough, so no adjustment needs to be made in that case.) The rule of thumb is one degree of temperature for each minute of mixing on second speed by machine. In ten minutes, the temperature will have increased by 10°F. So the sum is: $225 - (80 + 80 + 10) = 55°F$—the temperature of the water that will yield a 75°F dough.

Most French and American village bakers follow this formula. Some use ice, some use chilled water from an automatic refrigerated water dispenser. (Italian village bakers do not seem to keep careful track of their dough temperatures. They do, however, usually mix the dough on first speed so that it does not become overheated.)

Thus the village baker can slow down or speed up the fermentation process by altering the temperature of the dough.

ROOM TEMPERATURE

Room temperature is not, however, entirely immutable. The ambient or proofing temperature can be modified if the dough is put closer to the oven or in a proof box to speed its activity, or put in a cool area, or even retarded in the refrigerator to slow it down. If the environment is too dry, the loaves may be sprayed with water as they rise and a bulk *levain* or dough may be covered with plastic wrap or canvas to prevent a crust from forming.

DOUGH HYDRATION

The term *dough hydration* refers to how wet or dry the dough or *levain* is mixed. One of the key differences in sourdough bread baking in Italy, France, and America is the relative firmness of the sourdough starter in its various stages. If the baker knows the optimum firmness for a particular method, he can more easily achieve a predictable finished product. Most good recipes will attempt to describe the firmness or wetness of a dough but these are relative terms; it is up to the baker to venture a judgment.

In order to control or slow down the fermentation's activity, most sourdough refreshments (the practice of building a *levain* with more flour and water on which the active ferments can feed) are mixed firm—much firmer than most bread doughs are mixed. To increase this control, the *levain* can be mixed even firmer. In order to activate or increase the fermentation, the refreshment can be mixed wetter, the lack of resistance allowing the dough to rise faster. Incidentally, differences in the firmness of a dough result in variations in the loaf as well. For instance, similar methods of making San Francisco sourdough will yield different types of bread depending on whether the six-hour refreshment schedule is followed with wet or firm refreshments.

THE USE OF SALT OR SWEETENERS

Salt retards the fermentation and sweeteners speed it up, so a baker can use salt to hold back overly active *levains* and starters, or use honey or malt extract to hasten their activity. Either can be used in a straight dough as well, but only in very small amounts. Any additions made to a straight dough (more than a half a teaspoon in a six-cup batch or more than .5 percent for a commercial batch) will noticeably affect the flavor. In a *levain,* starter, or sponge, additions of salt will be less noticeable in the finished loaf because the salt will have had more time to be acted upon in the fermentation process. Even in controlling starters, it is always better to use techniques such as mixing a dough firmer or cooler that are less shocking to the process than to add salt. To preserve the intensity of the culture, most formulas for homemade sourdough call for some of the starter to be pulled back for future use before the salt is added. In commercial production, a piece of dough is often pulled back from the dough after the salt has been added, giving the baker more control. Other bakers retard their *levains* in the refrigerator to control their activity. Still others may have ongoing starters that they keep separate from any batches of dough and thus never need to add salt to the starter itself.

There are three methods of mixing bread dough: the sourdough method, the sponge method, and the direct method. All are used commercially and all may be adapted to home bread baking.

The sourdough method, known in France as *la méthode au levain,* is the oldest and most organic. To ferment the dough bakers use wild yeast captured from the air in the form of bacteria. A sourdough process takes twenty-four hours, excluding the time required to make the starter, which is a matter of days.

No doubt the method was discovered by accident—a bowl of porridge was forgotten and, when rediscovered a few days later, was seen to be bubbly and was emitting a wonderful, yeasty smell. What inspired leap of the imagination prompted the next step we will never know, but the step itself was (and still is) quite simple. Mix the starter with more flour and some water until you have a dough. Over the years, millennia actually, the procedure has become distinctly less haphazard. Bakers learned to make starters and to maintain their supply but the developments in the technique have been improvements in the handling rather than changes in concept.

The straight-dough method (which French bakers call *la méthode directe*—the direct method) was first used around 1810 with brewer's yeast and then with commercial baker's yeast around 1900. At first most bakers ignored the innovation; they later saw it as a boon to their laborious production schedules because bread could be made in six or seven hours instead of twenty-four and their customers seemed to like the lighter breads it produced.

The sponge method (in France described as *pain sur poolish*) is a compromise. In spite of feeling that bread made by the direct method with yeast was lifeless and devoid of character and flavor, the bakers did like its speed. So they came up with a prefermentation process by which fractions of the ingredients of a batch of dough were mixed early. This *poolish* or sponge, made with yeast and some of the flour and water, but none of the salt (so that the fermentation is not held back) starts the fermentation before the dough itself is mixed.

Because the sponge method normally uses less yeast than does a direct method, the first fermentation can rise much more slowly. The slower activity allows the baker to achieve some of the texture and crustiness of a bread made with sourdough yet retain some of the lightness of a straight yeasted dough.

The use of old dough, *vieille pâte* (referred to as the *pâte fermentée* method in France), is a glorified straight-dough method. It is not really a separate method, just a combination of methods using a yeasted starter. By including a piece of retarded, yeasted dough taken from a previous batch and allowed to rise for a time, the baker can add subtle qualities of texture and flavor to what most resembles a straight-dough method. The process will not yield any of the shiny, sour crumb nor the added shelf life of breads made with the sourdough method.

But many of today's village bakers in France are using the technique to achieve an interesting texture and a thin, crackling crust in their *pain ordinaire*. It can also provide a fast, efficient method for making *pain de campagne* and *pain de seigle*, without having to use a completely sourdough process.

The Direct Method
La méthode directe

The direct method—a one-step combination of yeast, flour, and water, with or without flavorings, to make a dough—is used by most commercial and most home bakers. It can yield acceptable bread but does not afford the challenge and sense of achievement that inspire the village baker in his *métier*. For the home baker, recipes may be found in any reliable cookbook and the results are often quite good. Many village bakers found their calling in a loaf of bread made by this simplest of methods. From there they went on.

In French bread baking, the direct method is used for one of the two principal types of bread eaten every day: *pain ordinaire*. (The other, *pain au levain*, is the one made by the sourdough method.) The basic recipe for a wonderful *pain ordinaire* can be found on page 69 and it is followed by recipes for variations of method that yield breads of increasing complexity of texture and flavor. (By the expression "complexity of flavor" I am referring, not to the taste of specialty breads in which ingredients such as eggs, milk, butter, fruit, spices, and so on are included, but to nuances of the flavor of bread made essentially with flour, water, yeast, salt, and perhaps a small quantity of sweetener.)

DIRECT-METHOD BREADS

The Sponge Method
Pain sur poolish

The sponge method may be a compromise, but it embodies the best of both worlds: the lightness of the direct method and the flavor of the sourdough method. Like sourdough, the process may be hastened or retarded as convenient.

The word *poolish* would seem to indicate that the method originated in Poland. It was adopted and perfected by the bakers of Vienna who found that it helped them achieve a more interesting texture in breads enriched with butter, milk, and sugar. In France between 1840 and 1920 it was the only method used because it made up for a scarcity of yeast. When yeast became plentiful, the method lost favor and today is used principally for rye and whole wheat variations and only rarely for *pain ordinaire*. This is unfortunate, because the method offers bakers a way to manipulate their time schedules, acquire a more interesting flavor, and give a chewy texture to the crumb. In fact, many of the bakers who first used it found that it enabled them to make their *pain fantaisie* (bread sculpture) much more elaborate.

A crackling crust, well-developed texture, and an aromatic, nutlike flavor are some of the qualities of a bread made with the sponge method. A sponge can provide some of the flavor and shelf life of a *levain* bread without requiring the laborious treatment of the starter. The method will also help improve the elasticity and behavior of doughs made with weak flours (flours low in gluten, all-purpose flours, or flours that have been in storage or in transit too long).

By premixing all of the required quantity of commercial yeast into a liquid sponge *(poolish)* with some of the flour and water, the baker can start the fermentation of the bread dough before he actually mixes the dough. This sponge is allowed to rise "until it is ready" in baker's terms—and "ready" can be judged in several ways: by the amount the sponge has risen (usually two or three times its original volume), by its appearance ("bubbling like beaten egg whites"), or by whether or not it has dropped. A mature sponge will drop or fall and that maturity is what gives it the strength to boost the next stage of mixing.

The ambient temperature and the temperature at which the sponge is mixed will affect the fermentation, but it is the wetness or firmness of the sponge that really determines how long it will take before it is ready to be mixed into the final dough. A soupy or wet sponge will rise quickly, taking between two and five hours, because the flour and water offer less resistance to the yeast, enabling it to grow and, therefore, start to bubble almost immediately. A firm sponge—because it offers more resistance to the process of fermentation—can take longer to rise (between six and twelve hours).

In the second stage, the baker mixes the rest of the ingredients together with the sponge to make the final dough. Thereafter he proceeds as usual, making a few slight adjustments to the method to account for the particular rate of activity brought on by that fermentation.

The sponge method allows the village baker to fit a dough's rhythmic cycles into a prearranged schedule and to push and pull the fermentation phase to meet a day's production needs. The home baker, too, can fit a sponge bread into a tight schedule. The traditional proportions call for one-third of the flour and two-thirds of the water to be mixed with a given quantity of yeast. Byusing less water and less yeast, the sponge can be made to take between eight and ten hours, rather than the traditional four hours. Then, because the action has been slower over a longer period of time, the fermentation on the dough side of the process (after the rest of the yeast, the salt and the remaining flour and water have been added) can be done more quickly.

OBSERVATIONS ON THE SPONGE METHOD

Over the course of hundreds of years of practice, bakers found that they could formulate guidelines that are still useful for today's bakers.

- Normally the amount of yeast used in a sponge is a little less than that used in a direct-method dough: About 25 percent less yeast for a four-hour rising, 50 percent less for eight hours, and 75 percent less for twelve to fifteen hours.

- The water used to prepare the sponge should be cool in summer and warm in winter.

- Because the sponge is a liquid starter intended to increase the maturity of the fermentation, salt is never added since it would tend to weaken and retard the fermentation.

- The larger the proportion of sponge in the final dough, the shorter will be the first rising of dough the next day.

- A sponge that constitutes a large proportion of the final batch should be made more liquid than usual so that it does not become too acidic. A very acidic sponge will exert too much force and make the final dough excessively elastic.

- A long-duration sponge that also constitutes a large proportion of the final batch should use less yeast and cooler water to slow down the fermentation.

- A sponge should be allowed to reach, or even go beyond, its full maturity. In America this stage is called a "full drop." After a sponge has increased to three times its original size, it will collapse, indicating that the gluten has ripened and the acidity has fully developed. A fully mature sponge will help the flour in the dough side of the process to ripen more quickly.

The basic sponge recipe can be used in any bread that calls for three cups of flour in the full recipe or it can be doubled for a six-cup recipe. In fact, it can be used in a recipe of any size as long as the proportions are kept the same.

FOR THE SPONGE *(POOLISH)*

> 1 cup warm water
>
> 1 teaspoon active dry yeast
>
> 1 cup flour

THE DOUGH

> 1 teaspoon active dry yeast
>
> ¼ cup cool water
>
> 1½ teaspoons salt
>
> All of the sponge from the previous step
>
> 2 cups flour

TO MAKE THE SPONGE, place ¼ cup warm water in a small dish or cup and sprinkle the yeast over the top. Mix it well until the yeast is incorporated. Let the mixture stand for between 5 and 10 minutes until it is creamy.

Combine the yeast mixture with the rest of the warm water in a medium-sized ceramic bowl or plastic container large enough so that it could hold triple the quantities of the original ingredients.

Add the flour by handfuls while stirring with a wooden spoon and making sure that all the lumps have been dissolved. The sponge will be a liquid with the consistency of a thick pancake batter.

Let the mixture sit, covered with a moist dish towel, for between 4 and 6 hours. When the sponge has risen to double or triple its original size and fallen, it is ready to use.

TO MAKE THE DOUGH, proof the yeast in the water as described above. Then add it, along with the salt, to the sponge and mix to incorporate the ingredients completely.

Proceed according to the instructions for *pain sur poolish* (page 80) or follow the instructions for whatever recipe you are using.

If you are using the sponge for another recipe, this list of ingredients for the dough will not apply. The list should be adjusted to the requirements of the recipe you are using; if your recipe has other enrichment ingredients, it is perfectly fine to use them.

Because the method uses less yeast, it creates a slower, more organic fermentation. The strong flavor and fast-rising qualities purposely built into commercial yeast are no longer so dominant. Instead new ferments arise from the action of the commercial yeast on the mixture of flour and water. This new fermentation, created by the prefermentation, is a slower, more natural process, not unlike that of the sourdough process itself. The dough, in ripening, can take full advantage of the flour which, because of its protein content, has an organic capacity for self-leavening. The result is a bread that has some of the textures and flavors of traditional loaves while still being light and delicate.

AUSTRIAN FLOURLESS SPONGE

A sponge or *poolish* can also be made without flour! At the Mugitch bakery in Vienna they use a mixture of water and yeast that is allowed to rise overnight. Like a regular sponge that contains flour, this mixture helps the yeast to burn out many of its fast-acting characteristics. When mixed into a regular bread recipe the next day, it helps give a moister, chewier texture. Village bakers can save money because they can use 10 percent less yeast, while still getting the same, or better, texture. Home bakers can use less of the mixture or use it full strength.

½ cup warm water

1 package (2½ teaspoons; ¼ ounce) active dry yeast

Put the water in a small ceramic bowl or large cup. Sprinkle the yeast on top, stir it in with a spoon, and let the mixture rest overnight.

The next day use it in your favorite bread recipe (one that would normally call for 1 package of yeast), being aware that the final rising of the dough may be shorter than normal. The crumb will be a lot more voluptuous, airy, and aromatic than it is when you make up the recipe in the usual way; see also the recipe for *Brezeln* on page 180.

SPONGE-METHOD BREADS

The Sourdough Method
Levain

A Frenchman once told me, "A piece of crusty *pain ordinaire* may be a spoon for your soup, but a slice of *pain de campagne* is like a plate." This was my first lesson in understanding the two most abundant and most loved types of French bread: sourdough *(pain au levain)* and everyday French bread *(pain ordinaire)*. The main difference is in their texture. *Pain ordinaire* is a daily bread that is light and crusty—a puff of air. Because it is made with commercial yeast and a fast, four- to six-hour process, its freshness lasts only hours. The crust is crackly and the inside fluffy, making it perfect for picking up sauce and for balancing the effects of any sauce on the palate and the stomach. *Pain au levain* is made by the rustic sourdough process, a long and natural method that produces a hearty, durable bread that will last up to a week.

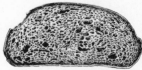

Pain de campagne

It's not surprising that the method yielding the most hearty and organic bread is also the oldest and takes the most time. The time demands are what make the method seem complicated. It is really very simple. The bread contains only three ingredients (four if you count the *levain* itself), flour, water, and salt, and the patterns of the dough's fermentation are easily understood.

The same Frenchman also told me that "the longer a bread takes to make, the better the bread." The natural sourdough method allows bread to be made in a slow, organic rhythm, making it hearty, flavorful, and moist. Breads made this way possess a built-in natural preservative—the organic sourdough starter itself gives the bread better keeping qualities.

Yeast as a separate ingredient is extremely new in the history of food. The first bread baker had, in effect, to capture what the French *boulanger* calls *levure sauvage,* wild yeast. That primitive ferment of flour and water was the only starter used for bread in antiquity and it is what we know today as sourdough starter or *levain.*

In centuries past baking was a weekly event in many homes. Between baking days, preparation of the next week's dough started when a little piece of this week's dough was kept in reserve to carry on the strain. It was held aside in the wine or root cellar where the temperature was cool enough to prevent its over-fermenting. A few days later the piece was mixed with more flour and water so that the starter's active ferments—now becoming sour and somewhat slower— could start their growth anew. This rebuilding with new flour gave them something to feed on and a strong, invigorating freshness. Because these starters should be delicately built into larger, stronger doughs, most natural breads are best made at home. The starter is remixed at its own pace, whenever it is ready, instead of having to fit into the schedule that the village baker must of necessity keep in running a business.

Most natural sourdough cultures can be built into a strong starter in about five days. Flour and water, the basic ingredients, are mixed together into a dough on the first day. Other ingredients, such as honey, ground cumin, or sour milk can also be added to encourage the bacteria. After two or three days—when the dough has become moist, inflated, and slightly sour—it is remixed (or refreshed) with more flour and water. These additions are made again once or twice in the course of building up the starter. The activity of the dough sets up a time pattern indicating to the baker that it is ready to be refreshed. Following the normal pattern, a dough needs to be refreshed after three days, again after another two days, and again the following day, that is, at three-, two-, and one-day intervals. By observation the baker learns to judge the activity of the starter and understand whether it should be refreshed early or late in its time pattern.

OBSERVATIONS ON SOURDOUGH

Through hundreds of years of practice and experiment, the techniques that regulate sourdough starters were developed. These are not exactly rules; they are, rather, observations of phenomena.

To begin with, a starter *(levain)* does not have to be saved from kith or kin, from generation to generation, charming as the idea may be. A good, strong, workable sourdough starter can be created from scratch in three to five days just with flour and water. Once you have an established starter and continue to use and replenish it, you will find that your bread becomes increasingly consistent and predictable. Not only will the starter get more reliable with frequent use, but also you will become more familiar with it.

Besides flour and water, other ingredients such as the natural yeast from unsulfured grapes, ground cumin, sour milk, fermented apples, and honey can be used to attract favorable strains of yeast from the air. All of these extra ingredients are catalysts used to help the *chef* (the initial dough or starter) to pick out of the air friendly strains of bacteria, so-called because they are the best ones for making bread rise.

I learned from a neighborhood sourdough baker in Aix-en-Provence what I call the Fresh Rule. It, too, was developed and perfected in the home: When the starter is fresh it has its greatest capacity to make the dough rise. The rule, also cited by Parmentier, means the opposite of what most of us think about sourdough bread. The excess acidity (sourness) in the starter diminishes active fermentation and, consequently, its ability to make dough rise. A *levain* kept fresh by being continually replenished with more flour and water is kept stronger. Bakers also manage to keep their starters fresh by mixing them firm and not soupy as is done in most modern home recipes for sourdough. A firm dough does not ferment as quickly.

An overly active *levain* can be controlled by mixing it with cooler water and more flour, by mixing it into a firmer dough, or by adding a little salt. An inactive *levain* can be stimulated when it is refreshed by the use of warmer water, extra water—to make a wetter dough—or the addition of a touch of honey or malt extract.

A bread batch made with a *levain* can be made by mixing just 10 percent of starter with more flour, water, and salt to make a bread dough. But the more complete method involves "building" a small (say two-pound) piece of risen *levain* with more and more flour and water at each remixing in several stages during the day. This follows the Fresh Rule and helps give a more predictable finished bread.

A *levain* bread requires more salt (2.2 percent) than the traditional French bread formula calls for. The added salt helps control the acidity of the starter.

Parmentier describes three characteristics of *levains*—based on their activity—as old, strong, and young. An old *levain* is past its readiness, too acidic. A strong *levain* is ready for use; it accelerates the fermentation of the dough and has a pleasing winelike aroma and a vital spirit. A young *levain* is at the beginning of its fermentation; it is in a gaseous (not acidic) state and gives a slow, gentle fermentation and therefore a pleasant taste to the resulting bread—unless it is too young to be of any use.

When active, a *levain* appears to be slightly inflated and more moist than when it was first mixed. A young *levain* (one that is well risen but not yet over the hill) will have expanded a little more than the original dough. But it still has some push left, so it springs back when touched. An old *levain* has risen and then fallen a little. It appears to be wet and overly sticky. It smells highly acidic and is tangy when tasted. A young, strong *levain* with its sweet aroma and slight viniferous acidity is what the baker is looking for. Almost by instinct a sourdough baker knows that a *levain* caught before it peaks and burns out with too much acidity will have strength in reserve to raise the bread.

PORRIDGE BREADS

Pain bouillie, page 105

Pane toscano antiquato, page 141

Pane francese antiquato, page 144

Pane di maïs, page 158

Muesli porridge cakes, page 184

SOURDOUGH BREADS

Starters

The basic sourdough starter begins with the simplest of ingredients, flour and water, and over the course of a few days, develops into a leavening that produces the second of the two major types of bread in France: *pain au levain*. Variations of the basic starter are used for other, more complicated breads. Other types of starters, made with different ingredients, are used for pancakes and specialty breads. *Pain de campagne* and honey starters are minor variations on the basic starter; milk starter is used for pancakes and for many American sourdough breads; yeast starter, which includes yeast as one of its ingredients, may be used to add complexity to *pain ordinaire;* and *lievito naturale* (or *biga*) is the Italian version of a yeast starter or sponge. More complicated is apple starter, for which an apple is fermented with sugar before any flour is added at all. Because the starters are, in themselves, basic ingredients for bread, detailed recipes are given here (except for apple starter, which is an integral part of *pain aux pommes* and so is included with the recipe on page 124.)

BASIC SOURDOUGH STARTER
LEVAIN

I small handful (¼ to ⅓ cup) white flour
Enough water to make a firm dough (approximately I or 2 tablespoons)

Make a mound with the flour on the worktable. Inside the mound make a small well and add the water. Slowly combine the water with the flour, working around the inside of the well with your finger, picking up small amounts of flour as you go. As more flour is brought into the middle of the well, the mixture will gradually be transformed from a paste into a dough. Use a plastic dough scraper or the back of a knife to clean your finger and the worktable. Then knead the little ball into a firm bread dough. Use a little extra water or flour if necessary.

This will be a very small piece of dough, about the size of a walnut, so knead it carefully with a few fingers of one hand on the worktable in the same way as one might knead a larger piece of dough with the heel of your hand. Knead the dough for between 5 and 8 minutes to develop the gluten. The dough should spring back when touched and not be too dry or too sticky.

Place the *chef* (what a *levain* or starter is called in its first stage) in a small bowl, cover it with a damp towel, and put it in a warm place out of drafts for 2 or 3 days. (As Parmentier said over two hundred years ago and any village baker would tell you today, exact times for the rising of any *levain* or sourdough starter are impossible to state. Any projected times will depend on the weather, the wetness and temperature of the *levain,* the freshness of the flour, and the manner in which it is stored.)

When it is ready, the *chef* will appear moist and wrinkled and will have developed a crust. Pull off a pinch of the crust; the interior of the *levain* should be inflated with tiny bubbles and it will have a sweet and pleasing aroma. It is now ready for its first refreshment, the addition of flour and water to provide more fresh food for the growing bacteria.

Throw away any hardened crust and mix the remaining piece, which will be the size of a hazelnut, with twice the original amount of flour and enough water to make a firm dough. (Proceed by making a well with the flour, diluting the *chef* with some water in the center of the well, and mixing as the *chef* was mixed and to the same consistency.) Set aside the dough as before.

After 1 or 2 days the *levain* (it is after the first refreshment that your piece of dough becomes a *levain,* natural leavening, or starter) will have a new, fresh, springy look. Remove any dried dough and remix as for the first refreshment, this time with 3 or 4 handfuls of flour (about 1 cup).

Cover the bowl with a damp cloth and leave it in a warm place to give the *levain* another 8- to 12-hour rising. Each baker's preference for and judgment about a young, strong, or old *levain* will determine the final rising time. (It is best when both young and strong.) When ready it will appear fully risen, and a small indentation made with a finger will not spring back. The resulting 1½ or 2 cups of *levain* are ready to be used in any 3- to 6-cup sourdough recipe. A small piece may be kept covered in the refrigerator for several days. Then it can be removed, refreshed as for the final refreshment above, set aside until fully risen, and then used in another batch of bread. Professionals may take the final 2 cups of *levain* and, by continuing to "build" or refresh it—doubling the amount of flour used each time (and always with enough water to make a firm dough)—obtain, after a few more days, a piece large enough to use in a larger batch of dough.

Recommended uses: pain blanc au levain (page 95), San Francisco sourdough (page 190), and *pane francese naturale* (page 190).

The *pain de campagne* and honey starters that follow are both made in exactly the same way as is the basic sourdough starter. In fact, any firm *levain* can be started in this way. Advanced bakers who want to experiment can add to the basic starter, with the water and flour, any of the following ingredients: one-quarter teaspoon of malt extract, a few crushed, unsulfured, unwashed organic grapes, a tablespoon of fermented porridge or grain, one teaspoon of goat's milk, or one teaspoon uncultured buttermilk. Each extra ingredient in the basic *chef* will give a unique flavor to the final bread.

All such starters should be mixed the same way, with Parmentier's precaution that the exact time of regeneration (the time the *levain* takes in order to be ready to go on to the next refreshment) is impossible to calculate; the baker must make his own judgment of the activity of the *levain*.

PAIN DE CAMPAGNE STARTER

½ cup whole wheat flour

1 tablespoon milk

⅛ teaspoon ground cumin

Enough water to make a firm but moist dough

Mix and handle as for the basic sourdough starter on page 30. After the third refreshment and when it has risen sufficiently, this *levain* will be ready to be made up into a dough.

Recommended uses: pain blanc au levain (page 95), San Francisco sourdough (page 190), and *pane francese naturale* (page 146).

HONEY STARTER

½ cup white flour

¼ teaspoon honey

Enough water to make a firm but moist dough.

Mix and handle as for the basic sourdough starter on page 31. This starter will become very active more quickly than other firm starters will because of the honey. If it becomes too wild with activity, add a pinch or two of salt in the first and second refreshments.

Recommended uses: pain de seigle de Costa (page 118) and *pain de régime au levain* (page 104).

MILK STARTER (MILK SOUR)

¾ cup flour

1 cup milk

In a medium-sized bowl mix the flour and milk together to make a batter like that used for pancakes. Cover the bowl with a damp cloth and leave it in a warm, draft-free place for 3 or 4 days. When the batter starts to bubble and give off a slightly sour aroma, it is ready for the first refreshment.

Mix the starter down with a wooden spoon. Add 1 cup of lukewarm water and mix it for several minutes until it becomes a very soupy batter. Gradually add ½ cup of flour, while mixing. Continue mixing for several minutes until it is entirely incorporated. Again, the starter will be a liquid batter like that used for pancakes. If it appears to be too thick, it may be thinned with a little water. Covered and stored as for the original batter, this first refreshment will take anywhere from 1 to 3 days to rise depending on the weather and the place of storage.

When the starter has nearly tripled in volume and started to fall, it is ready to be remixed for the second and final refreshment. It will appear bubbly, more liquid than when originally mixed, and will give off a slight alcoholic aroma. Refresh and let it rise in the same way as for the first refreshment, with 1 cup of water and ½ cup of flour.

After 1 day it will at least double, and perhaps triple, in volume, and at this stage 1 or 2 cups can be removed and used in a bread or pancake recipe. Whether some is used or not, the starter can now be placed in a Mason jar with an airtight lid and stored in the refrigerator.

The starter is best when used on a weekly basis. Each time you use 1 cup of starter, it must be replenished with 1 cup of water and ½ cup of flour. Add the water first and stir it to a liquid consistency. Then slowly add the flour and stir until it is fully incorporated. Leave the starter out of drafts in a warm spot for 3 to 4 hours, then place it back in the refrigerator for storage.

If the starter is not used for 10 to 14 days, it will still be good. But it will have to be refreshed in order to give it new life. Any excess liquid that comes to the top of the starter should always be poured off. Then simply refresh it with 1 cup of water and ½ cup of flour, as described above.

The starter can be kept indefinitely if it is used and refreshed frequently (every week or two). If it goes bad, you will know because the resulting bread will show any one or a combination of the faults of an excessively sour starter: the crust will not be a deep, rich color, the loaf will not achieve a good volume, the crumb will be tight grained, or the flavor will be too sour.

Instead of just using the milk sour straight from the jar, home bakers should mix a sponge or *levain* the night before. It may be mixed firm (like a bread dough) or wet (like a sponge); the firm starter will take longer to be ready than the wet sponge. This "refreshed" starter, allowed to rise for between 6 and 8 hours when firm and 3 or 4 hours when soupy, helps to give a lighter texture and a fuller color to homemade sourdough breads.

Recommended uses: Miners' Sourdough Pancakes (page 37), *pane integrale* (page 160), Berkeley Sourdough (page 195).

YEAST STARTER
COMPAGNON

This starter, which is left out to sour in a controlled way, is simply a recipe for *pain ordinaire* or straight French bread with less yeast. By putting it in the refrigerator after its first eight-hour rising, its acidity is held back, although it will still continue to rise. Too much acidity would limit its ability to raise the dough. If used correctly, this yeast-based starter can create some of the uneven texture and moist crumb of bread made with a natural sourdough starter.

> Approximately ¾ cup warm water
>
> 1 teaspoon active dried yeast
>
> 1 teaspoon salt
>
> 2 cups all-purpose or bread flour

Place the warm water in a medium-sized bowl and sprinkle the yeast on top. Incorporate the yeast with a wooden spoon and let it sit for 6 to 8 minutes. Sprinkle the salt into the flour. Then start adding the flour, a handful at a time, while mixing with a wooden spoon. When all but about ½ cup of the flour is added, scrape the bowl with a plastic dough scraper and pour the dough mixture out onto a worktable. Knead the dough, using the remaining flour to be sure the dough doesn't stick to the table or your hands. Knead for 8 to 10 minutes, until the ingredients are well incorporated and the dough is smooth and quite firm.

Let the dough rise in the bowl, covered with a damp towel, in a warm place for 8 or 10 hours.

Library Resource Center
Renton Technical College
Renton, WA 98056

Punch the dough down, round it up into a tight ball, and place it in an air-tight plastic container. Let it rise for between 24 and 36 hours in the refrigerator. It will then be ready to use.

This starter can be used in any bread recipe by replacing 1 cup of the flour in a 6-cup recipe with 1 cup of the *compagnon* starter. You must also reduce the yeast by about half the amount called for in the recipe.

To incorporate the starter, first chop it into little pieces. Proof the yeast as the recipe calls for and, in a large bowl, combine the yeast mixture, the rest of the water, and the chopped-up starter. Add a few handfuls of flour to the bowl and stir the mixture to dilute the starter, making a thick batter.

Proceed with your recipe. Let the dough rise, as called for in the recipe, for at least 45 minutes. Remember that the final rising will take at least twice (and perhaps three times) as long as normal because of the addition of the starter and the reduction of the yeast. The interesting texture of the finished bread will more than make up for the extra rising time.

Bake the loaf according to your recipe, but in an oven that is about 25 degrees hotter.

Recommended uses: pain blanc au levain (page 95), *compagnon au levain* (page 93), *pain de seigle—pâte fermentée* (page 113), *pane alle olive* (page 161), and *fougasse* (page 122).

LIEVITO NATURALE (BIGA)

This is the Italian version of the sponge method. Because this sponge takes between fifteen and twenty-four hours to rise, it must be mixed very firm and with a very small amount of yeast; some sponges made according to the American or French methods are mixed to a soupy consistency and will rise in four hours. This Italian sponge can give some of the uneven, moist texture of a pure sourdough method, but instead of a sour flavor the bread will have a yeasty, champagnelike taste.

> 1 cup warm water
>
> 1 scant teaspoon active dried yeast
>
> 4 cups all-purpose flour

Place the warm water in a medium-sized bowl and sprinkle the yeast on top. Incorporate the yeast with a wooden spoon and let it sit for 6 to 8 minutes. Start adding the flour, a handful at a time, while mixing with a wooden spoon. When all but about 1 cup of the flour is added, scrape the bowl with a plastic dough scraper and pour the dough mixture out onto a worktable. Knead the dough, using the flour that is left to be sure it doesn't stick to the table or your hands. The dough will already seem quite dry, but you should try to add as much of the flour as possible; the result will be much firmer than any bread dough.

Knead the dough for 8 to 10 minutes, until the ingredients are well incorporated, and it is smooth and almost stiff.

Let the dough rise in the bowl, covered with a damp towel, in a warm place for between 15 and 24 hours. The dough will rise and then fall back onto itself in a moist, sticky mass.

Recommended uses: pane toscano (page 141)—substitute three cups of this *biga* for the *bouillie* and adjust the quantities of water to make a medium wet dough, *pane francese* (page 145), *grissini* (page 156), *ciabatta* (page 151).

APPLE STARTER

A more complicated starter derived from a ferment of apples and sugar is used for a unique bread that contains pieces of sautéed apples right in the dough. I see no reason why the starter could not be used for other breads, perhaps a rye bread and breads containing raisins and nuts. It is mentioned here because, as complicated as it is, some ambitious bakers might like to try it. The recipe for *pain aux pommes* and the complete instructions for the starter may be found on page 124. Anyone so adventurous might also try using the starter to make *pain de seigle de Costa* (page 118).

OLD-DOUGH ADDITION (VIELLE PÂTE)

A shortcut that some French bakers resort to so that their *pain ordinaire* (or other breads) will have some of the flavor and texture of a sourdough bread is the addition of a small piece of dough held over from a previous baking and allowed to ferment for anywhere from four to twelve hours; the method is known as *pâte fermentée*. Most village bakers add however much old dough that would equal an amount of 10 percent of the amount of flour in the batch. Home bakers could use three quarters of a cup in a six-cup bread recipe.

The designation "old" means merely that the dough is left over from a previous batch, usually of *pain ordinaire*. In fact, because it is not excessively sour, it would in other circumstances be called a young dough.

The old dough can also be left overnight in the refrigerator so that it is prevented from overrising and exhausting its strength. This makes it very similar to the *compagnon* starter described earlier. The difference is that, in the *compagnon*, the strain is continued from day to day. In the old-dough method a piece of straight, yeasted dough is used to add extra push to a subsequent batch.

Detailed instructions for the use of old dough can be found in the *pain de son* recipe on page 101.

MINERS' SOURDOUGH PANCAKES

MAKES ABOUT 6 OR 8 PANCAKES

THE SPONGE

> 1 cup milk starter (page 33)
>
> ½ cup milk
>
> ½ cup all-purpose flour

THE BATTER

> All of the sponge from the previous step
>
> 3 tablespoons vegetable oil
>
> 2 tablespoons sugar
>
> 1 egg
>
> ½ teaspoon salt
>
> ½ teaspoon baking soda (optional)

TO MAKE THE SPONGE, mix the starter, milk, and flour together in a bowl and let the sponge sit, out of the refrigerator, for 8 hours or overnight.

TO MAKE THE BATTER, mix down the sponge in the bowl. Add the oil, sugar, egg, and salt and beat well.

Preheat a griddle or skillet and grease it lightly. Just before putting the pancakes on the griddle mix the baking soda, if you are using it, with a little water and stir that mixture into the batter.

MOTHER BUNN'S YUM-YUM SOURDOUGH *CRÊPES*

MAKES BETWEEN 12 AND 15 FIVE-INCH *CRÊPES* OR 8 TO 10 WAFFLES

> 4 cups milk starter (page 33)
>
> 5 eggs
>
> 1½ tablespoons sugar
>
> 1 teaspoon baking soda
>
> 1 teaspoon salt
>
> About ½ cup buttermilk

Combine all the ingredients except the buttermilk and beat well. Add enough buttermilk to thin the batter to a consistency suitable for *crêpes* (similar to that of heavy cream).

This recipe makes a good batter for waffles if you omit the buttermilk and, instead, add a couple of tablespoons of vegetable oil.

CHAPTER 3

Technique and Procedure

THE VILLAGE BAKER MAY USE mixers, molders, and professional ovens but, like the home baker, must still use his hands and his mind to make the bread. He guards the fermentation of the dough by guiding it carefully through the stages of its development, just as home bakers do in their own kitchens. Both share the artisan's approach to bread (what the French would call *la fabrication artisanale,* best translated as the craftsman's approach): They use their minds to visualize the processes of baking and to measure the ingredients, their eyes to observe the activity of the dough, and their hands to shape the dough into bread.

The techniques of handwork for the home baker are simply part of the craft of bread baking that was originally developed in the home. The most important part of handwork for bakers is the use of the fingers and the heel of the hand: the fingers to touch and test the dough, to grab it, to pick it up, and to control it while rounding it on the bench; the heel of the hand to seal the dough after it has been rolled up into a loaf. Techniques of handwork for the village baker are much the same. What the home baker will find, however, is that his handwork must be altered to make up for the lack of development in a dough that has been mixed by hand rather than by machine. Thus handwork becomes even more important for the home baker. No matter where it is made a loaf of bread is, however, the result of a process that entails a number of clearly definable procedures. In describing these procedures, I will also be describing the work of the generic French village baker. Because the differences between home baking and commercial baking are generally those of technique (volume aside), I shall discuss them in a section at the end of the chapter.

·❖·❖·❖·❖·❖·❖·❖· Hand Kneading or Mixing ·❖·❖·❖·❖·❖·❖·❖·

In bread making, where technique counts for so much, even the elementary step of combining the basic ingredients may be taken in different ways. At home, because a baker is actually kneading the bread on a worktable, the activity is referred to as kneading; in the village bakery, because most bakers use mixers, they usually refer to the process as mixing, even though the mixing arm is in fact kneading the dough. Furthermore, professional bakers—because they use mixers to produce large batches—rarely hand mix any bread dough. The exceptions might be a small batch of experimental or specialty bread or a small batch of starter or *levain*.

Nevertheless, the two main methods of hand kneading—the fountain method and the bowl method—are techniques that both the home baker and the village baker should have in their repertoire.

The Fountain Method
La fontaine

For the fountain (or well) method, the flour is placed in a mound in the middle of a worktable, and a well to contain the mixing liquid is made in the middle

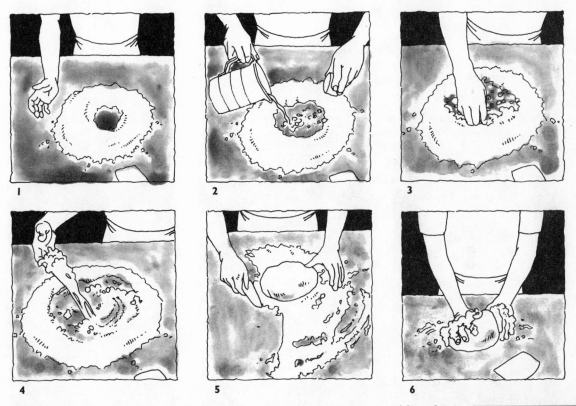

of the flour. If a starter is used it is broken up, placed into the middle of the fountain, diluted with a little of the water, then mixed with a little of the surrounding flour to make a paste. If yeast is used, the yeast and water mixture is first placed in the middle of the fountain and the rest of the water added.

Gradually the baker, using two or three fingers, swirls the liquid around the perimeter of the fountain, picking up flour to make a thick paste. At this point, while there is still about half of the flour left around the edges of the fountain, the baker uses sweeping motions of the hand to whip up the dough. Keeping one hand clean helps the baker to keep the operation tidy and also helps in containing the walls of the fountain.

The rapid motion of whipping the dough develops the gluten. The more the dough is whipped at this stage, the better the gluten will be developed and the dough will need less actual kneading when the rest of the flour is incorporated.

After the mixture has been developed in this stage, it becomes so elastic that it can be stretched like taffy from the middle of the fountain. Then more of the flour can be slowly brought in until an actual bread dough is attained.

The hands and bench are then cleaned with a plastic dough scraper or the back of the blade of a small knife and a little of the remaining flour. Finally, the dough can be kneaded on the worktable in the traditional manner of turning, folding, and pushing with the heel of the hand.

The Bowl Method

I developed this method myself as an alternative to the fountain method. It achieves the same results and is much easier and tidier for beginning bakers.

When the bowl method is used, the flour is gradually added to the liquid in a medium-sized bowl. If a starter is used, it is diluted in some of the water, then the rest of the water is added to the bowl. The baker starts adding flour to the liquid, a handful at a time, while mixing with a curved plastic dough scraper.

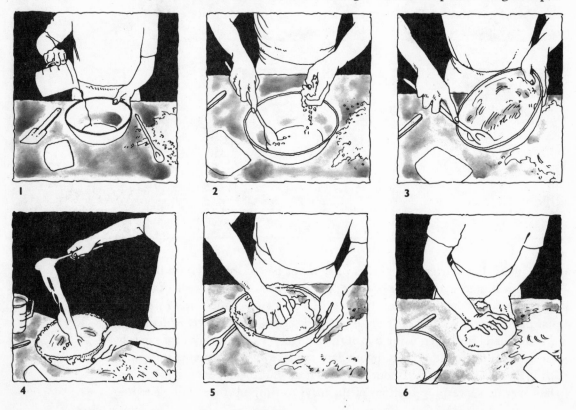

(A wooden spoon can be used, but the large surface of the dough scraper helps to control a larger amount of the dough, especially in the batter stage.)

When half of the flour has been added, the baker can start using wide, sweeping motions of the arm to whip the dough (imagine you are pulling taffy). When the batterlike dough is picked up with the dough scraper and beaten in a circular motion, back onto itself, the gluten in the flour is developed. (Keep one hand free of dough.)

After about ten minutes of mixing, the batterlike dough will become noticeably elastic and the dough strands that are pulled out of the bowl will want to spring back like taffy. It is hard to overdo this action in hand mixing. Usually the baker's arm will become tired before the dough becomes overmixed.

After the dough has been developed in the batter stage, more flour can be added gradually until all but about a cup is incorporated. Use this remaining flour to coat the worktable and to finish off the kneading.

The dough is scraped from the bowl and onto the worktable. The hands and bowl are then cleaned with the plastic dough scraper and some of the remaining flour and the dough is kneaded on the worktable in the traditional manner.

Parmentier described the fountain method over two hundred years ago so we know it has probably been around for a long, long time. When village bakers mixed bread by hand in a rectangular wooden trough they used to add the flour first. Then they would make a fountain in the flour, at one end of the mixing trough, in which to pour some of the mixing water and to dilute their *levain* (natural wild yeast). The rest of the water was added, and the baker started the laborious practice of incorporating the flour and water, then hand kneading it. (Much of the work was done with the legs, back and, finally, by the arms, in lifting out masses of dough and throwing it back onto the dough still left in the trough.) Hand kneading in the mixing trough was backbreaking work but, thanks to the mechanical mixer, no village baker needs to do it today.

The rest of the village baker's task—hand scaling (weighing each piece of dough), rounding pieces into *boules* (round balls) or squaring them into logs in order to undergo another rising, hand shaping, and loading the loaves into the oven—all these still survive and are practiced today.

Dough Consistency

French bakers recognize three basic consistencies of dough: firm, moist, and a combination of the two, which is a crossbreed and therefore called *bâtarde* in French.

FIRM DOUGH (LA PÂTE FERME)

The firm dough is rarely used, except for specialty doughs such as *le pain Brié,* or for large loaves such as crowns and some regional, twisted loaves. (In Italy a firm dough is used for sculpture and for *pane duro.*) A firm dough consists of between 52 percent and 55 percent water, that is, about two cups of water to every six cups of flour. Some home bakers make the mistake of mixing their doughs too firm; this gives good shape and expansion to the loaf, but a tight, dry texture.

REGULAR DOUGH (LA PÂTE BÂTARDE)

This dough is used for most breads. It is easily handled without an excess of flour. A regular dough consists of between 60 and 62 percent water, that is, about two and one-half cups of water to every six cups of flour.

MOIST DOUGH (LA PÂTE DOUCE)

It is used particularly for bread sculpture and those breads that need considerable development and lightness. Such dough needs strong flour and active mixing. Difficult to work, it requires the use of flour when being handled. A moist dough consists of about 65 percent water, that is, about two and three-quarters cups of water to every six cups of flour.

VERY WET DOUGH (LA PÂTE TRÈS MOLLE)

French bakers rarely use more than 65 percent water. But some Italian bakers use a very wet dough to obtain bread with a moist, irregular texture; such a loaf must be baked thoroughly so that the crust becomes crisp and appealing instead of rubbery and insipid. A very wet dough consists of about 70 percent water, that is, about three cups of water to every six cups of flour.

❖❖❖❖❖❖❖❖❖❖❖❖❖❖❖❖❖❖ *The Basic Steps* ❖❖❖❖❖❖❖❖❖❖❖❖❖❖❖❖❖❖

The progression of steps in the methods used by the village baker—whether in France, Germany, Italy, or America—can best be seen by looking at the French village baker's classified list of procedures. When making French bread, every village baker in France and most in Europe and America use some aspect of the following stages of the basic method:

Le pétrissage: mixing the ingredients

Le pointage: first rising

Donner un tour: punching down or knocking back

Le pesage: scaling the loaves

La détente: intermediate proofing

Le façonnage: shaping the loaves

L'apprêt: final proofing

Le coup de lame: slashing the loaves

La cuisson: baking the loaves

Most home bakers will also follow those same procedures, with the possible exception of scaling the loaves (the weight of bread sold to the public has long been rigorously regulated). The principal difference is that the home baker will be doing more of the work by hand.

Mixing or Kneading
Le pétrissage

By turning, folding, stretching, and kneading the dough in a mechanical mixer, the village baker mixes the four basic ingredients and turns them into bread dough. (The term "mixing" is used by most village bakers in America to describe the combined processes of placing the ingredients in the mixer, incorporating them, and kneading the dough.) The main aim of mixing is to develop the gluten in the flour to create an elastic network that will trap the carbonic gases created by the yeast. Mixing starts the process of bread baking by starting the fermentation. The French village baker knows—by craft and by experience—that the fermentation, and the resulting bread, will be most affected by the development of the dough in the mixing stage. The baker therefore tries to attain certain qualities that will help him achieve a well-developed dough: extensibility (the dough's ability to be extended in a fine network of gluten), elasticity (the dough's ability to spring back when stretched), plasticity (its ability to be molded and hold its shape), and tolerance (its capacity to endure slight faults such as overmixing, rough handling, or too long a final proofing).

In the trade there are three basic methods of mixing bread dough. One grew out of hand mixing and the others grew out of mechanical mixing.

THE CLASSIC METHOD (*LA MÉTHODE CLASSIQUE*)

This is an old method that is rarely used in France or America today. The flour, water, salt, and leavening (whether a starter or yeast) are mixed together by hand or with a mechanical mixer on low (first) speed; this takes about ten minutes. Traditionally, there was a *repos,* or pause, of two or three minutes during the course of the mixing—not included in the total time—that helped to hydrate the dough and relax the gluten in the flour. The delicate mixing of the classic method leads to a very slow, inactive, but natural fermentation and can never produce a highly extensible, fast-acting bread dough, so the rising time must be prolonged. A dough mixed by the classic method must be given several long risings of the whole dough and be "knocked back" repeatedly. The technique originated in the days when breads were made only by hand and it can be used today to give a more rustic, creamy texture to the crumb.

MODERN, ACCENTUATED MIXING (*LE PÉTRISSAGE ACCENTUÉ*)

This method, introduced in France in the late 1950s, calls for a wetter dough to be mixed at twice the speed (eighty revolutions of the dough arm per minute as compared with forty revolutions for the classic method) and for a longer time. This creates a very homogeneous dough. To make up for the extra heat generated by the mixer, the mixing water must be very cold. High-speed mixing creates a more active fermentation because the dough is very highly developed, allowing it to entrap the gas engendered by the reaction of the yeast. Because the fermentation is so active, bread may be made in four or five hours instead of the six or eight hours necessary in the classical method. The resulting bread has a greater volume, a more refined and crackling crust, and a whiter crumb. But it is less flavorful and much less substantial.

It is almost impossible to duplicate the accentuated mixing method at home, but bread made in a food processor or a home mixer will exhibit some of the qualities typical of the method. For a recipe that gives an approximation, see page 71.

IMPROVED, OR AMELIORATED, MIXING (LE PÉTRISSAGE AMELIORÉ)

Fortunately for the American village baker there is a compromise between these two extremes, a method that appeared around 1970 in France. The dough is mixed initially for three minutes on the first speed to incorporate the ingredients, then for ten or twelve minutes on the second speed. I have found that this is the best method to use with strong American flours; depending on the mixer, an eight- or ten-minute mix on second speed is adequate. The amount of ascorbic acid necessary is 1 to 2 grams per quintal of flour (1 quintal equals 100 kilos) which is about ⅛ to ¼ teaspoon per 100 pounds of flour. The first rising is between 1 and 1½ hours and the makeup is around 1½ hours. The bread has less volume than do loaves made by the accentuated mixing technique, but it tastes better and stays fresh for a few hours longer.

These three methods shed light on the relationship between home baking and commercial baking: Bread that is mixed by hand may be made according to the rules and technical demands of the classic method; commercial production, in which the dough is mixed mechanically is best served by the accentuated and ameliorated techniques.

The First Rising
Le pointage

The time between the mixing of the dough and the time it is made into loaves is called *le pointage*. In the classic method the first rising takes between two and four hours, during which the dough may be punched down and allowed to rise again. In the modern method the first rising may be as short as fifteen minutes, but most home methods (and many village bakers' methods) call for one hour. The baker is, however, always the final judge and bases his decisions on observation of the dough's activity, usually making the test with a touch of the finger. If the dough springs back quickly it probably needs more time; if it does not, and the indentation made with the finger remains, the dough is ready to be taken on to the next stage.

Very often the baker will shorten or lengthen the duration of the first rising to fit in with his daily schedule. The overall time of fermentation (from the end of mixing to the time the loaves are put into the oven) should be maintained according to the method. Thus, whenever the *pointage* is adjusted, the baker must also adjust the other rising times.

Punching Down or Knocking Back
Donner un tour

I once asked a Parisian baker why certain breads need to be punched down or "knocked back" during *le pointage*. He said: *"Pour donner la force"* (to give it the force), referring to an actual and metaphysical observation of the activity of the fermentation. An excess of force increases the elastic properties of the dough, making it less easily worked. But some force is necessary. It seems that certain doughs need to be punched down to stimulate their activity. The punchings or turns start the dough rising anew, giving it a fresh, stronger boost or push each time. (This step is sometimes referred to as *le rabat,* the French expression for the activity of beating the bushes to scare out game.)

The classic knocking back procedure was used in homes and in the first village bakeries when large batches of dough were mixed by hand. After the first rising, the dough was handled as follows: The baker, starting at one end of his wooden dough trough, would cut off eight- to ten-pound pieces of dough, gently fold them over by hand, and stack them to one side of the trough. The process helps to push air out of the dough and gives a new boost to the natural, but slow fermentation. When mechanical mixers came into use, the knocking back was accomplished by one or two slow turns of the mechanical mixing arm, by punching the dough with the fists, or by turning the whole batch over in its resting bin.

For the home baker the method for knocking back is simple. After a dough has risen in bulk for the first time, whether it has been in a bowl or on a table, simply punch the dough with the fists several times to flatten it. Then tuck the edges of the dough mass back onto the center, making sure there are no air pockets left in the dough. Turn the dough over, cover it once more, and let it rise again. The second rising usually will take a little more than half the time of the first rising.

Scaling
Le pesage

Cutting the dough into pieces of a precise weight is done either by hand with a metal dough scraper or *pâte coup* or by a mechanical dough divider. The purpose of *le pesage* is to make loaves of a uniform size and weight.

Because they do not punish the dough, the best mechanical dividers (*divi-seuses*) are hydraulic rather than working like pistons. Even so, after mechanical dividing, the dough—having been compressed and tightened—must rest before being shaped.

When scaled by hand, the dough is put on the bench in an oblong mass. Then a strip of dough between four and six inches wide is cut off the long dough mass. A piece of dough, the size of which depends on the size of the final loaf,

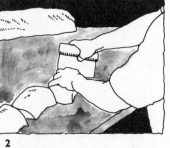

1   2   3

loaf, is cut off and placed on a balance scale. Little pieces of dough can be added or taken away and, when the scale goes just over the balance point, the dough is put on the bench or on floured boards to rest.

Bread loses moisture in the oven, so the weight of each loaf must be augmented by between 10 and 15 percent in the scaling stage. For example, a ten-ounce *baguette* (300 grams) must be scaled at twelve ounces; a one-pound loaf scaled at one pound, three ounces, and so forth.

When a small batch of bread dough (enough to make between twelve and forty-eight loaves) is hand scaled by one baker, the loaves may be laid on the bench or on flour-dusted wooden boards and then immediately shaped by hand or machine. But when a large batch (enough to make between ninety-six and 120 loaves) is hand scaled by one person (a process that might take between forty-five minutes and an hour), each loaf should be either rounded up or hand squared to prevent it from overrising at this stage.

Home bakers rarely need to think about scaling because most recipes call for dividing the dough into a certain number of pieces and this will determine the size of the loaves or rolls. Even so, if needed, small pieces of dough (for rolls, for example) may be weighed individually or may be gauged by eye or weighed in the hand.

Hand Squaring
La tourne

Scaled dough pieces are hand rounded for the intermediate proofing when the loaves are to be round. The pieces are usually squared for the intermediate proofing if they are eventually to be made up into oblong or *baguette* shapes, or if they will be passed through a mechanical molder.

To hand square a loaf so that it can undergo an intermediate proofing, the dough is first flattened with both hands to dispel all the air. The bottom half of the flat disc of dough is then folded over onto the top half to form a half moon, with the flat side toward you. The sides of this half-moon-shaped piece are folded in (about an inch on either side) toward the center and then flattened with the palms. Finally the rounded top piece is folded down half way into the dough piece and sealed with quick but delicate blows of the heel of the hand.

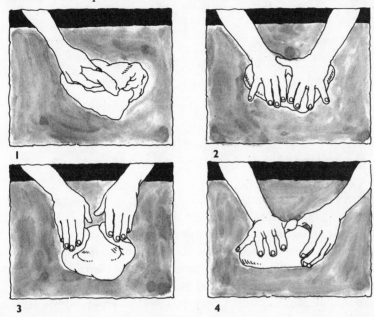

This gives a neat little square package that, when placed seam-side down on a floured board or on the workbench, can undergo another rising—preventing overrising at this stage of the fermentation because all the air has been pushed out of the dough. This gives each piece of dough another phase of development before it is shaped into a loaf. The extra fermentation not only develops the flavor in the final loaf, but also helps to produce a more appealing texture.

Rounding
La tourne en boule

All good, well-developed bread doughs have at least one thing in common. They contain enough water so that, unless they are dusted lightly with flour when being handled, the dough will stick to the hands, the body, the mixing bowl, and the workbench. This stickiness is used in rounding dough and in shaping loaves. The tendency of the bread to stick—especially to the bench—is what aids the baker in rounding bread into a ball. Only the hands or the top of the piece of dough are lightly floured. As a result of friction and the moisture in the dough, a bond forms between the bench and the underside of the dough both of which are unfloured.

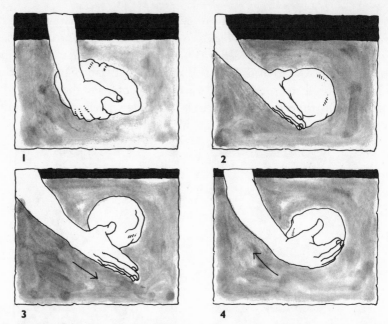

1   2

3   4

The piece of dough, whether it be a roll, a loaf, or a larger mass, is dragged along the worktable so that the upper part of the piece tightens as it is being pushed and the resistance of the dough underneath, which is reacting to the push above, will cause the dough to round itself into a tight ball.

I once saw a sourdough baker in Santa Barbara perform, in a four-step process, what I feel is the definitive exhibition of one-handed rounding. First an irregular piece of dough weighing one pound is taken up with the right hand and tucked under two or three times with a twisting of the hand and a little resistance from the worktable. The hand is then placed flat out, like a proffered handshake, on the right side of the piece of dough, pressure being applied to both the side of the dough with the palm and to the bench with the bottom (pinkie side) of the hand. The dough is pushed away from the body and enough tension built up to cause the dough to curl under itself and come together. By this time the dough and hand are out at arm's length on the bench. The hand is then cupped behind the ball of dough. With the thumb up and the pinkie part of the hand pushed into the worktable, the dough is dragged back with enough tension to cause its outer skin to shape itself into a tight, smooth, round ball.

Intermediate Proofing
La détente

Loaves that have been scaled in a hydraulic divider, or hand rounded, or squared after scaling become tight and unworkable because the gas has been flattened out of them. So they must relax for a period that the French *boulanger* calls *la détente* (literally, "the relaxing of tension"). Depending on the method used, *la détente* lasts between fifteen minutes and one hour. The relaxing loaves are placed in an airtight cabinet (sometimes with a little steam) or covered with plastic wrap or a large piece of canvas to prevent them from drying out and forming a crust. They are relaxed enough when they can be shaped without tearing.

Shaping the Loaves
Le façonnage

Before the loaves are shaped into their final forms, each piece of dough must be flattened in order to dispel any gas that might cause an irregular texture or unwanted air pockets. This knocking back once again starts the fermentation at a new stage.

Rounding a roll

1

2

Shaping a roll

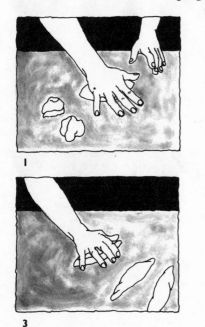

1

3

2

4

TECHNIQUE AND PROCEDURE

49

Shaping a loaf

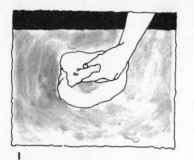

1

2

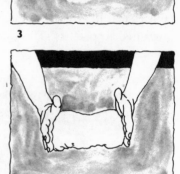

3

4

5

6

Shaping a *baguette*

1

2

3

4

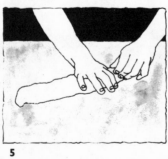

5

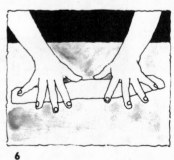

6

Pain aux pommes

Final Proofing
L'apprêt

American bakers sometimes use the term "makeup" to denote the actual shaping of the loaves. But to the French *boulanger,* the term *l'apprêt* (which may also be translated as "preparation" or "makeup"), refers to the period of fermentation that extends from the *façonnage* or shaping to the time when the loaves are loaded into the oven. Calvel calls the makeup "the period of waiting that allows the fermentation to produce a volume of carbonic gas appropriate to a good push of gas in the beginning of baking and finally a well-developed bread" (page 55).

The most ancient methods for proofing French bread are still practiced in village bakeries today. The tradition survives from the time when all breads were sourdough, when they were all made of extremely wet doughs that would not hold their shape without some sort of support, and when they were all baked, not on trays, but on the floor of a brick oven. The *banneton* and the *couche* help to hold the loaves during the long final proofing that is necessary for a sourdough

bread. The *banneton* is a basket lined with Belgian linen, a high-quality artist's canvas that will withstand everyday usage. A wet loaf of rounded dough is placed in each basket. The baskets are stacked, often on a dolly with wheels to make it easier for the baker to move the loaves away from or toward the heat of the oven to control the speed of the fermentation. At home bakers can use a regular basket that measures around eight or nine inches in diameter and about four inches high, place a white dish towel in the basket, and dust it lightly with flour.

The *couche* is a sheet of Belgian linen (ordinary canvas duck or a plain dish towel will work at home) about one meter wide. The proofing *baguettes* are laid on the *couche,* separated from one another by an upward loop of the canvas between each loaf.

Slashing the Loaf
Le coup de lame

The artistic signature of each baker is the *coup de lame,* made just before the loaf is placed in the oven. To give an attractive appearance each loaf is cut so that it has a planned and predictable spot at which to burst. *Le coup de lame* creates what the French call *la grigne,* a network of torn bread fibers visible where the

La grigne

loaf breaks. *La grigne* is practical as well as aesthetic. It is much better for the structure of the crumb for the loaf to burst on top rather than on the bottom or on the side.

For a *baguette* the two rules about the *coup de lame* concern direction and angle: The cuts should be straight and overlapping (parallel with the length of the loaf), with the blade held at a very shallow angle from the horizontal so that it cuts under the surface of the loaf rather than down into it. The straight, overlapping cuts on top allow the loaf to open longer and wider; the angular cuts made into the loaf allow the heat and moisture of the oven to penetrate the loaf more easily.

For a *baguette,* cut thus:

right—   wrong—

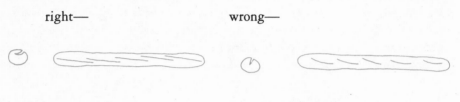

For an oval loaf, thus: For a round loaf, thus:

Baking the Loaf
La cuisson

Because bacteria grow quickly when exposed to heat and humidity, the first moments in the oven give the dough an accelerated push in volume. The push lasts for the first five to seven minutes in bread containing commercial yeast and the first ten to twelve minutes in a natural sourdough bread. Eventually the yeast is destroyed by the heat.

For centuries bread was baked on the floor of an oven lined with bricks. That is still the best way to achieve a superior loaf. American bakers say that loaves baked on the floor of an oven, rather than on trays, have "bloom"—a full-bodied appearance that can only be achieved when the heat rises through the loaf from the bottom up. (The word "bloom" is also used by some bakers to denote a full, rich color.)

Modern convection ovens, as time- and energy-efficient as they may be, seem to attack the loaf with heat from all sides. But they have their place. Modern rotary rack ovens, with perforated trays and low-pressure steam (necessary in the first few minutes of the bake-off for a shining, crackling crust), can do a remarkable job for some breads. The modern feeling in America as well as in France seems to be that it is permissible to bake *baguettes, pain fantaisie,* and enriched pan breads in a convection oven on trays. But the rustic hearth breads—

especially sourdough—are best baked right on a deck-oven floor. A deck oven is similar to a pizza oven in that the floor is lined with bricks; it can be fired by gas, oil, or electricity.

Home bakers would do best to use a gas-fired home oven for breads because the heat is more controllable. Whether you have an electric or gas oven, it would be useful to place an oven thermometer in the oven both before and during baking. This makes it easier to observe any variations in temperature and make whatever adjustments necessary.

As far as judging when a bread is ready to be baked, as always, experience helps. A loaf put into the oven a few minutes before it is "ready" (that is, when it still springs back quickly at the touch of a finger) will have an extra bloom (but if put in the oven too early it might explode in an irregular fashion). A loaf put in the oven a few minutes after it is ready will sag and lack a full, deep color. Also, by an instinct so long-followed that it has become a rule, the baker will bake a "young" loaf in a cooler oven to prevent any irregular bursting and an "old" loaf in a hotter oven to give it some extra push.

BAKING STONES

In some recipes, pizza or bread is baked on a stone in the oven. To use a baking stone, place it on a wire shelf in the oven before preheating it. Loaves that are to be baked on a stone are usually given their final proofing in *bannetons* or in *couches*. When such loaves are ready, sprinkle a little cornmeal or flour on a rimless cookie sheet and turn each loaf onto it by inverting the basket. The loaves in *couches* are either lifted gently or rolled out onto the cookie sheet. The loaf can then be slid right onto the baking stone to bake. If you don't have a stone you can always use a metal tray that has been greased lightly or one that has been lined with parchment paper.

·············· *Tips on Technique for Home Bakers* ··············

The examples given in the book attempt to show how recipes that contain similar proportions of the basic ingredients can—if various subtle techniques, various types of flours, and different types of natural and yeasted starters, old dough, and sponges are used—yield vastly different tastes and textures in the final loaf. Eventually, each baker will arrive at a variation that suits his or her fancy as well as timetable. It is advisable to try the simple, yeasted variations first (indicated by the package of yeast symbol) and then to go on to the sponge, old dough, and sourdough variations later. In using one recipe several times, the baker will begin to produce bread that has not only the characteristics of the type, but also the characteristics of the baker's own style. I would caution that, before you consider altering a specific recipe, you become familiar with it in its

All of the tips listed on the following page can help home bakers attain bread with a better texture.

original form. That familiarity will give you much more control over the process, permit you to make quite subtle changes, and build the confidence to go on to more complicated methods.

Although I advise bakers to follow recipes as they are given, I have to admit that many of the directions are approximate. Water and proofing temperatures are given merely as guides, as are rising times. Traditionally, home bakers have used a sense of feel and their experience rather than accurate measures, especially of time and temperature. The directions given in the recipes are accurate, but only at normal ambient temperatures (perhaps "ideal" would be a better description: daytime temperatures of between 70°F and 75°F). French bread, for instance, is best developed when the dough itself is at 75°F. Use cooler water on very hot days and warm water on cold days. Rising times are affected by so many variables: ambient temperature, humidity, draughts, moisture of the dough, temperature of the dough, development of the gluten and, who knows, perhaps the phases of the moon. Herein lies the creativity of each baker, who is left to test the dough and judge its readiness at each stage of its development. A delicate touch of the finger will usually show how the dough is doing: In the early stages of a rising, the dough will spring back immediately; it springs back much more slowly toward the end of a particular stage of rising. The baker can also judge the bread simply by its appearance, by how much and how fast its volume has increased.

When home formulas are used, longer proof times, several punchings back of the dough, and intermediate proofing stages are often necessary to make up for lack of force that would have been generated by mechanical mixing. At home, the yeast needs as much encouragement as it can get. The culture of the starter, the development of the gluten, the entire activity of the fermentation must be stimulated, principally because dough that has been mixed by hand in small quantities is never afforded the full development that would create a full, extensible dough. In commercial production, with its mechanical mixing, over-mixing is quite possible. It would be rare to overmix a dough by hand.

One way in which to prolong the rising times is to work with a cooler dough—one made with cooler water to begin with—and then set it to rise in a fairly cool place.

Among the more noticeable differences between commercial and homemade bread is that of texture. Texture is affected by the development of the gluten, the amount of water in the dough, the amount of yeast or type of starter used, and the length of time it is allowed to spend proofing. To get something more interesting than the tight grain and small bubbles usually obtained at home in a bread made with yeasted dough, one can make a number of adaptations.

- Develop the gluten as much as you can at the beginning in the batter stage of mixing the dough. After the proofed yeast and water mixture has been put in a bowl, start adding the flour a handful at a time, mixing each addition with a wooden spoon. As more and more flour is added, the mixture will become a thick batter that can be whipped in wide, sweeping motions. The mixture can be beaten together until the gluten almost breaks down, causing irregular bubbles to appear in the dough.

- Use less yeast than is called for in the recipe (try half the amount) or use a starter and very little yeast. The dough will then take longer to rise (perhaps twice the time in all stages) and the texture of the bread improved.

- Try using a flourless sponge (see page 26). The yeast in a recipe is mixed with a little bit of water and allowed to rise for several hours or overnight before the other ingredients are added. The result is a moist, chewy texture.

- After a bread dough is mixed and allowed to rise for one hour, it can be covered and placed in the refrigerator to rise overnight. The next day allow the dough to rise for two or three hours at room temperature. Then shape the loaf, set it to rise, and bake it as usual. The crumb will have more of a sourdough texture and less of a yeasty flavor than a normal yeasted bread.

- When first mixing the ingredients, use the quantity of water called for in the recipe. Then, before you have added the last cup of flour, flatten the dough on the worktable and make indentations in it with your fingertips. Into these holes pour an additional two or three tablespoons of water. Then fold the dough up and knead it on the table. Eventually you'll be able to work the dough with wide, stretching motions of one hand as if you were pulling taffy. After four or five minutes the dough will become quite elastic and surprisingly malleable. Use a little of the remaining flour to clean your hands and the work surface and then knead the dough for a few more minutes until it is smooth and satiny. This technique, described by French bakers as *le bassinage,* gives you a wetter dough; it will be easier to work because it has been mixed firm rather than very wet from the beginning, as would happen if all the water and the extra dry ingredients were to be incorporated at once. An example of this technique has been included in the recipe for *fougasse* on page 122.

Wet doughs are more easily handled in commercial production but, because they produce a superior loaf, many of the recipes in this book call for doughs mixed much wetter than those most home bakers are used to. The wetness helps to give a moist, voluptuous crumb to many of the loaves.

Wet doughs can be mixed according to either the bowl or the fountain method (described on pages 39–41). There are two main things to remember about them. First, try to develop the gluten when the dough is in the pasty, batter state and you won't have to knead it as much later. Second, when all of the ingredients have been combined, save a handful or two of flour on the work-table and knead the dough lightly, just enough to coat it with the flour. This forms a dry, safe film around the dough so it can be more easily handled.

The easiest way to mix a wet dough is with a food processor. The methods for *pain ordinaire* (accentuated mixing) on page 71 and *pane francese* on page 145 are good examples.

◇◇◇◇◇◇◇◇◇◇◇◇◇◇◇◇◇◇◇◇ The Bread Machine ◇◇◇◇◇◇◇◇◇◇◇◇◇◇◇◇◇◇◇◇

Many of the simple recipes in this book can be made, with remarkable results, in a bread machine. It is true that the best breads often take the personal care and observation of the baker, along with specialized forming and baking techniques. Nevertheless, any tool or piece of equipment that can help people make bread at home is a wonderful addition to our daily lives. (That is why I often use the food processor for some of my bread recipes that contain extra water.)

Most people who have used bread machines are familiar with all the suggested procedures of mixing bread in them. So all one need do is to follow the techniques prescribed for your particular bread machine when adapting any of the three-cup recipes found in this book. (Six-cup recipes may be cut in half.) If you want to use a soupy starter (sponge), just pour it in with your flour mixture. If you want to use a piece of old dough or a firm starter, just make sure that it is chopped up well before adding it to the machine. If you are mixing one of the wetter breads, such as *stirato* or *francese con biga*, reduce the amount of water used—at least for the first few times. Later you can try to make a wetter dough.

You will have to experiment with rising times. Of course, you can always pull a bread dough out of the machine after mixing it and then follow the rising times and shaping instructions given in the particular recipe.

You may not be able to achieve some of the subtle variations of crust and texture that are possible when the recipes are made by hand. But you might come up with some other qualities of taste and texture and, in so doing, create your own unique family bread. After all, that is what home and regional bread baking is all about.

EQUIPMENT FOR THE HOME BAKER

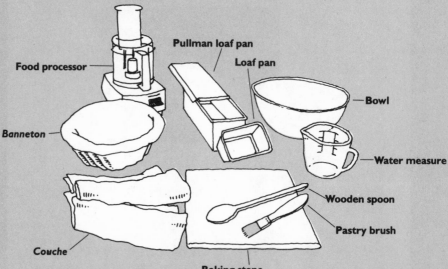

Food processor

Pullman loaf pan

Loaf pan

Bowl

Banneton

Water measure

Wooden spoon

Pastry brush

Couche

Baking stone

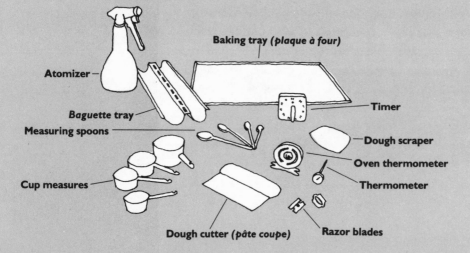

Atomizer

Baking tray (*plaque à four*)

Timer

Baguette tray

Measuring spoons

Dough scraper

Oven thermometer

Thermometer

Cup measures

Dough cutter (*pâte coupe*)

Razor blades

PART II

Recipes for the Home Baker

With these recipes from France, Italy, Germany, and America, I attempt to show how the knowledge of one simple recipe format—a three- or six-cup method for *pain ordinaire*—can be manipulated by method, technique, and ingredient to yield an infinite variety of breads. Although most of the recipes yield *baguette*, *boule*, or *bâtard* shapes, they can be made into any shape.

Many of the world's regional breads come in shapes that are indigenous to that region and therefore help to define a specific type of bread. I see no reason that the American home baker cannot, by using the glossary of shapes and decorations on page 284, form any of the recipes as he or she desires.

CHAPTER 4

The Breads of France

ALL OVER FRANCE THE REGIONAL diversity of bread is the result of different types of flour, different consistencies of dough (from soft to stiff), different techniques used in proofing, and different shapes and sizes. French village bakers show us what is possible with the ancient recipe for bread, four ingredients, and numerous variations of rising techniques. Each regional bread has its own texture, flavor, and appearance.

All the regional breads of France have developed organically out of the locally grown raw ingredients. Where rye *(seigle)* is grown, for example, we should not be too surprised to see rye bread as the predominant loaf. This is why we find rye breads in the north of France and in Germany where the durable grain can endure the harsh, damp climate.

In rural areas of the south, such as the Cantal mountains of the Massif Central, refined white flours from the mills of Lyons or Paris have been at a premium for hundreds of years. So local bakers use *farine bise,* the darker, stone-ground wheat flours. These coarse, unrefined flours produce rustic country loaves that complement the earthy Cantal cheese, peasant *charcuterie,* and savory stews that are found on local tables.

Some of the flavors and textures that are characteristic of Provence are captured in the breads there because the local honey is used as a catalyst in starting *levains.* Honey made by bees that feed on lavender and other native herbs adds to the dough a distinctive flavor that is augmented by the regional strains of sourdough culture that are pulled out of the air. That is why a sourdough bread from Provence will taste very different from one made in, say, the Jura.

Pain ordinaire is what the French call French bread. It is a simple bread with a short shelf life. *Pain sur poolish* and *pain au levain* are breads with greater character, made according to more complicated methods; their process is what gives them a hearty character. *Pain de seigle* (rye), *pain méteil* (half rye, half wheat), *pain de mie* and *pain au lait* (made with milk and butter), and *brioche* (made with eggs and butter) are all breads enriched by other ingredients and therefore not classifiable as *pain ordinaire.*

The recipe for *pain ordinaire* was developed by the French chef Carême early in the nineteenth century and is still used by every baker in Paris, all twelve hundred of them. The recipe is no secret: a hundred pounds of flour, sixty pounds of water, two pounds of salt, and one pound of yeast. If you have baked French bread at home from any of a dozen recipes, you probably know it as six cups of flour, two and one-half cups of water, one tablespoon of salt, and two packages of active dry yeast.

I first learned that the recipe was universal after studying one morning with Monsieur Robert in the Boulangerie-Pâtisserie le Feyeux in the Pigalle district of Paris. On being given the recipe, I felt that I had discovered the "secret" of French bread. But later that night in my pension on the rue du Four, I used my pocket calculator to compare the new recipe with the one I had been using in America. I was astonished to discover that the recipes were identical: I already possessed the "secret" to *pain ordinaire*.

On reflection I realized that the secret was not in the recipe but in the way it was used. The next day I learned from Monsieur Robert some of the classic techniques used to make a common bread extraordinary:

- The French *boulanger* uses water to create a very soft dough. *"Très mou"* was the phrase Monsieur Robert kept using to describe his "very soft" mixture as it was kneaded gently on the double-arm *pétrin* that looked like a giant wishbone beating air into the dough. Every few minutes he'd stop the *pétrin* and pull out a strand of the satiny dough with his fingers. It was like soft, damp taffy. By letting me touch the dough, he taught me what I couldn't learn by just looking.

- By adding salt only five minutes before the end of the mixing stage, the baker allows the gluten that is in the flour to be developed. Salt inhibits the development of the gluten and, once added, salt tends to tighten the dough, increasing its elastic and plastic qualities (its ability to stretch and be molded); it also helps it become extensible (its ability to expand) and therefore entrap the gas that makes it rise.

- In mixing the dough with cool water, to offset the heat created by the friction of the mixer, Monsieur Robert was able to achieve a dough with a temperature of 75°F rather than the 80°F that is customary for most American breads in order to give them adequate development. The cooler temperature prolongs the fermentation, giving time for the natural flavor of the flour to develop. It also allows the loaf to do most of its expansion in the oven, where the injection of low-pressure steam helps the crust expand like the surface of a balloon. This creates the thin, crispy crust so characteristic of Parisian-style *baguettes*.

- Although Monsieur Robert uses the accentuated, twenty-minute mixing method of the modern French baker, he described another method that I could use in America. He told me I could mix the dough on low speed for between ten and twelve minutes and allow the dough to rise longer to acquire a more flavorful *baguette*.

In America the answer to the question "What is a *baguette?*" might be: "A long, skinny French bread with a fluffy crumb and a crisp crust." In France, where bakers who wish to call their bread *pain ordinaire* are permitted to use only four ingredients, flour, water, yeast, and salt (ascorbic acid and fava bean flour can also be used in minute amounts), the answer would also entail descriptions of size (between 250 and 300 grams—between ten and twelve ounces), shape, texture, color of crust, and how it might be used in various meals.

Thus, the answer to the question "What is French bread?" is fairly simple: "A bread of French origin made by various techniques but using only the four basic ingredients." The answer to the real question "What is a French *baguette?*" is more detailed. The French *baguette* is a long, skinny bread, the shape of which provides a greater proportion of crust to crumb than do more conventionally shaped breads. It is made from only the four basic ingredients, combined according to the direct method, that is, without the use of a sponge or sourdough. Thus it will keep for only about six hours. The crust is golden in appearance and crisp to the touch and bite. The crumb is moist, voluptuous, and well suited to its role as an accompaniment to the soups, sauces, *pâtés,* and terrines of French cuisine.

In France *la baguette* is everywhere. Of course you see it at the *bistro,* and at the café, and under the arms of shoppers on their way home from work. It is even served for breakfast. On my first trip to Paris—when I was a beginning professional baker and still believed that the sacred *croissant* was the breakfast food of choice—early one morning I saw in a café long slices of *baguette* slathered with unsalted butter and stacked high on a plate, log-cabin style. *Tartines* were what they were called, half *baguettes* sliced along the top instead of down the middle. You took what you wanted and paid for what you ate.

It was fascinating for me to see French bread in such abundance. That was the day I discovered that the French bread I had been baking in my own bakery in California was French bread in name only. I had never seen or tasted the real thing. To see it crisp and alive in front of me was my first step in learning how to bake better bread.

I learned that it was a simple bread. I loved it and was sure that the French felt the same way—that their daily bread was absolutely wonderful. Five years and three trips to Paris later, I learned that bread-loving Parisians regard the modern *baguette* as common, daily fare and pretty disappointing at that. The bread I adored for its crisp crust and lightness is disdained by many Parisians who feel that today's chic *baguette* lacks the substance and flavor they remember from childhood.

"The bread . . . the bread is like air," one unhappy Frenchman said while waving a piece of crust in front of my face. "Years ago every bread was wonderful in Paris. But now they give us air."

It reminded me of something that Lionel Poilâne once told me. "In Paris," he said, "the *baguette* is dead." Like many Parisians, he was recalling a day when every baker took the time to make great *pain ordinaire.*

The sophisticated method used to make the modern *baguette* is called accentuated mixing. It produces a light, crusty, beautiful *baguette* of little substance; the old *méthode classique,* with its slow, gentle mixing and a long rising time, creates a rich, deep flavor and a moist, chewy texture. But the classical method is rarely used today because most modern French bakers simply cannot afford to take the time.

Before the turn of the century nearly all breads were made from sourdough as *miches* or round, country loaves weighing between four and six pounds. As bakers responded to their clients' requests for more crust, they found themselves making thinner loaves. Out of this evolution in taste, the *baguette* was born. But bakers found that their regular sourdough loaves, made slimmer, turned out to be dense and unattractive. They were too heavy for emerging modern tastes. Fortunately the increased availability of commercial yeast enabled the French *boulanger* to create a lighter, more appealing loaf in the new *baguette* shape. And bread could be made in eight hours instead of twenty-four.

About the same time, the invention of the *pétrin,* the French mechanical dough mixer, did for the back of the *boulanger* what yeast did for his laborious working of the sourdough starter: It relieved his burden.

What did not change was the government's controlled price of the *baguette,* and with it the French people's undenied birthright—a crusty, inexpensive daily bread. So, although the baker's job became easier, it did not become any more profitable. Saved from his labor by innovation, he was still obliged by his government-controlled servitude to supply inexpensive fresh *baguettes* for a bread-hungry nation.

French baking has been controlled by the state since the development of the communal oven. By financing the construction and maintenance of the community ovens, the government was able to control the production of bread. Not only was bread taxed, but also its price regulated and its ingredients prescribed in a law called *la répression des fraudes.*

It was not until 1982 that the French government lifted its controls on the price of a *baguette.* The French *boulanger* was then free—after centuries of government regulation—to market his products for whatever price he could get. Ironically, virtually all *boulangers* held the line on their *baguette* prices. The market may have been deregulated, but the bakers themselves then regulated it. If only for the sake of their clients' devotion, bakers felt that the price of bread should be kept affordable.

It is no wonder that the *boulanger* sacrificed time in his method. Instead of making *pain ordinaire* in eight hours, he quickly learned to make it faster. It was the only way he could keep up with the demand and still make a profit.

The modern *baguette* can be made in four hours. But, as one *boulanger* once told me, "The faster the bread is made, the quicker it loses its freshness." This is why modern *baguettes* are sometimes baked four times a day in Paris. Most *boulangers* would agree that it is possible to make a six-hour *baguette* with enough substance to satisfy even the most demanding Frenchman.

Baguettes from adjoining neighborhoods or towns made from identical recipes and by similar techniques taste remarkably different. (Even *croissants* from one bakery may differ greatly in quality from day to day.) A discerning Parisian

might walk a few extra blocks from his Left Bank apartment—passing several *boulangeries* on his way—in order to buy the *baguette* baked exactly to his own taste. Traveling outside Paris, one can see *baguettes* of different sizes, shapes, textures, colors, and flavors. The crust of Parisian *baguettes,* for example, seems to be more crisp and crunchy than the crust of those made near the ocean. This is partly the result of the modern Parisian style of bread baking that meets the city dwellers' tastes, but it is probably as much related to variations in climate as to variations in technique.

An American baker living in Paris once took me to an ancient marble-countered *boulangerie* to taste what his *concierge* had called "the best *baguettes* in the neighborhood." The antiquated shop had none of the modern, high-tech racks and lighting to be found in the new *boulangeries* a few blocks away on the boulevard Saint-Michel. In fact, this rustic shop—where each morning one could enjoy the scent of burning wood and freshly baked bread rising from the bakeroom below—sold *baguettes* that looked pale, dusty, and unappealing. The loaves had none of the glitzy sparkle of those displayed at the modern shop on the boulevard.

The *concierge* was right. Those mottled, decrepit *baguettes* were the most flavorful and chewy loaves in the neighborhood because they were made by an old method, one that takes time. The longer a bread takes, the more the natural flavor of the flour will be enhanced and the more substantial a texture it will have. The attractive *baguettes* from the *boulangerie* on the boulevard are made to shine and crackle with visual appeal, but their flavor is nondescript and their freshness fades quickly. The use of fast-acting commercial yeast, high-speed mixing, and additions of ascorbic acid and other admittedly entirely legal ingredients all make it easier for the Parisian *boulanger* to quickly provide fresh bread that looks immensely appealing. The appearance of a modern *baguette* is improved by mixing of the dough to inflate it with air and by giving the loaves a quick jolt of steam injection in the first few minutes of baking, but the old method creates flavor. The character in a loaf comes from a slow, natural process, preferably one generated by sourdough rather than yeast.

My first two discoveries of *le vrai pain de campagne* ("the true country bread," a rustic loaf made with a sourdough starter) were made before I ever went to Europe. The picture of a dark and dusty loaf on the cover of the January 1978 issue of *Gourmet* magazine appealed to my primitive bread-baking instincts and inspired me to do something other than the ordinary French bread I had been pumping out from a recipe acquired from David Morris, then the owner of the Bread Garden Bakery in Berkeley, California. His was the recipe that, before I ever went to France, I earnestly believed was enabling me to bake real French bread.

(It was not that Morris's recipe did not have the potential to create great bread; the proportions for flour, water, salt, and yeast were exactly those of classic French bread. Only when I saw, on my first two trips to Paris, how the simple recipe was finessed and discovered how bakers nurtured and coaxed their dough to an artful and highly finished extensibility did the baker's craft begin to reveal itself to me. At the time I did not know what a *levain* was; still less that it was the French equivalent to sourdough. My only experiments with sourdough breads had been complete failures. In fact, like many people, I thought that sourdough had been invented in San Francisco.)

I was wanting a loaf with a wilder, more moist texture and a more flavorful crumb than those I had been making from the Bread Garden recipe. The only way I knew of obtaining a different texture was by using what I now call natural additives, ingredients not permissible in true French bread in France but which American bakers use to add depth of flavor, a more interesting texture, and better keeping qualities to a straight dough bread.

Never having had the patience to work with starters, I made a white bread enriched with oil and milk and shaped it into a plump, two-pound loaf. On it I placed a feeble replica of the decoration on the bread pictured in *Gourmet*, dusted it with flour, and overbaked it until it was almost burnt. What I came up with was a sad imitation. But my customers adored it; they, too, had never seen anything like it in America. Though the new loaf I had created was called Old World Bread, it was only old in appearance. The crust was dark but had no character. The inside or crumb (as I was learning to call it) was airy but it was squishy, like Wonder Bread. It satisfied my own tastes for about a year. By then I had learned more about starters and *le vrai pain* and that a sponge or *poolish* bread or one made of sourdough could bring out those characteristics of texture and flavor that, in American bread, were produced by additives such as milk, eggs, fat, and honey.

My other inspiration came from Ken Conklin, an artist friend who had spent a year living, working, and painting in the south of France near Cahors. He described what sounded to me like a large, medicine-ball-sized loaf called *seigle*. I learned later that it was a country rye bread.

"When we first brought it home and cut into it," Ken had told me, "the inside was spongy and moist, like cake." The bread was always baked on Wednesdays and the large eight- to ten-pound loaf lasted a week. The American artist family Ken lived with taught him how to cut the bulky bread as the locals did, by holding it against his chest and, with a large Opinel knife, carving off slices toward his body. Ken also adopted, as his favorite ways of eating the bread, two local customs, those of putting a slice in a bowl and pouring soup over it and of cutting a large slice for breakfast, piling it high with cold rice from the previous night's dinner, and pouring honey over the top.

Before hearing Ken's vivid descriptions, I had no idea that French bread was anything other than a long, skinny bread with a crispy crust. These inspirations made me realize that French bread could go way beyond *pain ordinaire*.

All of the recipes that follow are based on one or another of the three distinct methods that French village bakers use to create different types of breads: direct, sponge, and sourdough (of which the old-dough method and the porridge method are variations). In America the sponge and sourdough methods are called starter breads and the direct method, in which all ingredients are mixed at one time, is called the straight-yeast method. Although the starter methods are very similar, the one using natural sourdough is the most complicated; the reward is that it also creates a more rustic, chewy texture and a hearty flavor. Many books on home baking have transformed natural sourdough methods into sponge methods for the sake of simplicity. Here the methods are kept distinct in order to enlighten home bakers about the ways in which a village baker can create subtleties of texture and flavor in different loaves. The natural sourdough recipes are authentic presentations of what a village baker might do if asked to make a small batch of bread. These more complicated recipes are included in order to challenge the ambitious home baker who has become proficient with the other variations.

The different methods have been described in detail elsewhere (pages 21 through 29). In explaining them here I intend to classify them for the home baker and to give a clear and precise idea of exactly what each method entails in its degree of difficulty and in its rewards. Needless to say, it will be easier for bakers to start with the straight-yeast recipes, move on to the sponge and old-dough recipes, and then graduate to the natural sourdough recipes when ready for the challenge. The symbols that are used to denote each recipe in the following list—and throughout the book—will help bakers select the method that most suits their level of interest, expertise, and time schedule.

The Straight-Yeast Method (*la méthode directe*)*:* Most home bakers are familiar with the practice of making bread by mixing all of the ingredients at once. The simplest method of bread baking, the direct method always includes a first rising of the dough and a final rising of the loaf. (It may also include a punching back of the dough after the first rising and another rising in bulk to develop more flavor and better texture.) The yeast method can take as few as three hours or as many as eighteen, depending on the amount of yeast used and the number of times the dough is punched back. In some methods less yeast is used and the second rising (in bulk) takes place in the refrigerator. This will yield a more interesting, shiny, sourdough-type texture—and can be done with almost any bread—but it is still considered basically a straight-yeast method.

 The texture of straight-yeast breads is usually fluffy and homogeneous; the flavor, yeasty; the crust more crackerlike than chewy.

YEAST

SPONGE

The Sponge Method *(pain sur poolish):* A sponge can be made for any bread by mixing some of the flour and water and all of the yeast (less yeast may also be used) into a liquid batter. This is the simplest type of starter and it permits the fermentation to begin before the actual bread dough is mixed.

After a four- or five-hour rising, the sponge, which has often doubled or tripled in volume, is mixed with the rest of the ingredients into a bread dough. The dough is handled in much the same way as it would be in the straight-yeast method—except that often the final rising times are somewhat faster because of the maturity in development of the sponge.

The aroma of a sponge bread is less yeasty than that of a direct-method bread and more like the aroma of nuts. The texture is less even and the size of the air bubbles more irregular; it has some of the chewiness of sourdough with some of the lightness of the straight-yeast method.

OLD DOUGH

The Old-Dough Method *(pâte fermentée):* This is placed here because it is similar to a sourdough variation, but it is much easier. In this method a baker can use a yeasted piece of dough taken from a previous batch of bread to help give a deeper flavor and a more interesting texture to a bread made with yeast. The old dough works in much the same way as a natural sourdough starter but, because the leavening is made from yeast, the method doesn't have to take as long. It will never produce the moist, shiny texture of a sourdough bread, but the texture and flavor it does impart are much more interesting than those of a direct-method bread. For the home baker, it is a rewarding method to use.

PORRIDGE

The Porridge Method *(pain bouillie):* This method actually predates the sourdough method. In a porridge bread, certain types of grain, cereal, or flour are cooked with water into a porridge or gruel; or grain is soaked overnight; or flour is covered with boiling water and allowed to absorb the moisture. The soaking, boiling, or cooking of the dry ingredient activates its enzymes, creating a bacterial growth—or alcoholic fermentation—that helps the dough rise and gives the bread a moist, rustic texture and a strong, earthy flavor.

The process can be done with or without yeast, depending on the expertise of the baker. Most of the porridge-bread recipes in this book are made with an overnight mixture and a little bit of yeast in the final bread to give it some lightness and to simplify the process.

SOURDOUGH

The Sourdough Method *(la méthode au levain):* Similar to the porridge method from which it has been derived, the sourdough method relies on a small piece of dough, or *chef,* that has been mixed from flour and water and allowed to ferment, in this case for several days. This piece of dough, containing wild yeast, is mixed several times with more flour and water to build the size of the *levain* and the strength of the ferments so that it can be used to inoculate or inseminate the bread dough with the natural yeast to make it rise.

The textures obtained are moist and chewy, with an irregular cellular structure. The flavors can be very sour or (as the French prefer) only slightly acidic, depending on the intensity of the starter. The bread will stay fresh longer than will bread made from the direct, sponge, or old-dough method.

PAIN ORDINAIRE
CLASSIC YEASTED FRENCH BREAD

All serious bakers, students, and cooks should have this basic recipe for regular French bread in their repertoire. By making the bread three or four times and by committing the recipe to memory, anyone should be able to produce an individual, subtle version of this classic daily bread. The simple recipe can be done in three different ways: made by hand, with a food processor (or mixer), or with a piece of old dough as a starter. Once mastered, the formula can be varied—and this is done in other recipes throughout the book by altering the ingredient proportions, the technique, and the method—to yield almost any other type of bread.

MAKES TWO 10-OUNCE *BAGUETTES* AND ONE 1¼-POUND ROUND LOAF

> 2 packages (2 scant tablespoons; ½ ounce) active dry yeast
>
> 2½ cups water
>
> 6 cups organic unbleached white (or all-purpose) flour
>
> 1 tablespoon salt
>
> Glaze: 1 egg white whisked into ½ cup cold water

Proof the yeast by stirring it into one cup of warm water (115°F). When the mixture is creamy (after 10 minutes), pour it into a large mixing bowl and add 1½ cups of lukewarm water.

Start adding the flour, handful by handful, stirring after each addition, at first gently and then vigorously, with a wooden spoon. As the batter becomes thicker it will also become more elastic. You are actually trying to create strands of dough much like taffy that extend from the spoon to the dough in the bowl each time it is whipped in wide, slow, sweeping motions. After all but 1 cup of the flour has been added (this will take about 10 minutes), turn the dough out onto a worktable, sprinkle the salt over the dough, and knead it for about 5 or 6 minutes while adding the rest of the flour. Because the dough has been whipped up vigorously in the batter stage, it will not have to be kneaded as much in the dough stage. The dough should be moist and satiny.

Place the dough in a bowl large enough to accommodate its doubling in volume. The bowl can be greased or ungreased as you prefer. Cover the bowl with a moistened dish towel and let the dough rise in a warm spot, out of the way of drafts, for 1½ to 2 hours, or until it has doubled in volume. Punch it back and let it rise again for another 30 to 45 minutes.

Divide the dough into 2 pieces, then divide one of the halves in two again. Round each of the 3 pieces of dough into tight balls and allow them to rest on the table for 15 minutes, covered with a cloth so that the outside does not crust over.

Shape the two small balls of dough into *baguettes* by flattening each piece into a rectangular shape that measures approximately 6 by 3 inches. With the 6-inch side toward you, fold over a third of the dough down from the top and then seal the edge with the heel of the hand. Do this two or three times until the piece is in the shape of a log of about 8 inches long. Stretch each log out by rolling it on the table under the palms of your hands until it is between 12 and 14 inches long. (The technique is illustrated on page 50.) Then place each in an oiled, black *baguette* tray or on a cookie sheet that has been greased or lined with parchment paper.

Shape the larger piece of dough into a tight, round loaf by first flattening it, then folding the outer edges over into the middle. Repeat the process of folding the dough 4 or 5 times and sealing each fold by pressing down on the dough with the heel of the hand. With the folds underneath, drag the round ball of dough across the worktable with some pressure on top to make a tight loaf without any air bubbles. Place it on a baking sheet lined with parchment paper. (If you are using the baking stone method, place the loaf in a *banneton,* a basket lined with a dish towel that has been lightly dusted with flour, and refer to the baking stone instructions on page 53).

Let the loaves rise, covered, for 45 minutes or an hour, until they have doubled in volume.

If you are using a baking stone, place it in a cold oven and preheat the oven to 450°F for at least 1 hour. Otherwise simply preheat the oven to 450°F.

With a razor blade, slash each *baguette* 4 or 5 times diagonally on top and glaze them.

Invert the round loaf in the basket (if you are using one) gently onto a floured, rimless cookie sheet, slash it with a razor blade in a tick-tack-toe pattern and slide it onto the baking stone. This loaf is not glazed because the matte, floured crust looks more rustic. (If you prefer a shiny crust, the loaf can be glazed, but first gently dust off any excess flour with a pastry brush.) If the round loaf has risen on a parchment-lined baking try, slash it and place the tray directly in the oven.

Bake the *baguettes* for 20 to 25 minutes and the round loaf for 40 to 45 minutes. When they are done the loaves will look golden brown in color and sound hollow if they are thumped on the bottom. Place the loaves on a wire rack to cool.

The modern *pétrissage accentué* method used in French bakeries is virtually impossible to recreate by hand mixing. By using a food processor or home mixer, you can achieve some of the same qualities. The method, at home or in the village bakery, creates a bread of a light, fluffy texture and a thin, crisp crust, which are the results of using more water in the dough and intense mixing.

The recipe proportions are identical to those of the previous recipe, except that this recipe calls for more water and is halved to accommodate the size of the food processor. The recipe can be doubled by mixing two batches consecutively in the processor and then combining the doughs in a bowl for the final rising.

MAKES TWO 11-OUNCE BAGUETTES

> 1 package (2½ teaspoons, ¼ ounce) active dry yeast
>
> 1½ cups water
>
> 3¼ cups organic, unbleached white (or all-purpose) flour
>
> A pinch of powdered vitamin C
>
> 1¾ teaspoons salt

Proof the yeast by mixing it with ¼ cup of warm water (115°F). Then set it aside until it is creamy—about 10 minutes. To ensure that the rest of the water is at the right temperature for this method, place three ice cubes in a transparent measuring cup and fill it with very cold tap water to the 1¼-cup mark. When the ice melts, the water should be around 50°F. (Use less ice in winter.) The ice is necessary because the food processor will heat up the dough.

Food Processor Method

Fit a food processor with the plastic dough blade and place in it 3 cups of the flour. When the yeast mixture is bubbly, stir the vitamin C powder into it and then add it on top of the flour. Pulse the food processor 2 or 3 times. Then, with the processor running, add ½ cup of the water. Process for 30 seconds. With the processor still running add the remaining ¾ cup of water. Process for another 15 seconds. Then sprinkle the salt into the dough and process for a final 15 seconds.

If the dough does not come away from the sides of the bowl because it is too wet and soupy, add half of the remaining ¼ cup flour and pulse for a few times.

Pour the dough out onto a worktable and knead it for a few minutes while incorporating the remaining flour. (The food processor has already done 99 percent of the kneading.) At this stage, the dough should be very wet, elastic, and ideally at 75°F.

Place the dough in a large ungreased bowl, cover with a damp towel, and allow it to rise in a warm place for between 45 minutes and 1 hour.

(At this point you can save 1 cup of the risen dough for making bread by one of the *pâte fermentée* methods; see page 73 for *pain ordinaire* made with the

addition of old dough and the index for other recipes using this technique. This dough may be stored, wrapped in plastic or enclosed in a lidded container, in the refrigerator for up to 2 days.)

Divide the dough in half, shape each piece into a *baguette,* and place in an oiled, black *baguette* tray or on a parchment-lined baking sheet.

Cover the loaves and let them rise for between 1½ and 2 hours.

Preheat the oven to 450°F and spray the inside of the oven with an atomizer of water 3 or 4 times before inserting the loaves. Spray again after the loaves have been in for a few minutes and bake for between 20 and 25 minutes or until they are golden in color and sound hollow when thumped.

Place the loaves on a wire rack to cool.

Mixer Method

Proof the yeast and prepare the water according to the directions given above for the food processor method, but use only 2 ice cubes as the mixer does not generate as much heat.

Fit the mixer with the dough hook and place all but ¼ cup of the flour into the bowl. When the yeast is bubbly, stir in the vitamin C powder and add it to the mixer on top of the flour. Pour in half of the water (that is, 1 cup plus 1 tablespoon).

Mix on the lowest speed for 2 or 3 minutes to combine all of the ingredients. The mixture will be firm. With the mixer still running on the lowest speed, slowly add the remaining water. The dough will now be wet and moist.

Mix for 5 minutes at medium-high speed, then add the salt and mix for 2 more minutes. If the dough creeps up the dough hook, simply push it down with a dough scraper or with your hand. Empty the dough onto the table and knead in the remaining ¼ cup flour.

Proceed with the rest of the recipe according to the directions given for the food processor method, above.

A Note for the Advanced Baker

To make them easier for the home baker to handle, both the preceding recipes for *pain ordinaire* have less water than is ideal. Once you have tried either of the two recipes a few times, consider adding extra water to give the bread a moist, chewy texture.

For the classical, hand-mixed method (6 cups of flour), add up to ½ cup extra water.

For the food processor or electric mixer method (3 cups of flour) add up to ¼ cup extra water before mixing in the salt.

WITH OLD-DOUGH ADDITION
PÂTE FERMENTÉE

If you have a piece of French bread dough left over one day and want to save it in the refrigerator to use within the next day or two, try this variation. (The old dough can also be frozen, then taken out, thawed and used in the recipe. Just allow the dough to warm up and rise for an hour or two before using it.) This piece of already fermented dough acts as a starter and it gives the bread a more chewy character and a fuller flavor. The exact proportions are not critical. But be careful that the old dough is not more than 10 percent of your overall batch because excessive amounts will give unpredictable results. (See page 74 for *la couronne de Figeac,* a variation of *pain ordinaire,* in which a larger percentage of starter is used.)

The old dough does not have to be very old; it can be used the day it is made. It will be effective if it is given between six and ten hours to rise at room temperature or between fifteen and twenty hours in the refrigerator.

MAKES TWO 11-OUNCE *BAGUETTES* AND ONE 1½-POUND ROUND LOAF

> 1 package (2½ teaspoons, ¼ ounce) active dry yeast
>
> 2¼ cups water
>
> 1 cup 6- to 10-hour-old *pain ordinaire* dough (see recipe on page 69)
>
> 5½ cups organic, unbleached white (or all-purpose) flour
>
> 2¾ teaspoons salt
>
> Glaze: 1 egg white whisked into ½ cup cold water

While waiting for the yeast to proof in ¼ cup of the warm (115°F) water, break up the old dough in a large bowl and add the remaining 2 cups of warm water, a little at a time. After each addition of water, add a half handful of flour. Then stir the mixture, gently at first, then vigorously with a wooden spoon or a plastic dough scraper. Make sure that the old dough is well dissolved in the early stages, so that its effects will be well distributed through the new dough. Continue adding water and flour alternately and mixing vigorously.

After all but about 2 cups of the flour have been added (this will take about 10 minutes), add the yeast mixture and incorporate it together with another cup of flour. After a few more minutes of mixing, sprinkle the salt over the dough, turn it out onto the workbench and knead it for another 5 minutes while adding the last cup of flour. The dough should be moist and satiny.

Let the dough rise, covered, for about 2 hours, until it has doubled in volume. Punch it back and allow it to rise again for between 1½ and 2 hours, until it has almost doubled again.

After this second rising, divide the dough into 2 pieces. Cut one half into two again and shape them into *baguettes* by flattening each piece and rolling it up into a tight log. Stretch each log to the desired length—between 12 and 14 inches—by rolling it on the table under the palms while stretching it lengthwise.

Place the loaves in an oiled black *baguette* tray. Shape the remaining piece of dough into a round loaf and place it to rise in a *banneton* (a basket lined with a dish towel and dusted with a little flour) if you are using the baking stone method. The *baguettes* or the round loaf can also be baked on greased or parchment-lined cookie sheets.

Cover the loaves with a damp cloth and let them rise for 2 hours in a cool place.

Slash each *baguette* diagonally with a razor 3 or 4 times on top and glaze the top surface.

Gently turn the round loaf out of the basket onto a floured, rimless cookie sheet, score it with a razor blade in a tick-tack-toe pattern, and slide it onto the baking stone. Or bake it directly on the baking sheet.

Bake the *baguettes* in a preheated 450°F oven for between 20 and 25 minutes, the *boule* for between 40 and 45 minutes.

When they are done the loaves will look golden brown in color and sound hollow if they are thumped on the bottom. Place them on a wire rack to cool.

OLD DOUGH

LA COURONNE DE FIGEAC
FIGEAC CROWN LOAF

This loaf is crown-shaped with a rustic appearance. It is often seen in the more rural parts of France where peasants enjoy large, four- to six-pound loaves, but also desire a fair amount of crust. Hence the hole in the middle of the loaf.

The method shows that a bread can be made with more starter than that used in the old-dough method (*pâte fermentée*) as long as the baker realizes that the rising times must be reduced. It was in Monsieur Jean Haettel's bakery (described on page 78) that I first encountered this loaf. Although Monsieur Haettel's was a natural sourdough bread, this version uses yeast to make it easier for the home baker. The result is startlingly similar.

The bread may be made in either of two ways: Use one cup of *pain ordinaire* (French bread) dough or make a starter (see recipe below) that has the same consistency as a bread dough.

I cup very old (5- to 8-hours-old) yeasted *pain ordinaire* (page 69)

½ cup warm water

1⅓ cups unbleached, organic white (or all-purpose) flour

2 tablespoons rye or whole wheat flour

½ teaspoon sea salt (or table salt)

Break up the old dough completely until you have reduced it to tiny pieces and place it in a medium-sized bowl. Pour the warm water over it and mix with a plastic dough scraper or wooden spoon for 4 or 5 minutes, until the dough is almost entirely dissolved in the water. Place both flours in a mound on the worktable. Keeping 1 hand dry, start to add the flour to the liquefied dough a few pinches at a time, while continuing to mix with the spoon or dough scraper. The dough will start to take on a wet elasticity. When all but ⅓ cup of the flour has been used up, the dough will still be quite moist. Beat the dough as if you are mixing a batter, giving it between 100 and 150 strong, vigorous strokes with the spoon. Sprinkle the salt over the dough and mix it for another 2 or 3 minutes until the salt is incorporated.

Use the remaining ⅓ cup of flour to coat the worktable. Empty the wet dough out and knead it gently until the rest of the flour is incorporated. If the dough sticks to your hands, just rub it off with a little more flour and reincorporate it. The dough will be wet and satiny and will spring back when touched. Resist the temptation to add more flour.

Let the dough rise in the bowl covered with a damp towel until it has nearly doubled in bulk, about 1½ hours. Then punch it down and let it rise for another 30 to 45 minutes.

Punch the dough back, shape it into a round loaf by tucking the outer edges into the middle and sealing them with the heel of the hand and then dragging it across the table with both hands until it forms a tight ball.

Set the ball of dough on the worktable and, with your elbow, press down right into the center. When your elbow has reached all the way through the dough and onto the worktable, make circular motions with your arm and elbow that will slowly expand the diameter of the circle inside the dough. Then use both hands to stretch the doughnut-shaped loaf so that the hole is between 4 and 5 inches in diameter.

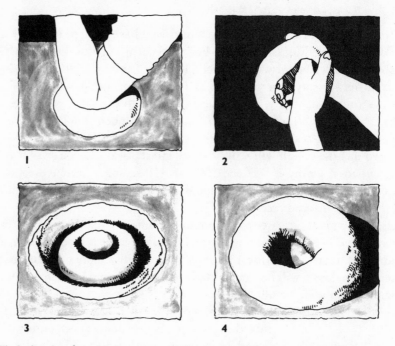

To help the dough rise use a 10-inch round basket that is about 4 inches deep, a very small teacup, and a linen or cotton dish towel. Place the teacup upside down in the middle of the basket. Place the towel inside the basket, shaping it to fit the contours of the inverted teacup and the inner walls of the basket. Dust the cloth-lined basket with about a handful of flour and place the crown-shaped loaf in it, with the teacup protruding through the center hole. Let the loaf rise, covered with another cloth, for about 1½ hours.

Place a baking stone in the oven and preheat the oven to 450°F. If you are not using a baking stone, the loaf can be baked on a parchment-lined baking tray.

Test the loaf by touching it with a finger. When the impression remains without springing back too quickly, the loaf is ready. Dust a rimless cookie sheet with flour and gently invert the basket on it. Peel away the towel carefully so the dough does not tear. Then slide the bread onto the baking stone and bake it for between 45 and 50 minutes.

The loaf is done when it sounds hollow when thumped on the bottom. At this point, turn the oven off and open the door, leaving the loaf on the baking stone for 5 minutes. This helps to give a thicker crust and dry out the moist dough.

Remove the loaf from the oven and let it cool on a wire rack. The loaf will stay fresh for several days.

Using a Starter

The recipe calls for an old piece of *pain ordinaire* dough, but if you do not have any on hand, you can make some.

> ¾ teaspoon active dry yeast
>
> ½ cup warm water
>
> 1 cup unbleached, organic white (or all-purpose) flour
>
> ½ teaspoon salt

Proof the yeast in a little of the warm water until it becomes creamy. This will take about 10 minutes. In a medium-sized bowl, combine the yeast mixture with the rest of the water and start adding the flour, a few pinches at a time, stirring with a wooden spoon, gently at first, then more vigorously when the mixture becomes a batter. After all but a few tablespoons of the flour have been added (this will take about 5 minutes), sprinkle the salt over the dough and knead it on a table for another 5 minutes while adding the rest of the flour. The dough should be moist and satiny. If the dough is too moist to be kneaded on the bench, add a few more tablespoons of flour, but be careful not to overdo it.

Set the starter dough aside, covered, to rise, the length of time depending on how soon you wish to make the bread. Set aside at room temperature, the dough will be ready within 5 to 8 hours. Otherwise, let it rise for between 3 and 4 hours and then punch it down, round it into a tight ball, and place it in a covered plastic container large enough for the dough to triple in size. Place the container in the refrigerator, where it will continue to rise very slowly, for between 24 and 36 hours.

Remove the dough from the refrigerator and let it rise at room temperature for between 2 and 3 hours.

BECAUSE EVERY VILLAGE BAKER has a different way of using the recipe for simple French bread, each baker's bread is distinctive. The bread made by Jean Haettel—a *boulanger* in the ancient town of Figeac—reminds one of dusty rocks or boulders, of outcroppings from the roots of trees, of burls that have risen up, expanded, and exploded. Strange as its appearance may be, a rustic bread such as Haettel's is far superior to slick modern breads. Two things make Haettel's bread more appealing than that of his fellow bakers: his use of unrefined flour and his unique method.

The day I visited Haettel, he picked up a gnarled and dusty loaf and pointed to a place where the crumb had broken through the crust. According to baker's lore, this is the spot where the loaves have "kissed" in the oven.

"You see the crumb?" he said. "It's gray. It's not stark white like modern bread."

The gray crumb makes it look as if the baker threw a handful of whole wheat or rye flour into the dough. But, unlike some local bakers who use a little rye flour to give a rustic color to their country breads (their *pain de campagne*), Haettel uses a white flour that has not had all the life and nutrients milled out. That is what makes his bread a shade darker.

In using unrefined flour to give his bread its rustic character, Haettel is not following modern practice. His technique too is ancient, even though he uses a mechanical mixer. Most modern French bakers mix their bread for twenty minutes on high speed, creating a fluffy, cotton-candy texture; Haettel mixes his bread slowly for only six to eight minutes. In this fashion, he'll explain, the dough is not inflated with excessive air. The technique allows the bread to ferment naturally, creating a more flavorful and chewy crumb.

After the dough has rested for twenty minutes, it is given several turns by hand (see the section on punching down or knocking back, *donner un tour,* page 45, for a description of the procedure). This is the ancient method for coaxing along the activity of a hand-mixed dough, giving it another push toward its second rising, before it is shaped into loaves.

Haettel's use of *levain* is also original. Most bakers will mix a small percentage of sourdough starter into their bread, perhaps sixteen pounds for a batch of, say, eighty pounds of dough. Because that very small quantity of natural yeast cells must grow and disperse through the larger quantity of dough, it will take anywhere from eight to twelve hours for the loaves to rise. Haettel uses more than the traditional quantities of *levain* or sourdough starter held back from one day's batch for the next.

In his bread, the long fermentation time necessary for a sourdough bread occurs at the beginning of the process: He allows the larger piece of *levain* to ferment for nearly twenty-four hours, creating a very active starter. The next day, when the dough is mixed, he adds only a little bit of flour. The loaves can therefore be given a very short, one-hour final rising before being baked, rather than the customary eight to twelve hours. This is the technique that allows Jean Haettel to rise at five every morning and have an authentic, rustic sourdough French bread ready for his customers at eight o'clock.

Bakers at the Ganachaud Bakery in the Twentieth Arrondissement of Paris use the *poolish* method to make their house specialty, *la flûte gana*. A high-quality organic flour is used in a four-hour sponge. To emulate ancient techniques, the dough is mixed gently and each loaf is shaped by hand, as can be seen through windows that reveal the rustic bake shop to customers. To create the well-developed, irregular texture of crumb, each *baguette* is first shaped by hand into an oblong loaf that is three inches wide by about six or eight inches long. After the logs of dough have sat on the well-floured worktable for between ten and fifteen minutes to relax, they are gently stretched to the desired length and placed in canvas *couches* for the final rising. In the following recipe the stretched *baguettes* are placed directly on *baguette* trays or on parchment-lined baking sheets to rise.

There are scores of variations for sponge-type breads. In some, the *poolish* is very liquid and so it rises quickly. In variations that use a firmer sponge, less yeast is normally used and the fermentation may take as long as twenty-four hours, because the drier dough will rise more slowly.

The proportions in the following recipe are one-third flour and two-thirds water, an easily remembered formula.

MAKES TWO 11-OUNCE *BAGUETTES*

THE *POOLISH* (SPONGE)

> 1 teaspoon active dry yeast
>
> 1 cup warm water
>
> 1 cup organic, unbleached white (or all-purpose) flour

THE DOUGH

> 1 teaspoon active dry yeast
>
> ½ cup water
>
> All of the *poolish* from the previous step
>
> 2 cups organic, unbleached white (or all-purpose) flour
>
> 1½ teaspoons salt
>
> Glaze: 1 egg white whisked into ½ cup cold water

MIX THE SPONGE OR *POOLISH* by first proofing the yeast in ¼ cup of warm (115°F) water. When it is creamy, combine the yeast mixture in a large bowl with the rest of the water, which should be at room temperature. Slowly add the flour by handfuls while stirring with a wooden spoon. When the ingredients are completely combined, set the liquid mixture aside, covered with a dish towel, for between 4 and 6 hours. When the *poolish* has risen and fallen it is ready.

TO MAKE THE DOUGH, proof the yeast in ¼ cup of warm (115°F) water. When the mixture is creamy, add it along with ¼ cup of cool water to the bowl that contains the 4- to 6-hour *poolish* and mix well.

Start adding the flour, handful by handful, stirring gently at first and then vigorously with a wooden spoon. Ideally each handful of flour should be stirred into your mixture with 50 strokes of the spoon. This is a much wetter dough than that for *pain ordinaire* so, if it is being mixed by hand, the task must be done with patience. The dough can be mixed in a food processor or with an electric mixer. See the directions on pages 71 and 72.

After all but a half cup of the flour has been added (this will take about 15 minutes), scrape the wet dough from the bowl and onto a floured worktable. Sprinkle the salt over the dough and knead it on the table for another 5 minutes while adding the rest of the flour. The dough should be moist and satiny.

Place the dough back into the bowl and let it rise, covered, for 2 hours. Punch it back and allow it to rise again for between 45 minutes and an hour.

Divide the dough into 2 pieces and shape them into *baguettes* by flattening each piece and rolling it up into a tight log that measures 3 inches by 6 inches. Allow the loaves to rest on a well-floured surface, covered by a moist kitchen towel, for about 15 minutes. When the loaves are fully relaxed, gently stretch each to a length of between 12 and 14 inches and place them in an oiled black *baguette* tray or on a parchment-lined baking sheet.

If you want a more rustic crust, you can proof the loaves in *couches* and then bake them on a baking stone. Let them rise for between 1 and 1½ hours.

If you are using the stone, set it in the oven and preheat the oven to 450°F.

When the loaves are ready, slash each *baguette* with a razor 3 or 4 times on top and glaze it. Bake the loaves for between 15 and 20 minutes, until they are golden brown.

Let the loaves cool on a wire rack.

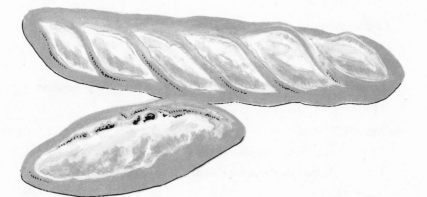

PAIN DE CAMPAGNE
COUNTRY-STYLE FRENCH BREAD

Pain de campagne is a traditional country loaf that is made throughout France in numerous variations. It is usually made as a large loaf of between four and six pounds, with a dark, almost caramelized crust that is lightly dusted with flour. The best loaves of French country bread are made with a natural sourdough starter *(levain)* that, along with the loaf's size, allows it to remain quite edible for close to a week.

Although this recipe takes six days, most of the time is spent in waiting for the several successive starters to rise. This is an authentic recipe that was used several hundred years ago by home bakers who made bread for their families once a week and baked the hearty loaves in a communal brick oven. When the method is used in some of today's French and American village bakeries, the entire process (including up to three refreshments of the starter) can be done in twenty-four hours. A piece of dough from the mixed batch is pulled back to serve as the *chef levain* (or chief leavening agent) that will continue the strain of active ferments for the next day's bread.

MAKES ONE 2-POUND ROUND LOAF

THE *CHEF*

½ cup whole wheat flour

Scant ¼ cup warm water

⅛ teaspoon ground cumin

½ teaspoon milk

THE FIRST REFRESHMENT

¾ cup whole wheat flour

2 tablespoons *chef* from the previous step

⅓ cup warm water

THE SECOND REFRESHMENT

¾ cup whole wheat flour

½ cup organic, unbleached white (or all-purpose) flour

½ cup (4 ounces; the size of a tangerine) *levain* from the previous step

½ cup water

THE DOUGH

3 cups organic, unbleached white (or all-purpose) flour

1½ cups (12 ounces; about the size of a large orange) *levain* from the previous step

1¼ cups very warm water

2½ generous teaspoons salt

The bread display at Gayle's Bakery, Capitola

TO MAKE THE *CHEF*, place the flour in a mound on the worktable and make a fountain or well in the middle. Into the fountain pour about two-thirds of the warm water and add the cumin and the milk. With 1 finger, start mixing the liquid with a little of the flour from the outer ring. Pull in more and more of the flour to make first a paste and eventually a firm dough. If the mixture is too dry, use some of the remaining water, adding it gradually until you have a pliable dough. The *chef* should be the same consistency as a bread dough, firm but somewhat sticky, and should spring back a little when touched.

After kneading the dough on your work surface for between 5 and 8 minutes, place the ball of dough in a ceramic or plastic container, cover it with a damp cloth, and let it rise in a warm place, out of the way of drafts, for 2 or 3 days. A heavy crust will form on top of the *chef,* but inside it will be inflated and moist. The consistency will be spongy. The aroma of cumin will still be evident and the dough will smell slightly sour but fragrant and appealing.

FOR THE FIRST REFRESHMENT, remove the outer crust of the *chef* and use a piece of the moist dough that is the size of a large walnut (about 2 tablespoons).

Pour the flour onto the workbench and make a fountain (see page 39). Break up the *chef* into little pieces and place it in the middle of the fountain. Pour in the warm water; stir and work the *chef* with your fingers until it is completely dissolved. Then, with several fingers of one hand, start pulling in some of the flour to make a paste in the middle of the fountain. Gradually work in most of the flour. You will see that the dough becomes more and more active as it is worked. Use the dry hand with some of the remaining flour to clean off the mixing hand and incorporate every little bit into the dough, which is now called a *levain.*

If the *levain* will not take all the flour, you can leave out a tablespoon or two. If the *levain* is too moist and does not come together as dough, add a little flour, a teaspoon at a time.

We describe the final dough as "firm," but it should not be too dry. Rather it should be moist and feel sticky and should stand up in a little ball and spring back when touched.

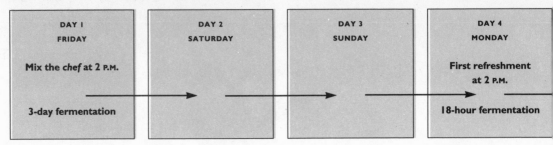

DAY 1 FRIDAY	DAY 2 SATURDAY	DAY 3 SUNDAY	DAY 4 MONDAY
Mix the *chef* at 2 P.M. 3-day fermentation			First refreshment at 2 P.M. 18-hour fermentation

Let the *levain* rise in the container, covered with a damp cloth, for between 18 and 24 hours. When ready the *levain* will have noticeably risen and fallen a little. It will still have a pleasing, alcoholic aroma. Inside it will be inflated with tiny bubbles.

THE SECOND REFRESHMENT is made in much the same way as the first. Use the entire *levain,* discarding any crust that has developed on top. Combine the 2 types of flour and hold back ¼ cup for kneading the final dough on the table. The dough should be moist to the touch but firm enough not to stick too easily to the hands.

Let the *levain* rise, covered in the container, for between 10 and 12 hours. At this stage you will see the *levain* take on a new life. After about 4 or 5 hours, it will sit up nicely in the container. By the end of about 10 hours it will have almost doubled in bulk, and, eventually, it will stop springing back when touched with a finger. At this stage it is ready to be mixed into a bread dough.

TO MIX THE DOUGH, make a fountain with the flour, add all of the *levain,* in little pieces, and then the water, a little at a time.

As the water is added, dissolve the *levain* in it and gradually pull in some of the flour to make a sticky paste. As the flour is added, the paste will become more and more elastic and should be stretched and pulled vigorously with the fingers of one hand. When all but about 1 cup of the flour has been incorporated, the dough will be moist and sticky. Clean your hands with the back of a knife blade or a plastic dough scraper and work those little bits into the dough.

Sprinkle the salt onto the wet dough and incorporate it by kneading it in, together with the remaining flour. Knead the dough for 5 more minutes until it is firm and springs back when touched.

Let the dough rise, covered with a damp cloth, for between 8 and 10 hours. The dough will become noticeably inflated and will have risen to nearly double its original size.*

The dough is now ready to be shaped and given a final rising. The most foolproof way to determine if the loaf is sufficiently risen and ready to bake is to set

VARIATION

See page 104 for a sourdough version of pain de régime made using this recipe for the chef and the first two refreshments. The ingredients in the final dough are, of course, different.

---

* If you want to make *pain de campagne* the next day, cut off a piece of the dough the size of a walnut and set it aside for between 4 and 8 hours at room temperature. This piece will constitute the *chef* for the first refreshment for your next batch of bread. The time patterns of that batch are impossible to predict but they will be abbreviated because of the freshness of the *levain.* The first refreshment will rise for around 8 hours; the second for around 4 hours.

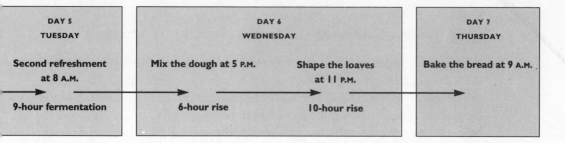

DAY 5 TUESDAY	DAY 6 WEDNESDAY		DAY 7 THURSDAY
Second refreshment at 8 A.M.	Mix the dough at 5 P.M.	Shape the loaves at 11 P.M.	Bake the bread at 9 A.M.
9-hour fermentation	6-hour rise	10-hour rise	

aside, when you make up the loaf, a small piece of dough that is about the size of a walnut. Round it up tightly and put it in a Mason jar filled with room-temperature water. Make sure that the ball of dough does not stick to the side of the jar and that you have set the jar right next to the loaf so the temperature is the same. When this test piece of dough rises to the top of the water, the loaf is ready to bake.

Shape the dough into a round loaf by flattening it and then folding the edges over 4 or 5 times into the center, each time sealing it with the heel of the hand. Place the loaf in a *banneton,* a basket lined with a dish towel and dusted lightly with flour, and set it to rise in a warm place for between 8 and 10 hours. The times given for the rising periods for the dough and then the loaf may seem a bit vague but they are best left up to the baker's judgment because it is hard to predict the activity of any one person's refreshments. The overall proofing time should be around 16 hours. If you shape the dough after it has been allowed to rise for 6 hours, the loaf will probably need another 10 hours in the final proof. You may apportion the rising times evenly, taking 8 for each, or 10 hours for the dough and 6 for the loaf.

The final rising will take forever if the dough temperature is too low and the consistency too moist. If the dough is below 75°F, allow the loaf to rise in a *very* warm place, perhaps in the oven with only the pilot light on. (Remember to remove the loaf before preheating the oven.)

To bake the loaf, place a baking stone in your oven and preheat it to 450°F. When it is ready, gently empty the loaf onto a rimless cookie sheet that has been sprinkled with a little flour or cornmeal. With a sharp razor blade, slash the top of the loaf in a tick-tack-toe pattern. Slide the loaf onto the baking stone. If your oven bakes very hot, you may want to turn the heat down to 400°F or 425°F after the loaf has gone in.

Bake the bread for 1 hour or until the loaf is golden brown and sounds hollow when thumped on the bottom. To give it a thicker crust, leave the loaf in the oven with the door open and the gas off for 5 minutes more.

Cool the loaf on a wire rack.

SPONGE

PAIN DE CAMPAGNE SUR POOLISH
SPONGE-METHOD COUNTRY-STYLE FRENCH BREAD

Village bakers who want to make country bread without all the laborious work use a yeasted sponge instead of a natural sourdough starter. The same method can be used at home, and the bread can be made in one day. If you want a more interesting texture and a more flavorful crumb in the final loaf, the process can be extended to a second day by letting the sponge rise overnight in the refrigerator.

MAKES I LARGE, 2¾-POUND LOAF

THE *POOLISH*

> I package (2½ teaspoons; ¼ ounce) active dry yeast
>
> I ½ cups water
>
> I cup organic, unbleached white (or all-purpose) flour
>
> ½ cup rye flour
>
> ½ cup whole wheat flour

THE DOUGH

> I teaspoon active dry yeast
>
> I to I ¼ cups water
>
> All of the *poolish* from the previous step
>
> 3 cups organic, unbleached white (or all-purpose) flour
>
> I cup whole wheat flour
>
> I tablespoon salt

TO MIX THE SPONGE OR *POOLISH*, begin by proofing the yeast in about ¼ cup of warm water. When it is creamy, mix it into a large bowl along with the rest of the water, which should be at room temperature. Combine the 3 kinds of flour and slowly add the mixture by handfuls to the yeast while stirring with a plastic dough scraper or with a wooden spoon. The sponge will be the consistency of a thick pancake batter. Let this sponge sit in the bowl, covered with a dish towel, at room temperature, for between 6 and 8 hours or in the refrigerator overnight.

(If the *poolish* has been set aside in the refrigerator, take it out an hour or so before you are ready to continue the recipe and use very warm water (110°F) for mixing the dough. If the *poolish* has been left out to rise at room temperature, use tepid water.)

THE HOME BAKER
86

TO MAKE THE DOUGH, proof the yeast in ½ cup of the water. Mix the rest of the water with the *poolish* in the bowl. Combine the 2 flours and start adding the flour mixture, handful by handful. After each addition of flour, stir vigorously with a wooden spoon for 50 strokes. After about 5 minutes of mixing, add the yeast mixture, stir it in, and then continue adding the flour by the handful. When all but 1 cup of the flour has been added (this will take about 10 minutes longer), sprinkle the salt over the dough and stir for a few minutes to incorporate it. Turn the dough out onto a table and knead it for another 5 minutes while adding the last cup of flour. The dough should be moist and satiny.

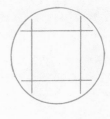

Let the dough rise, covered, for about 1½ hours, until it has doubled in volume.

To shape the dough into a tight, round loaf, first flatten it, then fold the outer edges over into the middle. Repeat the process of folding the dough 4 or 5 times and sealing each fold by pressing down on the dough with the heel of the hand. With the folds underneath, drag the round ball of dough across the worktable with some pressure to make a tight loaf with no air bubbles on top.

The loaf is best proofed in a *banneton* (a basket that measures 8 inches in diameter by 4 inches high and lined with a dish towel and lightly dusted with flour) and then baked on stones in the oven. But it is perfectly acceptable to proof and bake the loaf on a parchment-lined baking tray. Let the loaf rise for between 1 and 1½ hours. Slash the loaf with a razor 3 or 4 times in whatever design you prefer.

Preheat the oven to 450°F, along with the baking stone if you are using one.

To bake the bread, slide it onto the baking stone using a floured, rimless cookie sheet. Immediately turn the oven down to 400°F. The loaf will take between 60 and 70 minutes to bake. Shut off the heat and leave the oven door open for the last 5 minutes of baking to develop a thick crust.

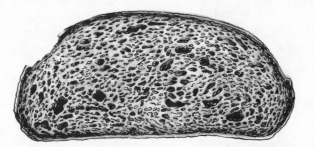

2 RUE THIERS, BRANTÔME

EARLY ONE MORNING IN BRANTÔME, I watched Maurice Duquerroy, sitting right in front of his brick oven, taking a nap. He said he did that every morning when the large loaves needed a few more minutes baking. He sat upright at his little desk with his arms folded on his chest. He explained to me, before he nodded off, how he watched the clock in front of him to make sure he would not oversleep and burn the loaves.

Monsieur Duquerroy lives every hour of his waking life for bread. His day begins at around 3:00 A.M. when he rises and descends the stairs to his *fournil* or bake room. He might take a peek at his rising bread on the way to fire the wood-burning oven. The oven, still hot from the previous day's baking, needs only about forty-five minutes of steady firing with oak branches and twigs and scraps of wood from local cabinet makers to become hot enough for the first batch. For each successive batch, the oven needs only one quick burst of heat from the burning of small twigs for about twenty minutes to bring it up to temperature.

During the firing, Duquerroy uses a cast-iron cone-shaped device called a *gueulard* that fits on a metal seat just inside the mouth of the oven and feeds the hot flames into the baking chamber from the firebox down below. The *boulanger* carefully directs the heat with the *gueulard,* first toward the right wall of the oven, then toward the left, so that it is evenly dispersed.

Library Resource Center
Renton Technical College
Renton, WA 98056

After the bread is baked, the *boulanger* then refreshes his starter once for the next day's bread. As the bread is cooling, Duquerroy arranges the loaves on shelves, on top of his equipment, and even on the floor for the first rush of customers.

At around 7:00 A.M. Madame Duquerroy comes down to open the shop and sell the bread. Then Monsieur Duquerroy fills his white Citroën station wagon with plastic and cardboard boxes stuffed to overflowing with the breads that he will deliver out in the countryside, to restaurants and other shops.

Back in his bakery by 11:00 A.M., Monsieur Duquerroy takes a well-deserved nap for an hour or two. After a provincial lunch of local *pâté,* cheese, salad, wine, and some of his own bread, he goes back to work for five or six hours. His starter, having been refreshed once, can, when it is divided, make several consecutive batches of bread (the size of a batch is determined by the size of the brick oven). Each batch is timed to be ready at two-hour intervals to afford Duquerroy the time to load and unload the oven as well as bake the bread. Over the course of the day the *levain* for the successive batches becomes more and more sour as a result of its extra two-hour rising, so Monsieur Duquerroy uses a progressively smaller portion. Accordingly, he adjusts the rest of the ingredients for each batch so that they all come out tasting much the same.

After weighing out each loaf *(le pesage),* shaping them *(le façonnage),* and setting them to rise *(l'apprêt),* Monsieur Duquerroy eats dinner at around 8:00 P.M. and then retires for the night.

When I told him that I had seventy-five employees in my bakery, he was astounded.

OLD DOUGH

Part of the leavening for this variation is provided by a cup of previously made French bread dough. Many of today's village bakers are using the technique for country, rye, or even white bread variations. A piece of a basic *pain ordinaire* dough is set aside to rise for between six and eight hours at room temperature, or for between twelve and fifteen hours in the refrigerator. If the old dough has been refrigerated, allow it to come up to room temperature before using it.

MAKES ONE 1¼-POUND ROUND LOAF AND TWO 10-OUNCE *BAGUETTES*

> 1 package (2½ teaspoons; ¼ ounce) active dry yeast
>
> 2¼ cups warm water
>
> 1 cup 6-hour-old dough (page 69)
>
> 4 cups organic, unbleached (or all-purpose) white flour
>
> 1½ cups rye or whole wheat flour (or a combination of the two)
>
> 1 tablespoon salt

Proof the yeast by mixing it with ¼ cup of the warm water. Set the mixture aside. Break up the old dough in a large bowl and add the remaining cup of water a little at a time as you continue to dilute the old dough. Combine the white, rye, and whole wheat flours and add 2¾ cups of the mixture, a handful at a time, to the water and old-dough mixture, beating gently at first and then vigorously with a wooden spoon after each addition. This will take about 8 minutes of mixing. Add the yeast mixture and continue to add flour by the handful until you have only 3 or 4 handfuls left. This will take another 3 to 4 minutes. Sprinkle the salt onto the dough and incorporate it. Turn the dough out onto your workbench and knead in rest of the flour. Continue kneading for another 3 or 4 minutes, developing a satiny dough. The total mixing time will be about 15 to 18 minutes.

Let the dough rise, covered, for 1½ hours, until it has doubled in volume. Punch it back and set it aside, covered, to rise again for 30 minutes.

Divide the dough into 2 pieces, then divide one of the halves in two again. Round each of the 3 pieces of dough into tight balls and allow them to rest on the table for 15 minutes, covered with a cloth so that the outside does not dry out and crust over.

Shape the 2 small balls of dough into *baguettes* by flattening each piece into a rectangular shape that measures around 6 by 3 inches. With the 6-inch side toward you, fold over a third of the dough down from the top and then seal the edge with the heel of the hand. Do this 2 or 3 times until the piece is a log about 8 inches long. Stretch each log out to the desired length by rolling it on the table under the palms of your hands until it is between 12 and 14 inches long. Then place each in an oiled, black *baguette* tray or on a cookie sheet that has been lined with parchment paper.

Shape the larger piece of dough into a tight, round loaf by first flattening it, then folding the outer edges over into the middle. Repeat the process of folding the dough 4 or 5 times and sealing each fold by pressing down on the dough with the heel of the hand. With the folds underneath, drag the round ball of dough across the worktable with some pressure to make a tight loaf without any air bubbles on top. Place the loaf on a baking sheet lined with parchment paper. (If you are using the baking stone method, place the loaf in a *banneton,* a basket lined with a dish towel that has been lightly dusted with flour, and see the baking stone instructions on page 53).

Set the loaves aside, covered, in a warm place to rise. The round loaf will take 2 hours and the *baguettes* will take 1½ hours.

If you are using a baking stone, preheat the oven with the stone in it for at least 1 hour at 450°F.

Slash the *baguettes* with a razor blade 4 or 5 times at an angle along the length of the loaves. Bake without glazing them for 20 minutes.

Gently turn the round loaf from the *banneton* onto a rimless cookie sheet that has been dusted with flour. Cut the top with a razor blade in a cross or a circle and slide it onto the baking stone. (Or bake it directly on the parchment-lined baking tray.) It will take between 40 and 45 minutes to bake. Leave the loaves in the oven with the door open and the heat off for the last 5 minutes if you prefer a hearty crust.

Place the loaves on a wire rack to cool.

Compagnon

The word *compagnon* or companion comes from the Latin, *cum panis,* which signifies a person with whom we share bread. In the early years of village baking as a trade in France, along with an *apprentissage* or apprenticeship for student bakers, there was a *compagnonnage* (a guild) for journeymen bakers, the term being derived from the companionship of those who baked the bread and a camaraderie among those who watched over the craft.

Not much information exists on the bread itself, but it appears that this version of French bread is a development derived from the old, pure sourdough techniques with a little yeast added to give it a light, modern appeal. The *compagnon* starter is really just a piece of *pain ordinaire* dough that is left in the refrigerator for thirty-six hours. *Compagnon* can also be made by the direct method and for that version I recommend that the dough be mixed in a food processor.

MAKES ONE 1½-POUND OR 2 SMALL 14-OUNCE OVAL LOAVES

1 package (2½ teaspoons; ¼ ounce) active dry yeast

1¾ cups water

3½ cups organic, unbleached white (or all-purpose) flour

1¾ teaspoons salt

Glaze: 1 egg white beaten up in ½ cup cold water

Proof the yeast by sprinkling it into ¼ cup of very warm water (115°F). Stir the mixture and it set aside for 10 or 15 minutes. Place 3 ice cubes in a glass measuring cup and fill the cup to the 1½-cup mark. When the ice melts, the water should be around 50°F. If you are making the bread in winter, use less ice.

Measure 3 cups of the flour into a food processor that has been fitted with the plastic blade. When the yeast mixture is creamy, pour it over the flour. Pulse the processor 2 or 3 times. Then, with the motor running, slowly add half of the water and process for 30 seconds. With the processor still running, slowly add the rest of the water. Sprinkle the salt onto the dough and process for another 15 seconds. The dough will be wet and soupy. Add all but about a handful of the remaining ½ cup flour, a little at a time, and pulse a few times.

Now the fun begins. Coat your worktable with the remaining flour. Pour the dough out onto the table and beat it vigorously about 100 times with a wooden rolling pin, folding the dough over onto itself several times. This flailing helps to break down the gluten and give the finished loaf a very uneven texture. If the dough is really too sticky, add a little more flour. By the time you

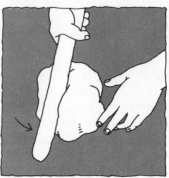

have finished, the dough will be moist, elastic, and satiny. It will feel cool to the touch and its temperature will be between 70°F and 75°F.

Let the dough rise, covered, for 45 minutes. Punch it back and let rise for another 30 minutes.

Flatten the dough and roll it into a tight, oval loaf or divide it in two and make 2 small loaves. Draw the ends of each loaf out into points by rolling them with the palms of the hands on the workbench. Place the loaf (or loaves) on a parchment-lined baking sheet, cover with a towel and let rise for 1½ hours.

Slash each loaf with a razor thus:

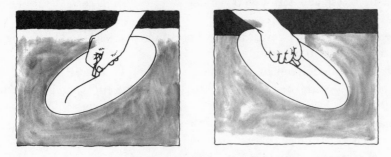

Glaze the loaves and place them in a preheated, 450°F oven. Immediately spray the oven with an atomizer filled with water. Bake a large loaf for between 35 and 40 minutes and 2 small loaves for between 25 and 30 minutes.

The loaves are done when the crust is golden brown and they sound hollow when thumped on the bottom.

Cool on a wire rack.

OLD DOUGH

COMPAGNON AU LEVAIN
STARTER- AND YEAST-METHOD COMPAGNON

MAKES TWO 1¼-POUND OVAL LOAVES

> 1 teaspoon active dry yeast
>
> 1½ cups water
>
> 2 cups *compagnon* starter (page 34)*
>
> 3 cups organic, unbleached white (or all-purpose) flour
>
> 1½ teaspoons salt
>
> Glaze: 1 egg white beaten up in 3 tablespoons cold water

Proof the yeast in ¼ cup of the warm water. Then break up the *compagnon* starter (right out of the refrigerator) in a large bowl and add the remaining 1¼ cups of water, hot out of the tap (130 to 140°F). Mix until the starter is dissolved somewhat and the water has cooled a little (so it is below 115°F), then add the yeast mixture. Start adding the flour, handful by handful, stirring gently at first, then vigorously with a wooden spoon. (The dough can also be mixed with the fountain method; see page 56 for notes about handling wet doughs and make sure that the starter is well broken up in the early stages, so that its effects can be distributed evenly through the new dough.)

After all but 2 or 3 handfuls of the flour have been added (this will take about 10 minutes), sprinkle the salt over the dough and knead it on the work-

* Instead of the *compagnon* starter, you can use 2½ cups of *pain ordinaire* dough. Let the *pain ordinaire* dough rise, covered, in a cool place for 6 hours. Then punch it down and let it rise again, covered and in the refrigerator, for between 24 and 36 hours.

bench for 4 or 5 more minutes while adding the rest of the flour. The dough should be moist and satiny and will be wetter than a normal *pain ordinaire* dough.

Let the dough rise, covered, for 1 hour. Punch it back and allow it to rise again for another 30 minutes.

Divide the dough in half. Flatten each piece, fold it over itself once, sealing the join lightly with the heel of the hand, square the edges, and fold it into a tight log. Each loaf will be about 8 inches long and 3 inches in diameter. Seal the final seam tightly with the heel of the hand and, with the palms, taper the ends of each loaf slightly.

Let the loaves rise, covered, for 1 hour on a parchment-lined flat, black cast-iron baking sheet or baking tray.

When the loaves are ready to be baked, slash each loaf twice down the length of the top like this:

The two cuts should be angled toward the outside of the loaf to create the proper burst in the oven.

Glaze the loaves and bake them in a preheated, 450°F oven. After the first 15 minutes, turn down the heat to 400°F and continue baking the loaves for between 20 and 25 minutes longer.

VARIATION

Use very cold water in the dough and extend the final rising of the shaped loaves from 1 to 2 or 3 hours. This will give the bread a more voluptuous, chewy texture.

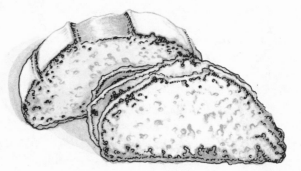

SOURDOUGH

PAIN BLANC AU LEVAIN
WHITE SOURDOUGH BREAD

Pain blanc au levain is widely available in France. Very irregular and chewy in texture, it is light because yeast is added to the dough. Monsieur Maurice Duquerroy (see page 88) made a memorable version. Try it with a sourdough starter which can be a straight *levain* allowed to rise for between eight and ten hours but not so long that it is overrisen, or a piece from a final loaf (which will, therefore, have the salt added). This starter is then given one refreshment with more flour and water and allowed to rise for another five hours before being mixed into the final dough.

MAKES ONE 1½-POUND ROUND LOAF AND TWO 11-OUNCE *BAGUETTES*

THE REFRESHMENT

> 1¼ cups organic, unbleached white (or all-purpose) flour
>
> ½ cup warm water
>
> ¾ cup sourdough starter (page 31) or an 8- to 10-hour piece from
>   yesterday's loaf

THE DOUGH

> 1 package (2½ teaspoons, ¼ ounce) active dry yeast
>
> 2 cups warm water
>
> 4½ cups organic, unbleached white (or all-purpose) flour
>
> All of the refreshed *levain* from the previous step (about 2½ cups)
>
> 1 tablespoon salt (1 scant tablespoon if the original starter comes from a
>   salted bread dough)
>
> Glaze: 1 egg white whisked into ½ cup cold water

TO REFRESH THE STARTER, make a fountain with the flour and in the middle put the starter or old dough that has been broken up into little pieces. Pour in the warm water and dissolve the old dough completely by mixing it with the water and slowly pulling in the flour, little by little, from the rim of the fountain until you have a paste that can be stretched and pulled with 2 or 3 fingers of your mixing hand. Make sure that the old dough is well broken up in the early stages and evenly distributed through the new dough. Add the rest of the flour, a little at a time, and clean off the mixing fingers with a plastic dough scraper and then with some of the remaining flour. As the dough begins to come together, knead it on the table for 5 or 6 minutes until it becomes firm but elastic.

Let the dough rise, covered, in a warm place for between 4 and 5 hours.

TO MAKE THE DOUGH, first proof the yeast in ½ cup of the warm water and set it aside until it is creamy. Make a fountain with the flour. Break up the refreshed *levain* and dissolve it in the rest of the warm water in the center of the

1   2   3

VARIATION

PAIN POLKA

Virtually any bread dough can be made in this pain polka shape. The loaf is often made with a bread such as pain blanc au levain because the texture and crust are suitable for a flat bread.

After the final rising, flatten the round loaf with the palms of the hand so that the loaf measures between 12 and 14 inches in diameter and 1½ inches high. Score the loaf in a criss-cross pattern as shown in the illustration. Make sure the cuts go into the loaf at least ¼ inch.

Let the dough rise for another 20 minutes.

Bake in a preheated 450°F oven for between 25 and 30 minutes, either on a baking stone or on a parchment-lined tray. When the loaf is done, turn off the oven, open the door and leave it inside for between 5 and 8 minutes to develop a thick crust. Cool on a wire rack.

flour, making sure that the *levain* is well diluted. Gradually pull in the flour from the edges. As the mixture becomes pasty and elastic, develop the gluten by whipping the wet dough with wide sweeping motions of one hand. Add the yeast mixture and then pull in most of the rest of the flour. When only about 1 cup of the flour is left, sprinkle the salt over the dough. Gradually add the last of the flour and knead for 3 or 4 minutes. You will have a soft, very wet dough. You do not have to knead it much at this stage because the gluten was well developed in the paste stage.

Let the dough rise, covered, for 1 hour. Punch it back and allow it to rise again for another 30 minutes.

Shape the dough into 1 round loaf and 2 *baguettes*. (Detailed instructions are on page 70.) The loaves may be set to rise in *couches* or *bannetons* for the baking stone method or directly on baking trays.

Let the loaves rise, covered with a damp cloth, for between 1½ and 2 hours in a cool place. Slash each *baguette* diagonally with a razor 3 or 4 times on top and the large loaf in a criss-cross pattern. Glaze all the loaves.

Bake the bread in a preheated 450°F oven. The *baguettes* will take between 15 and 20 minutes and the round loaf will take 40 minutes. The loaves will be golden brown when done and sound hollow when thumped on the bottom.

Cool on a wire rack.

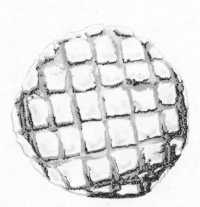

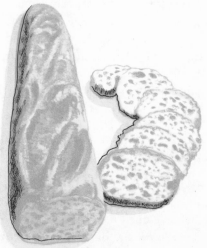

All breads used to be more healthy than they are now. The oldest methods of crushing grains between two stones and sifting the flours through the fingers meant that the nutrients of the natural grains that are pulverized, refined, and bleached away in modern milling procedures were still part of the flour.

Coarse, multigrain breads can still be found in many mountainous regions of France, Italy, Switzerland, and Germany. In Zurich, Basel, Geneva, Munich, Heidelberg, Vienna, Salzburg, and Strasbourg, for example, many bakeries have reputations for strictly whole-grain breads, made in numerous variations. They make small quantities of white bread and only to appease a few fussy customers. Many American bakers make a few whole-grain loaves to satisfy their few customers who request sturdy and nutritious breads. Even then, the quality may be suspect.

The characteristics of an entirely whole-grain bread are often imitated in America: The grains themselves are used but the bread is also loaded with excessive quantities of caramel coloring (a form of burnt sugar) and molasses, ingredients that not only disturb the balance of the bread—distorting its wholesomeness—but also obliterate the natural flavor of the grains that dedicated home or village bakers are trying to celebrate.

Other ingredients also bastardize health breads. Especially in America, bakers have found that enrichments, such as sweeteners, fats, eggs, and milk help to imitate the rich, moist texture of a sourdough. The best way to make a whole-grain bread of character is to use either the sourdough or sponge method rather than depending on the addition of the spurious ingredients we are ostensibly trying to avoid.

On my first visit to Strasbourg, in France, I discovered bakeries in which sturdy whole-grain breads were built into a flamboyant sculptural panorama to lure customers in from the streets. Madame Sheer at Charles Woerle's Boulangerie au vieux Strasbourg told me that whole-grain bread was not a part of a regional heritage. The new interest in health had been stimulated by the natural whole-grain breads made in neighboring Switzerland and Germany.

Lionel Poilâne claims to have identified more than eighty specific French breads. I learned from Madame Sheer that more than 1,260 identifiably different breads are made throughout Europe. "There are as many breads," she said, "as there are cheeses." Many of them are healthy breads with various combinations of grains. The key to all the variations of *pain de régime* is the relative proportion of different grains that are made into flour. Any sturdy grain flour—whole wheat, corn, millet, soy, rye, and barley, to name a few—can be used in varying percentages to change any recipe for bread to yield a more nourishing, wholesome bread. (Add to this the fact that most grains can be cracked, rolled, or malted—soaked in water, roasted, and then cracked—and one can easily imagine the scores of combinations possible.)

The baker must be aware that the heavier flours will affect the activity of the dough. Because grains other than wheat contain no gluten and their ability to take on water is different, they will alter the rhythm of the fermentation. The baker must, therefore, stand prepared to make adjustments to the quantities of water, the rising times, and other basic steps in the process of making bread.

In keeping with the tradition of using all of the purest ingredients, fine sea salt is used in the following recipes for health breads. If instead you choose to use ordinary table salt in the formula, it will not make any noticeable difference in the flavor of the final loaf.

PAIN COMPLET
WHOLE WHEAT BREAD

The simplest recipe for a whole wheat French bread is a variation of the basic six-cup recipe for *pain ordinaire*. Whole wheat flour replaces white flour and milk is used instead of water. To make the loaf a little lighter you can make the bread with equal quantities of white and whole wheat flour.

MAKES ONE 1¼-POUND LOAF

> 1¼ cups milk
>
> 2 packages (5 teaspoons; ½ ounce) active dry yeast
>
> ¼ cup warm water
>
> 3 cups whole wheat flour
>
> 1½ teaspoons fine sea salt
>
> Glaze: 1 egg whisked with 1 tablespoon milk

Scald the milk and let it cool for about 20 minutes, until it is just warm.

Proof the yeast in the ¼ cup warm water, and set it aside until it is creamy (about 10 minutes).

Pour the flour onto the work surface and make a fountain in the middle, ensuring that the sides of the fountain are high enough to hold all the liquid. Pour in the yeast mixture and the warm milk. Mix the liquid together using the fingers of one hand and then gradually pull in small quantities of flour while swirling the mixture around. Continue mixing the liquid and pulling in flour until you have a stringy paste of a batter. Sprinkle in the salt and continue mixing. Use the dry hand to push some of the dry flour into the moist dough. Eventually (after about 10 or 12 minutes), you will be able to clean off the working hand with the back of a knife or a plastic dough scraper. The dough will start to come together so that it can be kneaded on the bench. Knead the dough for about 5 minutes until it is moist, elastic, and springs back when touched.

Let the dough rise, covered, for 1 hour. Punch it back and let it rise again for another 30 minutes. Flatten the dough and shape it into a pointed oval loaf: Fold the dough over onto itself and then roll it up into a tight log, sealing the ends with the edges of the hand. Draw the ends of the loaf out into points by rolling the dough under the palms.

Place the loaf on a baking sheet covered with parchment paper and let it rise for 1 hour.

Preheat the oven to 425°F. Glaze the loaf to give it a shiny, crackling crust and bake it for 35 minutes, until it is deep brown in color and sounds hollow when thumped on the bottom. Cool on a wire rack.

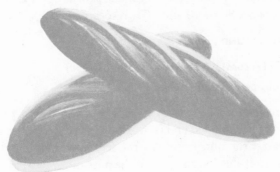

PAIN COMPLET AUX RAISINS
WHOLE WHEAT–RAISIN BREAD

Raisins can also be added to *pain de campagne* or *pain de régime* doughs (the recipes are on pages 86 or 90 and 103 respectively). The dried fruit is incorporated after the dough has been fully kneaded. If you wish to add nuts as well, reduce the raisins to 1 cup and add 1 cup walnut pieces.

MAKES TWO 1½-POUND ROUND LOAVES OR 12 4-OUNCE ROLLS

1 recipe (4½ cups) whole wheat dough (page 98)

2 cups raisins

Glaze: 1 egg whisked with 1 tablespoon milk

Follow the recipe for *pain complet* (or *pain de campagne* or *pain de régime*) and, after the dough has been mixed and completely kneaded, flatten it out onto the workbench. Scatter the raisins on top of the flattened dough and push them in with the fingers. Then roll the dough up with the raisins inside. Round the entire piece into a ball and let the dough rise for 1 hour.

To make rolls, cut the dough into twelve 4-ounce pieces (the size of tangerines) or, to make 2 loaves, divide the dough in half and round each piece into a *boule*.

Depending on which dough you have chosen to embellish with raisins, proceed with the final proofing and baking according to the principal recipe. Glaze the loaves and rolls with the egg and milk mixture before baking in a preheated 425°F oven. Bake the loaves for between 40 and 45 minutes and the rolls for between 10 and 12 minutes.

PAIN COMPLET AUX NOIX
WHOLE WHEAT–WALNUT BREAD

Nuts, too, can be added to *pain de campagne* and *pain de régime* doughs (the recipes for which are on pages 86 or 90 and 103, respectively).

MAKES TWO 1½-POUND LOAVES

> 1 recipe (4½ cups) whole wheat dough (page 98)
>
> 2 cups roughly chopped walnuts

Follow the recipe for *pain complet* (or *pain de campagne* or *pain de régime*) and, after the dough has been mixed and completely kneaded, flatten it on the workbench. Then scatter the nuts on top of the flattened dough and push them in with the fingers. Roll the dough up with the nuts inside, round the entire piece into a ball, and let it rise for 1 hour.

Divide the dough into 2 pieces. Flatten each piece, round each into a *boule*, and follow the directions for the final proofing and baking that are given in the principal recipes. The loaves will take between 35 and 40 minutes to bake in a 425°F oven.

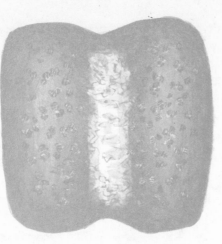

OLD DOUGH

PAIN DE SON
BRAN BREAD

I learned this bread from Monsieur Robert at the Boulangerie-Pâtisserie le Fey-eux in Paris. Not strictly a whole wheat bread, *pain de son* is a classic example of a variation on real French bread in that bran flakes are included in a *pain or-dinaire* dough but there is no sweetener. The old dough provides just enough acidity in the loaf to give the bran an interesting flavor.

Use a piece of *pain ordinaire* dough that has risen at room temperature for 4 hours or in the refrigerator for between 12 and 24 hours.

MAKES TWO 1-POUND LOAVES

1¼ cups plus 2 tablespoons very warm water

1 teaspoon active dry yeast

1½ cups 4-hour-old *pain ordinaire* dough (page 69)

2 cups organic, unbleached white (or all-purpose) flour

1½ cups wheat bran

1½ teaspoons fine sea salt

Place ¼ cup plus 2 tablespoons warm water in a cup. Sprinkle the yeast on top and stir to incorporate. Set the mixture aside until creamy. Break up the old dough in a large bowl and stir into it the remaining 1 cup of warm water. Start adding the flour, handful by handful, stirring at first gently and then vigorously with a wooden spoon. Make sure that the old dough is well broken up in the early stages, so that its effects can be evenly distributed through the new dough. After all but 1 cup of the flour has been added (this will take about 5 minutes), stir in the yeast mixture and the bran. Sprinkle the salt over the mixture and stir for a few more minutes until all ingredients are incorporated. Pour the shaggy mass of dough out onto the worktable and knead it for between 5 and 8 minutes, using at most another handful or two of flour. Because of the bran the dough should feel a little dry and it will be firmer than a normal white flour dough. But if pressed hard with the palm it will stick.

Let the dough rise, covered, for 1½ hours. Punch it back and set it to rise for another 30 minutes.

After the second rising, divide the dough into 2 pieces, flatten each piece, folding it over once, square the edges, and roll it into a log. Each time you fold

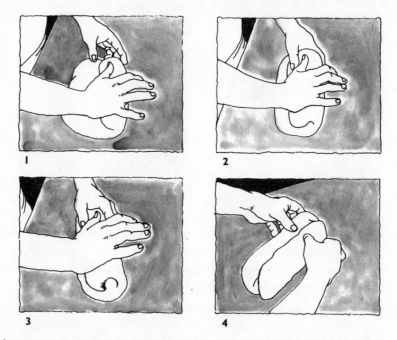

the dough over itself, seal the seam with the heel of the hand. When the dough is completely rolled up, seal the last seam very loosely with the heel of the hand.

If you plan to use a baking stone, place it in the oven and preheat the oven to 450°F.

Set the loaves to rise on a flour-dusted board or rimless cookie sheet, with the seam-side up and covered to avoid crusting, for between 35 and 40 minutes. When the loaves are ready to be baked, slide them gently onto the baking stone, seam-side up, without slashing or glazing them. (They can also be baked on a parchment-lined baking tray.) If they have been shaped correctly the loaves will open with a nice tear along the loosely sealed seam. Bake the bread for 35 minutes, or until it is golden brown. Cool on a wire rack.

SPONGE

PAIN DE RÉGIME SUR POOLISH
WHOLE-GRAIN (SPONGE) BREAD

A recipe using the sponge method yields an entirely satisfactory texture. It is also a considerably quicker version of French health bread than one using the sourdough method, so I have given the simpler version first.

MAKES ONE 3-POUND ROUND LOAF

THE *POOLISH*

> 2 packages (2 scant tablespoons; ½ ounce) active dry yeast
>
> 2 cups warm water
>
> I cup organic, unbleached white flour
>
> ½ cup organic rye flour
>
> ½ cup organic whole wheat flour

THE DOUGH

> ¾ cup warm water
>
> All of the *poolish* from the previous step
>
> 1½ cups organic whole wheat flour
>
> I cup organic, unbleached white flour
>
> I cup organic barley flour
>
> I cup organic crushed 6-grain cereal (a mixture of buckwheat, rye, oats,
>
>   barley, triticale, and wheat; any mixture of an organic, 4- to 6-grain
>
>   crushed cereal can be used)
>
> I tablespoon sea salt

TO MIX THE SPONGE OR *POOLISH*, first proof the yeast by sprinkling it into 1 cup of the warm water and stirring to dissolve. When it is creamy, place it in a large bowl and mix in the rest of the warm water. Combine the flours and begin adding them slowly by handfuls to the yeast mixture, stirring with a wooden spoon. Set the sponge aside in the same bowl in which it was mixed, covered with a dish towel, for between 2½ and 3½ hours. When the *poolish* has risen and fallen, it is ready to use.

TO MAKE THE DOUGH, stir the warm tap water into the *poolish*. Combine the 3 flours and the cereal and start adding the mixture, handful by handful, to the sponge, stirring after each addition, at first gently and then vigorously with a wooden spoon. After all but 1 cup of the flour mixture has been added (this will take about 10 minutes), sprinkle the salt over the mixture and knead the dough on the workbench for another 5 minutes while adding the last of the flour. The dough should have a firm consistency but still feel sticky. Resist the temptation to add more flour.

Let the dough rise, covered, for 1½ hours, until it has doubled in size. Flatten the dough and shape it into a round loaf.

This bread is best proofed in a canvas-lined basket and then baked on a stone in the oven, but it can also be placed on a parchment-lined baking sheet. Set it aside, covered, to rise for between 45 minutes and 1 hour.

If you are using a baking stone, place it in the oven and preheat the oven to 425°F. Slash the loaf in a tick-tack-toe pattern with a razor blade. The loaf will take between 55 and 60 minutes to bake.

PAIN DE RÉGIME AU LEVAIN
SOURDOUGH WHOLE-GRAIN BREAD

This is a sourdough version of *pain de régime*. To make this variation, follow the principal recipe for *pain de campagne* that begins on page 82, making up a *chef* and giving it two refreshments, until you have 1½ cups of fresh, active *levain* that has completed its final rising. Make up the dough using the following ingredients:

MAKES ONE 2-POUND ROUND LOAF

1 teaspoon active dry yeast

1½ cups warm water

2 cups organic dark rye flour

¾ cups organic rye meal (or cracked rye grain)

¼ cup wheat bran

1½ cups whole wheat *levain* (pages 82–84)

1 tablespoon sea salt

To mix the dough, proof the yeast in ¼ cup of the warm water. Combine the rye flour, meal, and bran and make a fountain. Add all of the *levain,* which has been chopped up, and then the rest of the water, a little at a time.

As the water is added, dissolve the *levain* in it and gradually pull in some of the flour to make a sticky paste. As the flour is added, the paste will become a little firmer and should be stretched and pulled vigorously with the fingers of one hand. When all but about 1 cup of the flour has been incorporated, the dough will be moist and sticky. Clean your hands with the back of a knife blade or a plastic dough scraper and work those little bits into the dough.

Sprinkle the salt onto the wet dough and incorporate it by kneading it in, together with the remaining flour. Knead the dough for 5 more minutes until it is firm and springs back when touched.

From this point on, the procedure is exactly the same as that for making *pain de campagne,* as given on pages 84–85, except that, because of the addition of yeast, the first rising takes 1½ to 2 hours and the final rising between 4 and 6 hours. Very ambitious bakers who have successfully tried the recipe several times and who feel that their starter is active enough (and yet not too sour) to give a good push to the bread, may try the recipe without yeast. In that case they should adhere to the 16-hour total proofing time given in the *pain de campagne* recipe for the final rising.

PORRIDGE

PAIN BOUILLIE
PORRIDGE BREAD

Whenever you see a French recipe that begins with the instructions *"Faire une bouillie . . ."* you know you have come across a very old recipe because it starts off with a mush made by pouring boiling water over flour. The mush, which will ferment slightly overnight, is used the next day mixed into a bread. The most fascinating recipe I have heard of for *pain bouillie* is one from the Alpine region of France around the town of Villar-d'Arène. The *bouillie* is made with dark rye flour and set aside to rest for seven hours. The porridge is then mixed into a dough, without any yeast, and allowed to rest for another seven hours. When the dough is finally made into loaves, they are placed in an oven that has already been used for making bread and so the temperature is only about 200°F. The loaves bake for seven hours and the process produces a moist, dense, completely sourdough bread that lasts well over six months—or so the story goes. The bread is traditionally made in November and it keeps best when stored in wine cellars and hay lofts.

In the following recipe yeast and some white flour are included to make the procedure a little easier for the contemporary home baker.

MAKES TWO 14-OUNCE LOAVES

THE *BOUILLIE* (PORRIDGE)

> 2 teaspoons honey
>
> 1¾ cups boiling water
>
> 1 cup organic rye flour
>
> 1 cup organic cracked rye grain

THE DOUGH

> 1 teaspoon active dry yeast
>
> 3 tablespoons warm water
>
> All of the *bouillie* from the previous step
>
> 2 teaspoons fine sea salt
>
> 2 teaspoons caraway seeds
>
> 1 tablespoon raisins
>
> 2 cups organic, unbleached white (or all-purpose) flour

TO MAKE THE *BOUILLIE* (PORRIDGE), dissolve the honey in the boiling water and pour it over the rye flour and grain in a ceramic bowl. Let the mixture soak for a few minutes, then stir it with a wooden spoon until the flour is completely wet. Cover the bowl with a towel and set it aside overnight in a warm place.

TO MAKE THE DOUGH, proof the yeast in 2 tablespoons of warm water. Place the *bouillie* in a medium-sized bowl, sprinkle the salt over the porridge and stir it in. Crush the caraway seeds in a mortar, add the raisins, and grind the mixture to a paste. Stir in the remaining tablespoon of water. Add 2 teaspoons of this caraway flavoring to the *bouillie*. Gradually add 1½ cups flour, a handful at a time, while mixing with a plastic dough scraper. Mix in the yeast. Continue adding the rest of the flour by handfuls until it is all incorporated and you have a medium-firm piece of dough. Knead the dough on the worktable for between 5 and 8 minutes using a small additional quantity of white flour if necessary. The dough will be firm but if you press your fingers into it it will feel sticky.

Return the dough to the bowl, cover it with a moist towel, and place it in an unlit oven for between 1½ and 2 hours to rise.

When it has doubled in bulk, cut the dough into 2 pieces. Shape the pieces into flat loaves that are 5 inches square and 2 inches high by flattening and then

1

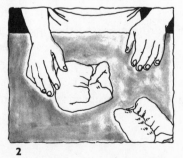

2

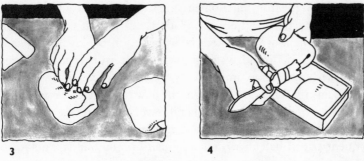

3   **4**

folding the edges toward the middle and sealing the joins with the heel of the hand. Oil 1 side of each loaf and place them, oiled sides abutting, side by side in a greased bread pan that measures 9 inches by 5½ inches by 3 inches.

Let the loaves rise, again covered with a moist towel, in an unlit oven for 30 minutes, until the dough has risen about ½ an inch above the top of the pan.

Give each loaf a straight, 2-inch slash on the top with a razor blade and brush the tops with a little salad oil.

Set the oven at 450°F and immediately place the loaves inside. Bake the bread in what is known as a rising oven for 25 minutes. Then reduce the heat to 400°F and bake the loaves for 45 minutes longer. They will be quite dark.

Remove the loaves from the pan and place them on a cooling rack. When cooled the bread is best sliced very, very thin.

Rye Breads

My Search for *Seigle*

Ken Conklin's description of the medicine-ball-sized loaf that he found in the town of Vers in the Cantal mountains was my first acquaintance with *seigle*. Ken's description made me wonder what such a bread could be like. He said it lasted a week and that the texture was like cake. Was it made of sourdough? How much rye could possibly be in the dough? All these questions went through my mind. Inspired, I spent two weeks in France in the spring of 1988 investigating *seigle*. I saw the whole spectrum of rye bread types, from *tourtes* (large, round flat loaves) to *baguettes*, from loaves made entirely of rye to those with only a handful of rye in the dough. Each baker's bread and each regional variation was distinctive. I learned from sampling those breads and talking to the bakers that my long-held belief about rye bread was true: It is almost impossible to make a direct-method rye bread that has an appealing flavor, character, or texture or any shelf life. Rye needs a certain amount of acidity (translated as age in the dough) to bring out its natural flavor. Almost every baker I spoke to used a *levain, poolish,* or the addition of old dough in his *seigle*.

My appetite for *seigle* had been whet some years earlier by the loaf that my wife and I had bought from the Boulangerie Costa in Aix-en-Provence. Leaving the shop, we wandered up the rue Paul-Bert, tearing off chunks of the tangy *seigle* and eating them as we walked. We stopped in our tracks, looked at each other, and Gayle said, "You have to go back and learn to make this bread."

We returned to the shop immediately and introduced ourselves to Monsieur Costa and his family. That day he taught me how to make his *levain* (pronounced "levaing" in the dialect of Provence) and gave me his recipe. But the precise method of making the bread itself was a mystery for many years. It seemed that on subsequent trips I had always tried to visit him on Sunday, his *jour de repos,* when his shop was closed.

The trip in 1988 started out in Strasbourg where the traditional rye bread is made into a large log about two and a half feet long and six inches in diameter. It is proofed in *bannetons* that are not lined with canvas so that striations of white flour are left on the crust from the imprint of the baskets. (This indicates that the bread can undergo a short, say one or two hour, final proofing time; any bread that must rise in a basket for between eight and ten hours would need the canvas lining so the dough would not stick to the basket.) The loaf is not slashed with a *lame* (a curved, flat blade, often fitted with a razor) as are most French breads; instead it is punctured with a *rouleau à pique* (a small rolling pin with many sharp nails protruding from it that is used for pricking puff pastry) to prevent the crust from breaking irregularly when the loaf is first exposed to the heat of the oven. (At home the procedure can be done by stabbing the top of the loaf frequently with an ice pick just before baking.) I did not manage to see the bread being made, but Madame Sheer at the Woerle bakery told me that it was made with *levain*.

Four or five days later and clear on the other side of France, right in the middle of what is called the Massif Central, I discovered numerous variations of rye in one day. And I bought almost every loaf I saw. In the town of Thiézac, between Vic-sur-Cère and Saint-Flour in the Cantal mountains, I found an oversized, hubcap-shaped loaf of pure *seigle*. As the baker described it, the bread is just another variation of the basic formula for French bread, but the procedure requires delicate and exacting care. The loaf is made entirely with rye flour, even in the refreshments, and absolutely no yeast. After the dough was mixed, three kilos (six and a half pounds) are pulled back and allowed to rise for at least one day and preferably two: The *levain* should be allowed to acquire the excess acidity that makes *seigle* interesting.

After one or two days the three-kilo piece is refreshed with eight liters (two gallons) of water and enough rye flour (around sixteen kilos, thirty-two pounds) to make a firm *levain*. After the *levain* has been mixed for six or eight minutes and comes away from the sides of the bowl, it is allowed to rise for between six and nine hours, usually overnight. The duration is not that important, the baker said, but the *levain* must be very, very acidic.

The next day the *levain* is mixed with forty liters (ten gallons) of water and enough rye flour (around eighty kilos, 160 pounds) to make a dough that feels moister than that of *pain ordinaire*. The texture owes as much to the inherent stickiness of rye as to the quantities of water used. The salt is added at this point, when the dough is mixed.

After being mixed for between twelve and fifteen minutes on the lowest speed, the dough is set to rise for about two or two and a half hours on the bench or in the bowl. It is then made up into loaves that are placed in floured *bannetons* for a final rising, which takes an hour. Like many variations of French rye breads, this dough is so active that it can be baked soon after it has been made up into loaves.

The bread is moist with a spongy, tight grain, like a dense but moist cake. The flavor is tangy, piquant, and almost bitingly sour with a heavy, salted flavor. But the salty taste is the result of the acidity of the starter, not the quantity of salt used. The *vendeuse* (the shopkeeper, who often seems to be the wife of the baker) told me that the bread went well with *charcuterie*, oysters, Cantal cheese, and—to great enjoyment—as a float in onion soup. The recipe for *pain de seigle de Thiézac* on page 116 is a slight variation of the entirely sourdough method.

Back up the road several kilometers I had visited a baker in Vic-sur-Cère who made a bread of white flour with a small addition of rye, appreciably less than 25 percent, to give it a creamy beige cast. The crumb was much more voluptuous and uneven in texture than that of the bread in Thiézac. The baker called it *pain de campagne* and, according to the *vendeuse*, it was made by the *pâte fermentée* method—a piece of *pain ordinaire* and a little bit of yeast being used in the dough. The texture, therefore, was not as spongy and shiny as that of a bread made only with *levain:* It had a little fluff to it. It was lighter in weight, color, and texture than a pure *seigle* made with *levain* and only rye flour.

The trip that day had started at eight in the morning in Saint-Flour and the rye *baguette* that I bought there contained about 60 percent rye flour and 40 percent white. Its texture was dense and drier than that of the other breads. It was also salty and seemed to have been made with a small percentage of *levain* that had not been built with refreshments.

By the time I arrived at Vers to find the fabled sixteen-pound medicine-ball loaf of *seigle* that started the search years before, I was exhausted: My little Siate sedan was filled with well over forty pounds of bread, in loaves of various shapes and sizes. I had spoken to half a dozen bakers and their wives. Running through my head were numerous descriptions of methods, techniques, and ingredient proportions, all about *seigle*. I found myself mumbling that I was sick of bread and when I drove past the bakery in Vers did not have the energy to stop. In honor of friends who had stayed there, I drove across the little bridge between the medieval town and the road and tried to find the garret where they had spent a wonderful summer ten years ago.

Unable to find the garret, but completely intoxicated by the aromas and

thoughts of rustic country rye bread, I pointed the red Siate down the road toward Cahors and then eventually to Carcassonne, knowing I had seen more *seigle* on that one day than I would probably see for the rest of my life.

Using Rye Flour

French law states that, to be called *seigle* or rye bread, breads must contain at least 50 percent rye flour. Those that do, as well as those that contain only a handful of rye, come in many varieties of shape, size, appearance, and flavor, characteristics that make French-style rye bread more interesting than regular wheat-based French bread. Rye bread can be like a dark, moist cake with tiny, regular air bubbles or have a light, beige color and a voluptuous uneven crumb. At its best, the flavor is tangy, the crust irresistible.

Seigle appears in sixteen-pound round loaves in rural mountain regions, as twelve-ounce *baguettes* in the Midi, ten-pound flat loaves in Thiézac, and dark, almost perfectly round, one-pound *boules* in Paris. (I encountered the Parisian style of *seigle* in 1983 at Monsieur Poilâne's famous bakery on the rue du Cherche-Midi. His loaves have a thick crust and a spongy, golden crumb that has the brilliant sheen of honey. The moist inside is more reminiscent of cake than of bread and it seems to stay fresh for up to a week.) Often, whether in large, flat loaves called *tourtes* or two-ounce rolls, it is studded with raisins; the distinctive, sour tang of rye creates a startling contrast to the sweet dried fruit.

Only the most experienced bakers have been able to use rye flour by itself in baking bread because it contains no gluten. Used, however, along with wheat flour in varying quantities, rye flour can give a moister crumb and depth of flavor and extend shelf life. Even *pain ordinaire* may contain up to 2 percent rye flour.

Pain méteil is a bread made of equal quantities of wheat and rye flour. Its origin may be traced back to the time when fields were seeded with a mixture of wheat and rye grains. Today the baker combines the two flours in his shop before mixing his dough for *pain méteil.*

The regional differences all derive from the amount of rye flour used and the method and particular care taken by each baker. The numerous variations in the percentages of rye flour that are used in French bread show its potential for loaves of differing styles and indicates the range of possiblities for the village baker in America. There is a rye bread loaf that would please almost any bread lover.

Where to Find *Seigle* in France

CHRISTIAN DANIAS
12 rue du Collège
15100 Saint-Flour, Cantal

"À LA TARTE DE VIC"
J. P. Pouilhes, pâtisserie-boulangerie
15800 Vic-sur-Cère, Cantal

POILÂNE'S
8 rue du Cherche-Midi
Paris

BOULANGERIE COSTA
19 rue Paul-Bert
13100 Aix-en-Provence

THIÉZAC
The village is so small that there is no need of an address;
just follow the scent of bread baking.

BOULANGERIE AU VIEUX STRASBOURG, Charles Woerle
10 rue de la Division-Leclerc
67000 Strasbourg

B. GANACHAUD—Maître Boulanger
150 rue de Menilmontant
Paris, 20th Arrondissement

BOULANGERIE HAETTEL
40 rue Émile Zola
46100 Figeac

SPONGE

PAIN MÉTEIL
WHEAT AND RYE BREAD

During the time when bread was baked in communal ovens, individual families mixed, shaped, and set to rise their own breads. When the loaves were ready to bake, each French housewife would marked her own loaves to distinguish them from her neighbors'. In some regions, the family's signature or symbol—a cross, a circle, an initial—was cut on each loaf. Elsewhere a stencil was made of the family symbol, the loaf dusted with flour, and the stencil removed. In other villages decorative patches of dough were placed on the loaves.

Pain méteil was, and in some regions still is, commonly made with the dusted stencil design on top. *Méteil* is French for "maslin," a British dialect word for a mixture of wheat and rye, either as grain or flour.

MAKES ONE 2½-POUND LOAF

THE SPONGE

> 1 package (2½ teaspoons; ¼ ounce)
>   active dry yeast
> 1½ cups water
> 1 cup rye flour
> ½ cup organic, unbleached white
>   (or all-purpose) flour

THE DOUGH

> 1 cup warm water
> All of the sponge from the previous step
> 3¾ cups organic, unbleached white (or all-purpose) flour
> 2¾ teaspoons salt

TO MAKE THE SPONGE, proof the yeast in ½ cup of warm water. When it is creamy, add it to a medium-sized bowl along with the rest of the water, which should be at room temperature. Slowly add the combined flours by handfuls, while stirring the mixture with a wooden spoon. Set the sponge aside, covering the bowl with a dish towel, for between 15 and 24 hours.

TO MAKE THE DOUGH, mix the 1 cup warm tap water into the sponge. Start adding 2¾ cups of flour, handful by handful, stirring the mixture, gently at first, and then vigorously with a wooden spoon. Beat in each addition of flour with 50 strokes of the spoon. This will take about 15 minutes. Sprinkle the salt over the dough and then knead the dough on a table for another 2 or 3 minutes while adding the remaining cup of flour. The dough should be of medium consistency but still feel sticky. Resist the temptation to add more flour.

Let the dough rise, covered, for 2 hours. When it has doubled in bulk, flatten it out and shape into a round loaf.

Set the loaf aside on a parchment-lined baking sheet, covered, to rise for about 1½ hours. The loaf is ready to be baked when the indentation made by a finger does not bounce back.

To mark your loaf in the traditional manner, make a stencil out of a piece of typing paper. Draw your family initial, making the letter ½ an inch wide, from the following alphabet:

ABCDEFGHIJKLM
NOPQRSTUVWXYZ

With an ice pick, puncture the loaf through the top crust about 1-inch deep, at least 8 or 10 times. This will serve the same purpose as slashing the loaf, except that the crust will not tear and mar the stencil design. Place the stencil on top of the loaf. Put a few tablespoons of white flour in a strainer with fine mesh and use it to dust the top of the loaf lightly. Remove the stencil.

Place the loaf in a preheated, 425°F oven for between 35 and 45 minutes.

PAIN DE SEIGLE (PÂTE FERMENTÉE)
RYE BREAD WITH OLD-DOUGH ADDITION

OLD DOUGH

The recipe for rye bread made with the addition of an old dough is similar to that for *pain de campagne.* If you are looking for an interesting texture, try this recipe; if you want a more tangy rye flavor, try the next one for *seigle sur poolish.* This method turns out best when the old dough has been refrigerated for between twenty-four and thirty-six hours. If you use the dough right out of the refrigerator, use slightly warmer water.

MAKES ONE 1¾-POUND OVAL LOAF

> 1 package (2½ teaspoons; ¼ ounce) active dry yeast
>
> 1½ cups warm water
>
> 1 cup 6- to 8-hour-old *pain ordinaire* dough (page 69)
>
> 2½ cups rye flour
>
> ½ cup organic, unbleached white (or all-purpose) flour
>
> 1½ teaspoons salt
>
> Glaze: 1 egg whisked with 1 tablespoon cold milk

Proof the yeast in about ¼ cup of the warm water. In a large bowl break up the old dough and add the rest of the water. Combine the flours and start adding the mixture, handful by handful, while stirring gently at first, and then vigorously with a wooden spoon. When the yeast is creamy (this will take between 5 and 10 minutes), add it to the dough and continue mixing with the spoon. Make sure that the old dough is well broken up in the early stages, so that its effects can be evenly distributed through the new dough. After all but 1 cup of the flour has been added (about 10 minutes), sprinkle the salt over the dough and continue mixing. After the dough begins to come together but is still quite moist, empty it out onto the worktable and knead it for a few more minutes while adding the last of the flour. The dough should be moist and satiny. It will be more sticky than a normal dough, but avoid the impulse to add more flour.

Let the dough rise, covered, for 45 minutes. To shape the oval loaf, flatten the dough, then fold it over once, and square the edges by folding them about an inch over into the middle. Roll the dough down toward you, 2 or 3 times, sealing it each time with the heel of the hand. When the dough is completely rolled up and in an oval log, seal the last join tightly with the heel of the hand and seal the ends with the pinkie edges of each hand.

Place the loaf on a tray lined with parchment and it let rise, in a warm place and covered with a damp cloth, for 45 minutes. Slash the loaf diagonally with a razor 3 or 4 times on top and glaze it. Bake the loaf in a preheated 450°F oven for between 45 and 50 minutes.

SPONGE

PAIN DE SEIGLE SUR POOLISH
SPONGE-METHOD RYE BREAD

Many bakers who make French-style rye bread—and who do not wish to use the sourdough method—prefer to use the sponge method rather than the old-dough method when they are concerned more with taste than with texture. The use of rye flour in the sponge helps to bring out more of the tangy rye flavor.

MAKES ONE 3-POUND ROUND LOAF

THE *POOLISH*

    2 packages (2 scant tablespoons; ½ ounce) active dry yeast

    2 cups water

    I cup organic, unbleached white (or all-purpose) flour

    I cup rye flour

THE DOUGH

    I ½ cups warm water

    All of the *poolish* from the previous step

    2 cups rye flour

    2 cups organic, unbleached white (or all-purpose) flour

    I tablespoon salt

    Glaze: I egg whisked up with I tablespoon milk

PREPARE THE *POOLISH* by first mixing the yeast into ½ cup of warm water. When it is creamy, add it to a large bowl, along with the rest of the water, which should be at room temperature. Slowly add the flour by handfuls while stirring with a wooden spoon. When the flour is incorporated and there are no lumps, set the sponge aside, covering the bowl with a dish towel, for between 2 and 3 hours. When the *poolish* has risen and fallen it is ready to use.

TO MAKE THE DOUGH, add the 1½ cups warm water to the *poolish* and mix it in. Combine the flours and start adding 3 cups of the mixture, handful by handful, stirring gently at first, and then vigorously with a wooden spoon. After each addition of flour, stir the mixture with 50 strokes of the spoon. This will take about 15 minutes. Sprinkle the salt over the dough, turn it out onto a table and knead it for another 2 to 3 minutes while adding the last cup of flour. The dough should be of firm consistency but feel sticky. If the dough is very sticky and unworkable, add up to ½ cup white flour

Round the dough up into a tight ball and let it rise, covered, for 2 hours. Flatten out the dough and shape it into a round loaf.

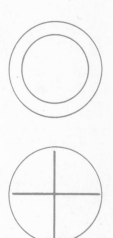

This bread is best proofed in *bannetons* and baked on stones in the oven, but it can also be placed on a parchment-lined baking sheet. Let the loaf rise for about 1 hour.

With a razor slash the top of the loaf to make either a cross or a circle around the top. For a smooth finish the loaf can, instead, be docked (punctured at least ½-inch deep) 8 to 10 times with an ice pick. Glaze the loaf and bake it in a preheated 450°F oven for between 40 and 50 minutes.

Pain de Seigle

SOURDOUGH

PAIN DE SEIGLE DE THIÉZAC
THIÉZAC RYE BREAD

The following recipe will produce a very close replica of the large loaf of rye bread that I bought in Thiézac in 1988. The method is identical to the authentic recipe, except for the additions of a little yeast and white flour in the final dough. For the first few times, I would recommend your including both the yeast and the white flour. They make the procedure easier and give a lighter loaf. Once you are familiar with the method, try it with all rye flour and no yeast to make a 100 percent sourdough rye bread.

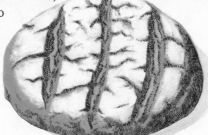

MAKES ONE 3-POUND ROUND LOAF

THE *CHEF*

¼ teaspoon honey

⅓ to ½ cup warm water

I cup organic rye flour

THE REFRESHMENT

All of the *chef* (I cup) from the previous step

½ cup warm water

I cup organic rye flour

THE DOUGH

I teaspoon active, dry yeast

2 cups warm water

All of the *levain* (2½ cups) from the previous step

2 cups organic rye flour

2 cups organic, unbleached white (or all-purpose) flour

I tablespoon salt

TO MAKE THE *CHEF*, dissolve the honey in the warm water in a small bowl. Add the rye flour a pinch at a time while stirring the mixture with a wooden spoon. The finished dough does come together but it will be moist and sticky.

Do not use all of the flour if that will make the dough stiff and dry, but an extra tablespoon or 2 of water may be added. If pressed hard, the *chef* will stick to the fingers. If pressed lightly with a floured finger, it will bounce back.

Let the *chef* rise, covered with a damp cloth and in a small dish or container, for between 24 and 36 hours. It will be bubbly and smell pleasantly sour when it is ready to use.

FOR THE REFRESHMENT, dilute the *chef* in the water in a medium-sized bowl and, as before, add the rye flour a pinch at a time, making a moist dough. It should be firm enough to be worked lightly, with a little flour, on the table without sticking excessively to the hands. (If the dough is grabbed hard with unfloured hands, it will stick and be messy.) Once refreshed, the *chef* becomes the *levain* or "natural starter."

Let the *levain* rise in a plastic container (or in the bowl in which it was mixed) and covered with a damp cloth for between 8 and 10 hours. The dough will nearly double in volume, appear inflated, and smell slightly sour.

TO MAKE THE DOUGH, proof the yeast in ¼ cup of the warm water. In a large bowl (rye doughs are messy so they are best mixed in a bowl), dilute the *levain* in the rest of the warm water. Combine the flours and add 1¼ cups of the mixture, a handful at a time, to the *levain,* mixing it in with a wooden spoon. When the yeast mixture is creamy, add it to the dough mixture.

Sprinkle the salt on top and continue mixing, adding another 1½ cups flour gradually. When the dough starts to come together but is still quite sticky, empty it out onto the table. Use a plastic dough scraper to clean all of the rye dough out of the bowl. The dough will be quite sticky. Knead it lightly (so it does not stick to the hands), while incorporating the rest of the flour. Do not try to add any more flour and knead the dough on the bench for only a few minutes after it has come together. The total mixing time should be only about 10 or 12 minutes.

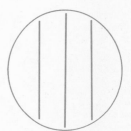

Let the dough rise, covered, for 45 minutes. Then flatten it and fold the edges over onto the middle several times, sealing it each time with the heel of the hand. Round the dough into a ball and let the loaf rise, covered, in a large *banneton* (cloth-lined basket that has been dusted with flour) if you plan to bake it on a baking stone, or on a parchment-lined baking sheet, for 45 minutes.

Slash the loaf lightly with a razor straight across the top 3 times and bake it in a preheated 450°F oven for 45 to 50 minutes. The loaf will be done when it sounds hollow when thumped on the bottom, but rye dough is very wet and needs a little extra baking. Turn the heat off and open the door of the oven for bewteen 5 and 7 minutes, leaving the loaf inside, to help dry out the moist crumb.

Monsieur Costa's bread has a wild, uneven texture and an aroma of honey and nuts. His loaves are oval in shape and flat, being no more than two or three inches high in the thickest parts. The crust is almost a quarter of an inch thick but is, nevertheless, still easily chewed. The flavor is pure essence of rye flour and so appealing that nothing else is needed to accompany it.

His bread is based on a white sourdough *levain* that is refreshed every day. The baker adds a piece to the final batch of each of his sourdough breads. To mix his *seigle,* Monsieur Costa uses six kilos (twelve pounds) of *levain blanc,* twenty-two kilos (forty-four pounds) of white flour, eight kilos (sixteen pounds) of rye flour, thirty grams (two tablespoons) of salt per kilo of flour, and enough water to make a firm dough. The first rising takes 1½ hours. Then the loaves are scaled, rounded, and allowed to rise for another three hours. They are then shaped and set to rise in *couches* for between 15 and 20 hours.

The following recipe is a near-perfect adaptation for the home baker of his wholly sourdough method.

MAKES ONE 1½-POUND OVAL LOAF

THE *CHEF*

> ½ cup organic, unbleached white (all-purpose) flour
>
> ¼ teaspoon honey
>
> Enough water to make a firm dough

THE FIRST REFRESHMENT

> ½ cup organic, unbleached white (or all-purpose) flour
>
> 2 tablespoons *chef* (a piece the size of a large walnut) from the previous step
>
> ¼ cup plus 1 tablespoon warm water

THE SECOND REFRESHMENT

> 1½ cups organic, unbleached white (or all-purpose) flour
>
> All of the *levain* (½ cup) from the previous step
>
> ½ cup water

THE DOUGH

> ½ cup *levain* from the previous step
>
> 1¼ cups warm water
>
> 2½ cups organic, unbleached white (or all-purpose) flour
>
> ¾ cup rye flour
>
> 2 teaspoons fine sea salt

TO MAKE THE *CHEF*, mound the flour up on your worktable and make a fountain. Dissolve the honey in a small cup that contains a tablespoon of warm water and pour that into the middle of the fountain. With 1 finger start mixing the liquid with a little of the flour from the outer ring. Pull in more and more of the flour, adding only enough water to make a firm dough.

Place the *chef* in a cup or small bowl, cover it with a damp cloth, and set it aside in a warm place out of drafts. Let the *chef* rise and ferment for between 2 and 3 days. When it is ready, the dough will be pleasantly sour, very sticky, and inflated with air. (It is better to use this *chef* several hours, or even a day or so, before it is ready, rather than too late. Because of the honey, the *chef* will become active very quickly. If it becomes too unbearably sticky, discard it and start over.)

FOR THE FIRST REFRESHMENT, mound up ½ cup white flour on your worktable and make a fountain. Crumble the *chef* and place it in the middle of the flour well. Pour in the warm water and stir until the *chef* is completely dissolved. Then, with several fingers only, start pulling in some of the flour to make a paste in the middle of the fountain. Gradually work in most of the flour. You will see that the dough becomes more and more active as it is worked. Use the dry hand to clean off the mixing hand with some of the remaining flour and incorporate every little bit into the dough, which is now called a *levain*.

Set the *levain* aside, covered, to rise for between 24 and 36 hours.

FOR THE SECOND REFRESHMENT, repeat the procedure described for the first and set the refreshed *levain* aside again, covered, for between 18 and 24 hours. By the time this *levain* is ready to be mixed into a dough, it has become deadly in its stickiness; be forewarned. Always remember the precaution of using this starter early in its rising cycle rather than late or it will become too acidic.

TO MAKE THE DOUGH, place the *levain* in a bowl and dilute it with half of the water. (If you prefer, you can use the fountain method instead of the bowl method for mixing the dough.) Combine the flours and add a little to the *levain*, breaking it up and making a paste. Dilute the paste with the rest of the water. Add 2 or 3 handfuls of flour, mixing vigorously to develop the gluten in the white flour. Sprinkle the salt over the wet, pasty dough and incorporate it. Then gradually add the rest of the flour, handful by handful, mixing vigorously all the while with a wooden spoon or plastic dough scraper. When the dough becomes somewhat workable and there is still a cup of flour left, empty the dough onto your worktable and knead it for another 5 or 6 minutes while incorporating the last of the flour. If you have a very firm dough, there is no need to incorporate all the flour; you can leave out up to ¼ cup.

Let the dough rise, covered and in a warm spot, for between 8 and 10 hours.

Shape the dough into an oval loaf and place it in an oval basket that has been lined with a kitchen towel and dusted with a little flour. Let the loaf rise, covered, for between 8 and 12 hours.

The loaf is best when baked on a baking stone but it can also be emptied from the basket onto a parchment-lined baking sheet just before being placed in the oven.

Slash the loaf with two long cuts about an inch apart in the middle, with the angle outward. Bake in a preheated 425°F oven for 1 hour.

SPONGE

LES BENOÎTONS
RAISIN-NUT RYE ROLLS

Benoîtons are traditionally made with raisins in a sour rye dough. These are made with raisins and walnut pieces. The irregularly shaped rolls are sweet and crunchy with a tangy rye flavor. For considerations of time and flavor, it is best to use the *seigle sur poolish* recipe on page 114 for the dough (although any rye dough will work).

MAKES I DOZEN 4-OUNCE ROLLS

½ recipe (1 ¼ pounds) *seigle sur poolish* dough (page 114)

I cup walnut pieces

I cup raisins

½ cup cornmeal

I tablespoon sugar

I teaspoon cinnamon

Glaze: I egg mixed with I tablespoon cold milk

After the dough has been completely kneaded, flatten it on the worktable and coat it with the nuts and raisins. Roll the dough over itself several times until it forms a log. Knead the dough on the table for several minutes to incorporate the nuts and raisins completely.

Let the dough rise, covered in a bowl or on the table, for between 2 and 3 hours.

To shape the rolls, flatten the dough and cut off pieces the size of a tangerine that will be roughly 4 ounces. You should have 12 or so irregularly shaped rolls. If any of the rolls is visibly smaller, take a small pinch off of a larger roll and add it to the smaller one. Do not round the rolls or in any way try to form them; the irregular shape is part of their appeal.

Mix together the cornmeal, sugar, and cinnamon and spread it out on the worktable. Gently pass each roll through the mixture, picking up a little bit. Then place the rolls on a parchment-lined baking sheet.

Glaze them with the egg glaze and let them rise for between 45 minutes and one hour.

Bake the rolls in a preheated 425°F oven for 12 to 15 minutes.

VARIATION

After the first rising, the entire batch of dough may be shaped into one loaf. Allow the loaf to rise for between 1 and 1½ hours and then bake it at 400°F for between 1 and 1¼ hours.

❖❖❖❖❖❖❖❖❖❖ *Specialty and Enriched Breads* ❖❖❖❖❖❖❖❖❖❖

Ingredients such as butter, eggs, milk, cheese, apples, nuts, raisins, onions, and virtually anything the baker can think of can be added to bread dough to make breads that go beyond the definition of straight French bread. These ingredients enrich the flavor and texture of the bread and, in some cases, increase its shelf life. Village bakers traditionally have let their customers know what is in the bread either by giving it a descriptive name or providing a list of ingredients.

Most bread bakers in France make many enriched products but the furthest they will go in providing enriched yeasted products would be *brioche* and, sometimes, *croissants.* Any products that go beyond yeasted breads—tart doughs made of *pâte sablée* or *pâte sucrée,* roll-in doughs such as those for *croissants* and danish and puff pastry, cakes or pastries made with fresh fruits and creams—are traditionally the province of the *pâtissier.*

Fougasse are flat breads made in the shapes of ladders or trees and studded with fresh herbs, cheese and nuts, or anchovies. They are traditional in Provence.

The following is a recipe based on a *poolish* made with a sourdough starter. Many village bakers in France make their *fougasse* out of straight *pain ordinaire* dough, without using a starter at all.

There are two ways to make the bread without the sourdough addition. You can use a piece of four- or six-hour-old *pain ordinaire* dough instead of the *levain*. Or you can substitute half a cup of flour for the *levain* and increase the yeast in the *poolish* to one teaspoon.

MAKES THREE 12-OUNCE *FOUGASSE*

THE *POOLISH*

    1 cup yeast starter (*compagnon*) (page 34)

    ½ teaspoon active dry yeast

    1 cup warm water

    1 cup organic, unbleached white (or all-purpose) flour

THE DOUGH

    All of the *poolish* from the previous step

    ½ cup cool water

    3 cups organic, unbleached white (or all-purpose) flour

    2½ teaspoons fine sea salt

    1 tablespoon fruity olive oil

    15 to 20 whole fresh sage leaves, with stems removed, or

    1 can (2 ounces) anchovy fillets, drained of their oil, soaked in milk, drained again, and dried with paper towels, or

    12 ounces Roquefort cheese, crumbled into ½-inch chunks and 1 cup walnut pieces

TO MAKE THE SPONGE (*POOLISH*), proof the yeast in ¼ cup of 115°F water. Chop up the *levain* and place it in a medium-sized bowl. Dilute the *levain* by adding the remaining ¾ cup of water and mixing with a plastic dough scraper. When the yeast is creamy, add it to the diluted *levain* mixture. Slowly add the flour by handfuls while stirring. The mixture will be soupy. Let the sponge sit in the bowl, covered with a dish towel, for 8 to 10 hours or overnight. When the *poolish* has risen and fallen, it is ready to use.

TO MAKE THE DOUGH, mix the *poolish* and ½ cup of the water together in the bowl. Start adding 2½ cups of the flour, handful by handful, stirring vigorously with a wooden spoon. After each addition of flour beat the mixture with 50 strokes of the spoon. This will take about 15 minutes.

Sprinkle the salt over the dough, stir in the olive oil, and turn the dough out onto the worktable. Knead the dough for another 5 minutes while adding the rest of the flour. The dough should be moist and satiny.

Flatten the dough and coat it with the sage leaves, the anchovy fillets, or the Roquefort cheese and walnuts. Incorporate the ingredients gently by folding the dough over onto itself several times.

Let the dough rise, covered, for 1 hour. Divide it into 3 pieces and round each piece up into a tight ball. Set the balls aside on a floured work surface and covered with a damp towel to rise for another 30 minutes to 1 hour.

When the dough has doubled in size, shape each piece by flattening it out into a rectangle measuring about 8 inches by 4 inches or into a triangle of about 8 inches on each side. Cut the pieces as shown in diagram a, then stretch them until they look like the second example, b:

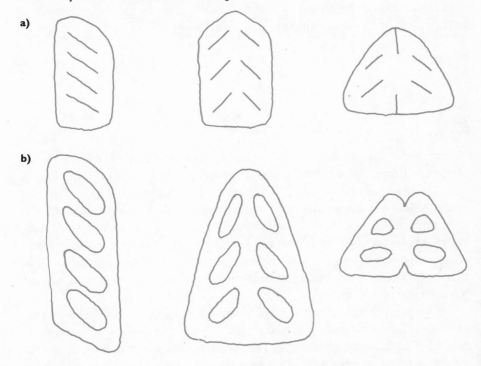

a)

b)

Let the *fougasse* rise on parchment-lined baking sheets for at least 1 hour. The loaves will be ready to bake when the imprint of a finger pushed into the dough fails to spring back quickly.

Brush the flat loaves with a little olive oil and bake them in a preheated, 450°F oven for between 15 and 20 minutes.

The French baker's term for adding more water to a dough after it has been nearly completely kneaded is *bassinage*. (The opposite procedure, adding more flour to a dough, is called *contre-frasage*.) Bassinage is done to correct the consistency of a dough or to create a wetter dough. Village bakers know that it is easier to create a very wet dough by first mixing it firm and then adding water toward the end of mixing.

The method can be used for the preceding recipe for *fougasse* (or for any recipe where a wetter dough is desired). After the salt and oil have been incorporated and there is still a handful or 2 of flour left, flatten the dough on the worktable. Poke the dough full of indentations. Pour the water (¼ cup for the *fougasse* recipe) over the dough so that it fills the indentations. Slowly fold the dough over itself several times and knead the dough gently at first. Use wide stretching motions with 1 hand, as if pulling taffy, to incorporate the extra water. After 4 or 5 minutes the dough will become quite elastic and surprisingly workable. Clean off the dough-covered hand with a dough scraper, clean the worktable and your hands with the rest of the flour, and finish off by kneading the dough for a few more minutes.

PAIN AUX POMMES
SOURDOUGH APPLE BREAD

Whenever I think of retiring to the country, I fantasize about buying an apple orchard in Corralitos, California, where I imagine myself building a brick oven fueled by branches of applewood. I can almost smell the aroma of an apple bread made from apple starter and my own homegrown organic apples. Well, the dream may never happen. But if someone else wants to make an aromatic, sourdough apple bread, here is the recipe. Although it is an involved, time-consuming process, this is one of the most unusual recipes I have come across in that it shows one how to make an authentic sourdough starter from fruit that has been allowed to ferment.

If the prospect of making a loaf of bread that is going to take the better part of two weeks is a bit daunting, you might like to experiment with a shortcut. Instead of making an apple starter from scratch, mix the dough using the ingredients listed on page 125 and substitute 2½ cups *pain ordinaire* dough for the *levain de pomme;* the rest of the recipe may be followed without any changes. The *pain ordinaire* starter will give a lighter, more yeasty flavor; the *levain de pomme* a more shiny sourdough texture and a pleasing apple-cider flavor.

MAKES FOUR 14-OUNCE *BÂTARDS* or *BOULES*

THE *LEVAIN DE POMME*

> 1 medium-sized apple cut into pieces
>
> 3 tablespoons sugar
>
> 2 tablespoons water

THE FIRST REFRESHMENT

> 1 teaspoon malt extract or 2 teaspoons honey
>
> ⅓ to ½ cup warm water
>
> ½ cup apple starter from the previous step
>
> 2 cups organic, unbleached white
>   (or all-purpose) flour

THE SECOND REFRESHMENT

> 1 teaspoon malt extract or 1 teaspoon
>   honey
>
> Approximately ⅓ cup water
>
> All of the *levain* from the previous step
>
> 1 cup organic, unbleached white (or all-purpose) flour

THE DOUGH

> 1 pound tart Granny Smith or Gravenstein apples (4 cups cubed)
>
> 3 to 4 tablespoons butter for sautéing the apples
>
> 1 package (2½ teaspoons; ¼ ounce) active dry yeast
>
> 1½ cups warm water
>
> 1 teaspoon malt extract or 1 teaspoon honey
>
> 3 cups organic, unbleached white (or all-purpose) flour
>
> 1 cup organic rye flour
>
> All of the *levain de pomme* (a little over 2 cups) from the previous step
>
> Glaze: 1 egg white beaten with ½ cup cold water

TO MAKE THE STARTER, combine the ingredients and let them rest, covered and in a warm place, for between 8 and 10 days. When the mixture has become highly alcoholic and carbonic gas starts to develop, it is ready to use.

If any mold, fungus, or other fuzz has developed on the apple mixture, carefully remove it. This should leave at least three-quarters of the mixture (½ cup).

FOR THE FIRST REFRESHMENT, dissolve the malt extract or honey in the warm water. Mash the pieces of apple to a paste and add the malt extract mixture. Add the flour by the handful while mixing with a wooden spoon. When the dough comes together, empty it onto the worktable and knead in the rest of the flour. Continue kneading into a firm dough for between 8 and 10 minutes.

Place the *levain de pomme* in a container, covered with a damp dish towel, in a very warm spot to rise for between 8 and 10 hours. If the *levain* looks splotchy and spooky, throw it out and start over. If it looks round and well risen, it is ready to be refreshed.

FOR THE SECOND REFRESHMENT, dissolve the malt extract or honey in the warm water. Break up the *levain* in a bowl and pour the malt extract and water mixture over it. Start adding the flour by the handful while mixing with a plastic dough scraper. Mix into a firm dough. If necessary up to 1 or 2 tablespoons more flour may be added to make the dough firm but not too dry.

Let this refreshed *levain de pomme* ferment for between 3 and 5 hours, in a container covered with a damp cloth as before. It should double in size.

TO MAKE THE DOUGH, begin by preparing the apples. Peel, core, and cut them into ½-inch pieces. Sauté them in the butter just for a few minutes until they have softened. Set them aside.

Proof the yeast in a little of the warm water and, when it is creamy (this will take about 10 minutes), add it, together with the malt extract, to the rest of the water in a large bowl. Chop up the *levain* with a dough cutter or knife and add it to the liquid. Combine the salt with the flours, and then start adding the dry mixture to the liquid by handfuls while mixing with a spoon. After you have added several handfuls of flour, you will need to stir the spongy mixture quite vigorously in order to dissolve the *levain* and make sure it becomes well incorporated in this early stage. Continue adding the flour until you have only several handfuls left and the dough has come together somewhat. This will take about 10 minutes. Empty the dough out onto a worktable, clean off your hands and the bowl with a plastic dough scraper, and, just before the final cup of flour is added to the dough, add the sautéed apples and incorporate them. Then knead the dough to a firm consistency with the rest of the flour.

Set the dough aside, covered and in a warm place, to rise for 1¼ hours until it has doubled in bulk.

Cut the dough into 4 pieces and shape each piece into a *bâtard* or a *boule*. Do not be concerned if the apples break through the skin of the dough when you are shaping it. Just try to poke them back in. Place the loaves on a parchment-lined baking sheet or, if you plan to use a baking stone, on a flour-dusted board.

Set them aside, covered and in a warm place, to rise for between 45 minutes and 1 hour.

Glaze the loaves and, with a razor blade, slash the *boule* in a tick-tack-toe pattern and give the *bâtard* 3 diagonal cuts.

Bake the loaves in a preheated 425°F to 450°F oven, either directly on the baking stones or on a baking tray, for between 35 and 40 minutes. For the last 15 minutes of baking, turn the oven down to between 375°F and 400°F.

A Note for the Advanced Baker

Having tried the recipe a few times, you may wish to reduce the yeast to 1 teaspoon and extend the rising times of the dough and the loaves from a total of 2 hours to around 5 hours to give more of a sourdough effect.

If you want to make the *pain au pommes* the next day, save a 1-cup piece of the final dough and let it rise for around 8 hours. Use that piece to create another "second refreshment." Take the recipe from that point to make your next batch.

BRIOCHE

Brioche and *pain au lait* (which follows) are the two most enriched breads to be found in the bread baker's domain. Neither is officially considered to be French bread in the strictest sense, but both can be offered by the *boulanger* as long as he lets his customers know what they are and what they contain.

Brioche is a rich, buttery egg bread that many French people enjoy for breakfast. I learned this recipe from a Portuguese baker who worked at the Moule à Gateau on rue Mouffetard in Paris.

MAKES FOUR 1-POUND *BRIOCHES À TÊTE*,
TWENTY 3-OUNCE *PETITES BRIOCHES À TÊTE*,
FIVE 14-OUNCE *BRIOCHES MOUSSELINES*, OR
FIVE 14-OUNCE *BRIOCHES DE NANTERRE*

4 packages (3 tablespoons plus 1 teaspoon; 1 ounce) active dry yeast

½ cup warm water

6 cups organic, unbleached white (or all-purpose) flour

4 teaspoons salt

½ cup sugar

6 eggs (cold if you are using a food processor; at room temperature otherwise)

1½ cups (3 sticks) unsalted butter, softened

¼ cup cold milk

Glaze: 2 eggs whisked together with 2 tablespoons milk

TO MIX THE DOUGH IN A FOOD PROCESSOR, divide the ingredients into 2 batches before placing them in the machine.

Proof all of the yeast in the entire ½ cup of warm water. Mix the flour, salt, and sugar together and set aside. Beat all of the eggs together lightly.

Place half of the flour mixture into the food processor and add half of the yeast mixture and half of the butter. Process for between 15 and 20 seconds until the ingredients are partially mixed. While the processor is running, slowly pour in half of the eggs and process for 30 seconds. Add half of the milk slowly, pulsing 2 or 3 times. The dough will be quite wet and elastic. Add a tablespoon or 2 of flour if necessary to help the dough come together, while pulsing the machine once or twice.

Remove the dough from the processor and place it in a large bowl. If you are making the entire recipe, repeat the steps for the second half of the ingredients. Combine the 2 batches into one piece of dough by kneading them lightly on the worktable.

TO MIX THE DOUGH BY HAND, treat the entire recipe as 1 batch. Proof the yeast in the warm water. Mix the flour, salt, and sugar together. Beat the eggs, which for hand mixing should be at room temperature, together.

Make a fountain with most of the flour mixture, setting aside ½ cup. Pour the beaten eggs and the yeast mixture into the middle. With one hand, start mixing the liquid around the sides of the fountain, slowly incorporating small quantities of the flour. In mixing slowly and patiently, so as to avoid any lumps or dry spots, this procedure will take between 10 and 12 minutes before the dough is in a single, shaggy mass. Knead the dough on the worktable for another 3 or 4 minutes.

When the dough is satiny but quite firm, start adding the softened butter in little nut-sized pieces, working it in by stretching and folding the dough back onto itself. When all of the butter is incorporated and the dough is very soft and shiny, add the milk, a few drops at a time, working it in in the same manner. Knead in the remaining flour mixture. The dough will be moist, elastic, and very responsive when touched.

From this point on the dough, whether made by hand or in the food processor, is treated in the same way. Lightly dust the dough with a little flour, round it into a ball as best you can, place it in a bowl, and cover it with a moist dish towel. Let the dough rise in a warm place for between 1½ and 2 hours. It should double in volume.

Punch the dough down, wrap it in plastic wrap, and let it rise in the refrigerator for between 10 and 15 hours. After this second rising, the dough is ready to be shaped into *brioches*. It may be cut and shaped immediately after it has been removed from the refrigerator or may be allowed to warm up for about 40 minutes first.

VARIATION
After the first rising, the dough or part of it may be well wrapped and stored in the freezer. It will keep for about 2 or 3 weeks but it is best used within 7 or 8 days.

To thaw a frozen piece of brioche dough, transfer it from freezer to refrigerator at least 24 hours before you plan to use it.

1   2   3

Brioches are made in various shapes and sizes. The *brioche à tête,* for which one uses a piece of dough about the size of a grapefruit (18 ounces or 2 cups), is baked in a fluted *brioche* mold that measures about 5 or 6 inches across the top and is about 2 inches deep. *Petites brioches à tête* (each made with a piece of dough the size of a tangerine—3 ounces or ⅓ cup) are made in identical, but smaller, molds that measure about 3½ inches across.

To shape them add a small "head" to each round ball of dough by pressing down on the roll about one-third of the way in toward the center (see figure 1); stand the roll upright, with its "head" on top, run a finger round the "neck" to make a depression, and push the "head" into it (see figure 2); set each roll into an individual mold (see figure 3).

The *brioche mousseline* is made of a piece of dough the size of a large orange or small grapefruit (15 ounces or 1⅔ cups) and baked in a small coffee can (13-ounce, 1½-cup capacity); the result is a single, cylindrical *brioche.* The *brioche de Nanterre,* for which one uses enough dough to come between one-half and two-thirds of the way up the pan (about 15 ounces or 1⅔ cup), is baked in a small, (6-by-3-by-2-inch) bread-loaf pan.

Brioche mousseline

4   5

Divide each 15-ounce piece of dough into 3 pieces and form each piece into a ball. Place the 3 balls side by side in the loaf pan and, with a pair of scissors, snip the top of each roll (see figure 6).

Brioche de Nanterre

To prevent the *brioches* from drying out and crusting over, glaze them immediately after they have been shaped. Set aside the rest of the glaze.

6

If the dough was removed from the refrigerator and immediately cut and shaped, the smaller *brioches* will take between 1½ and 2 hours to rise; the larger varieties will take up to 3 hours. If the dough was allowed to warm up first, the rising times will be between 1 and 1½ hours for the small and about 2 hours for the large loaves. The dough will still be cool when it is ready to be baked, but the *brioches* will all have nearly doubled in size.

Glaze the *brioches* again and bake them in a preheated 385°F oven (set between 375°F and 400°F). The large loaves will take between 20 and 25 minutes; the small between 15 and 17 minutes. The *brioches* will be a deep golden brown when done and will feel very light when lifted out of their molds. Remove them from their molds and cool on wire racks. If the larger loaves feel a little moist underneath, bake them for a few more minutes out of the mold.

PAIN AU LAIT
MILK BREAD DOUGH

A highly enriched, moist dough, *pain au lait* is used in the *viennoisserie* (the production room in a French bakery that specializes in enriched doughs) for snails, *pain aux raisins,* and various exhibitions of sweet pastries. This simple dough is easier to make than are other doughs used for the same type of pastries; in doughs such as those for *croissants* or danish pastry the butter is rolled in, by a process of flattening the dough and folding the piece several times, to create flaky layers. Therefore, *pain au lait* is more in the *boulanger*'s domain than are the so-called roll-in doughs. This dough may also be used for a simple pan bread or for milk rolls.

MAKES EIGHT 2-OUNCE CREAM-CHEESE SNAILS
AND EIGHT 2-OUNCE RAISIN-CINNAMON SNAILS

1 package (2½ teaspoons; ¼ ounce) active dry yeast

¾ cup water

3½ cups organic, unbleached white (or all-purpose) flour

1½ teaspoons salt

2 tablespoons milk powder

4 tablespoons sugar

3 eggs (cold)

6 tablespoons (⅓ cup; 3 ounces) butter, softened

This recipe is best done in the food processor because the dough is very wet. But it can also be mixed with the bowl or fountain methods (described on pages 39–41), if done with patience.

For the food processor method, proof the yeast in ½ cup of warm water. Place an ice cube in the remaining ¼ cup of water and set it aside. In a food processor fitted with the plastic blade, place the flour, salt, powdered milk, and sugar. Pulse to mix.

Add the yeast mixture and the eggs, which should be cold, and pulse 8 or 10 times to incorporate the ingredients. The dough will be quite crumbly. With the machine off, add the softened butter through the feed tube and process for about 20 seconds, until the butter is nearly all incorporated. With the machine on, slowly pour the remaining ¼ cup iced water through the feed tube and process for 45 seconds.

Carefully scrape the dough out of the processor bowl, adding a little flour if it is too sticky to handle. Place the dough into a large bowl that will accommodate it after it has doubled in size. Let the dough rise for between 1 and 1½ hours in a warm spot. After the dough has doubled in volume, punch it down, wrap it loosely in plastic wrap, and place it in the refrigerator for between 8 and 10 hours or overnight.

The next morning (or 8 or 10 hours later, depending on your schedule), take the dough out of the refrigerator and divide it to make 2 varieties of snails.

VARIATION

After the first rising, the dough or part of it may be well wrapped and stored in the freezer. It will keep for about 2 or 3 weeks but it is best used within 7 or 8 days.

To thaw a frozen piece of brioche dough, transfer it from freezer to refrigerator at least 24 hours before you plan to use it.

CREAM-CHEESE SNAILS

Half a recipe *pain au lait* dough (page 130)
Glaze: 1 egg whisked with 1 tablespoon milk

TOPPING

¾ cup farmer's cheese

2 tablespoons sugar

½ teaspoon vanilla extract

⅓ cup jam or preserves

Flatten the dough out on the worktable, having sprinkled a little flour on the table and on the top of the dough. Roll it out with a rolling pin until it measures 8 inches by 12 inches by about ⅜ inch thick. Cut the dough lengthwise into 8 strips, each 12 inches long. Stretch each piece to about 24 inches by holding each end with the fingers and pulling gently. With the piece on the worktable in front of you, place one palm over each end of the strip, then with gentle pressure push one palm away from you and one toward you, rolling the piece of dough so that it twists itself into an elongated corkscrew strip. Curl this piece up around itself in a circle starting in the center, tucking the end underneath.

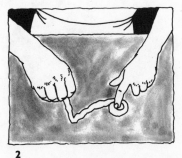

1   2   3

Place the snails on a parchment-lined baking sheet and glaze them.

Combine the cheese, sugar, vanilla, and 1 tablespoon of the egg glaze. Flatten the center of each snail with the fingertips, creating a pocket the size of a silver dollar. Place a tablespoon of the cheese mixture in the middle of each snail. On top of the cheese mixture put a tablespoon of your favorite jam.

Let the snails rise for between 1 and 1¼ hours until they seem puffy but have not yet collapsed. Preheat the oven to 385°F (set between 375°F and 400°F) and bake the snails for between 15 and 17 minutes or until they are golden and the jam is bubbly. (NOTE: Both of the glazes below are for use with both types of snails.)

PAIN AUX RAISINS
(RAISIN-CINNAMON SNAILS)

Half a recipe *pain au lait* dough (page 130)

Egg glaze: 1 egg whisked with 1 tablespoon milk

FILLING

¼ cup sugar

½ teaspoon cinnamon

⅓ cup raisins

CLEAR GLAZE

¼ cup water

¼ cup sugar

⅛ teaspoon vanilla extract

FONDANT GLAZE

1 to 2 teaspoons boiling water

⅔ cup powdered sugar

TO FILL THE SNAILS, roll the piece of dough out into an 8-by-10-inch rectangle, with the 8-inch side toward you on the worktable. Do not cut it into strips. Instead, coat the piece with egg glaze, leaving 1 inch along the bottom edge unglazed. Over the egg-coated portion sprinkle the sugar, cinnamon, and raisins.

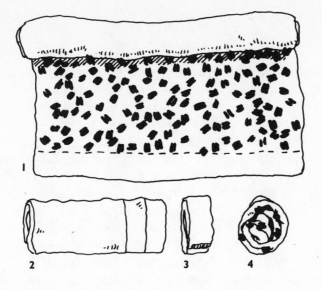

Starting at the top, roll the dough down toward you into a tight log, sealing the bottom edge tightly. Use a sharp knife or a dough cutter to cut 8 discs from the log and place them on a parchment-lined baking sheet, flattening each with the palm of the hand. Paint the snails with the egg glaze and let them rise for between 45 minutes and 1 hour. While the snails are rising, prepare the two sugar glazes.

TO MAKE THE CLEAR GLAZE, heat the water, sugar, and vanilla in a small saucepan, stirring until the mixture just starts to boil. Remove the pan from the heat and set the glaze aside to cool.

TO MAKE THE FONDANT GLAZE, pour the boiling water slowly over the powdered sugar in a small bowl while stirring the mixture with a wooden spoon. Pour in only enough water to make a creamy mixture that has the consistency of a pancake batter. Set it aside to cool.

When the risen snails are puffy and before they collapse, bake them in a preheated 385°F oven (set between 375°F and 400°F) for between 15 and 17 minutes or until they are golden. As soon as the rolls come out of the oven, paint some of the clear glaze onto the dough spirals, avoiding the filling.

When the rolls are cool, drizzle some of the fondant glaze over each pastry in a squiggly little pattern. (The easiest way is to dip your fingers in the glaze and let it drip off the ends onto the snails.) Serve for breakfast or a snack.

Canapés, toast points, and the delicate triangular tea sandwiches that the Italians call *tramezzini* are all made with *pain de mie,* a tight-grained bread. If you do not have a Pullman-loaf pan, you can use a heavy baking sheet weighted down by a brick or you can make a lid for a regular loaf pan out of a plank of wood and a long strip of the same wood stock.

Take a regular loaf pan (they come in two basic sizes, a large one measuring 9 inches by 5 inches by 2½ inches, and a small one measuring 7⅜ inches by 3⅝ inches by 2¼ inches) and place it, upside down, on a piece of unpainted, ¾-inch wood that is at least 2 inches wider and longer on all sides than the pan itself. With a pencil, draw an outline on the wood of the upper rim of the loaf pan. From a strip of the same or similar wood that measures 1-inch square, cut two pieces the same length as the two long sides of the outline of the loaf pan that was drawn on the wood. Nail these two pieces just outside the pencil lines so that the pan can slide freely inside the two wood "rails." Cut two smaller strips from the 1-inch wood. Nail these shorter strips in place to form a frame.

The frame is used to keep the top of the loaf flat and square as a lidded Pullman-loaf pan would do. After the dough has been shaped, it is placed in the loaf pan and set aside until it has risen to the top of the pan. The makeshift lid frame is then placed on top of the dough and weighted down with a heavy cast-iron frying pan or a brick after the loaf has been placed in the oven to bake.

This recipe is designed for the smaller pan; if you are using the larger pan, double the quantities but be careful not to use too much dough when shaping the loaf. The shaped loaf should come no more than three-quarters of the way up the pan.

MAKES ONE 1¼-POUND LOAF

- 1 package (2½ teaspoons; ¼ ounce) active dry yeast
- 1 cup warm water
- 3 tablespoons grated raw potato, with its juice
- 2 teaspoons milk powder
- 2 teaspoons sugar
- 1 tablespoon butter, melted and cooled
- 1½ teaspoons salt
- 3 cups organic, unbleached white (or all-purpose) flour

Using a large bowl, proof the yeast in ¼ cup of the warm water. When it is creamy, add the remaining ¾ cup water, the potato with its juice, the milk powder, sugar, melted and cooled butter, and the salt and stir to combine. Add the flour a little at a time while stirring the ingredients with a wooden spoon.

When the dough starts to come together, empty it out onto the worktable, scrape the bowl clean, and knead the dough for 8 to 10 minutes, using the remaining flour. At the end of the mixing process, the dough will be firm but not too dry.

Set the dough aside, covered, to rise for 1 hour.

Shape the loaf into a log about 7 inches long. Grease the loaf pan and its lid if you are using a Pullman pan or, if you are using a fabricated wooden lid, cut out a piece of parchment paper to fit on the top of the loaf. Place the loaf into the pan and let it rise, covered with a towel, for 30 minutes. When the dough has reached the top of the pan, gently cover it with the Pullman lid, or the parchment paper and wooden lid, or a heavy baking tray. Set the loaf aside for between 10 and 15 minutes longer.

Place the loaf in a preheated 425°F oven and cover the wooden lid with a cast-iron frying pan or a brick to hold it down. Bake the loaf for 20 minutes, then remove the frying pan and lid. Continue baking the loaf for another 20 to 25 minutes. When the loaf looks done, remove it from the pan and thump it on the bottom to see if it sounds hollow. If it does not, return it to the oven, either in or out of the pan, for a little more baking. Remove the loaf from the pan before cooling it on a wire rack.

When cool, cut the loaf into thin slices with a sharp carving knife or a serrated bread knife. For *canapés* or tea sandwiches remove the crust.

CHAPTER 5

The Breads of Italy

BECAUSE HE HAS WORK HABITS AND IDEAS about baking that are different from those of his French counterpart, the Italian village baker can teach us much about the craft of bread making. He uses a *biga*, or yeast starter, instead of sourdough to create texture, flavor, and a quicker process; more water in some breads to create a moist, billowy crumb; and slower mixing for a more rustic loaf. Of course, the final product will look, feel, and taste different—not only because of the different methods—but also because Italian bread has a different role in accompanying Italian food.

The key to the different method is the *biga*—a piece of dough that is actually a yeast starter—mixed firm and set to rise overnight. This is the ingredient that helps give Italian bread its wide, uneven texture and its earthy, yeasty flavor.

The use of sourdough seems to have disappeared in the Italian bakeries of today. It must have been used in ancient times, before the advent of yeast. One day a baker at the Due Fratelli bakery in Milan described to me a method for making *lievito naturale* (or natural yeast) for *pane francese,* rebuilding a natural starter every two hours, until a final fresh starter was obtained that would fuel the dough with the ferments that make it rise. This showed me that today's Italian bakers—though they themselves do not use it—are well aware of the ancient methods of sourdough bread baking.

Perhaps sourdough has been abandoned for production reasons, because Italians do not care for the taste, or because the bread is heavy and does not make a good accompaniment for Italian food. Whatever the reason, sourdough is rarely seen in the Italian village bakery and its replacement, the *biga,* has not only helped to give interesting textures and flavors but also has helped bakers to make breads in a shorter time. Because the *biga* rises for such a long time in its initial stage, the final loaves can be baked off very quickly after being shaped. In fact batches of bread can be backed up one after the other for sequential baking, almost straight off the mixer.

Also unusual are the quantities of water that Italian bakers use. In many styles of Italian bread, water used in amounts considered excessive by village bakers of other countries, helps give the moist, billowy crumb and golden crust that goes so well with Italian food. Raymond Calvel, the French expert on bread, feels that it is too easy to underbake those Italian breads, such as *pane francese, pane pugliese,* and *ciabatta*, that contain a lot of water so that the crust is often rubbery and insipid. Baked for the right amount of time, however (and leaving the loaves in the oven with the heat shut off and the door open for the final five or eight minutes of baking), these breads will have a crust that is "set," that is, it will not turn soggy a few hours later. The crust, golden and cracklingly crisp, therefore becomes a foil for the moist, chewy crumb and is a delicious utensil for lifting food from plate to mouth. Italian bakers do not use the chilled water that is so common in French village bakeries. Therefore, they must mix their breads for a longer time, on the first or slowest speed so that the dough does not become *brusciata* (or burnt out). This gives those breads a less modern, more rustic character.

These techniques, as well as Italian village bakers' use of ingredients such as polenta, olives, extra virgin olive oil, rosemary, and potatoes can all be used at home.

PIADINE
UNLEAVENED BREAD ROUNDS

Flat, unleavened cakes like Mexican tortillas, *piadine* come from Emilia-Romagna. Originally they were cooked over a flat, hot stone, called a *testo,* in an open fireplace. They go well with *minestrone* or any rustic bean and vegetable soup. Serve them also with a mixture of chopped *prosciutto,* ricotta cheese, and chopped fresh herbs, or with greens sautéed in olive oil and garlic.

MAKES FOUR 8-INCH *PIADINE*

I teaspoon lard

I teaspoon olive oil

½ teaspoon salt

About ¼ cup warm water

I cup organic, unbleached white (or all-purpose) flour

Put the lard, olive oil, and salt into a ¼-cup measure; fill the measuring cup with warm water and allow the lard to melt. Measure out the flour straight onto the worktable and pour the lard mixture into a well in the middle of the flour. Slowly add the flour from around the well into the middle. Knead the mixture for about 4 or 5 minutes until it is smooth. The dough will be firm but not too dry or crumbly.

Allow the dough to rest, covered by a damp towel, for 30 minutes.

Then divide the dough in quarters and roll each piece out into a circle 8 inches across.

Heat a cast-iron skillet over high heat until it is very hot. Rub the skillet down with a paper towel that has been daubed in lard. Cook each *piadina* in the skillet for 4 or 5 minutes or until it is brown on each side.

Panino is the name given to any small bread or roll, and it is also the name for any little sandwich on a roll.

Textbook examples of Italian regional breads may be seen in the proliferation of *panini* found all over the country. Most, but not all, of them are generally made of a firm, dense dough. (The recipe below is for an olive oil dough that produces rolls with a hard, crisp crust and a fine-textured crumb. *Pasta dura,* literally "hard dough," made according to a slightly different formula, is also commonly used, but so, too, is a dough that is even softer than *pane all'olio*—it depends on where you are.) It is from the shapes that one can determine the origins of these rolls.

In her book, *The Italian Baker,* Carol Field describes the shaping of a representative selection, including *coppiette* (which she likens to a starfish) and *montasu* (resembling scrolls) from Emilia, *mustafa* (an intricately curled knot), *bauletta* (literally "a little trunk") from Mantua, and *carciofo* (a petalled roll called an artichoke) also from Emilia. Other shapes one might encounter in Italy are those described as *coperto* (round), *cornetti* (*croissant*-shaped), and *treche* (braided). The *biovette* of Piedmont, that might be described as "butterflied" logs, are made of a somewhat softer dough.

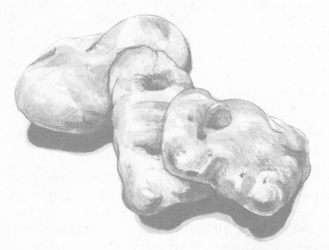

Maltagliatti. These rolls are made from *pane francese* dough that has been shaped into *baguettes* and cut into several pieces just before being baked.

SHAPING PANINI

What often takes a laborious description in words apprentices can see in a few minutes as they watch a master baker deftly transform lumps of dough into fanciful shapes. I shall give directions for only two of the numerous possibilities, the mano (hand), because it is common, and the banano (suggestive of a banana perhaps), because it is simple.

MANO

To make small rolls, use 6 ounces of dough (a piece the size of an orange) for each one; to make large rolls, use 12 ounces (the size of a large grapefruit).

1. Roll out each piece of dough into a long oval shape, between about 6 and 8 inches or 12 and 14 inches long. Using one hand and starting at one narrow end, roll up the dough toward the middle. Use the other hand to stretch out the dough so that you have a tight roll made up of 5 or 6 layers.

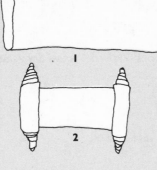

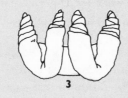 

2. Roll up the other end of the oval dough in the same way so that you have 2 parallel logs connected in the middle by a flat piece of dough.

3. Twist the 2 rolled-up logs toward the middle, bending the ends of each log to point the same way: the 4 fingers of a primitive hand.

4. When you flip the mano over, the flat connecting piece of dough in the middle will cover the base of all 4 fingers and emulate a palm. Small mani will take between 12 and 15 minutes to bake; the large one around 25 minutes.

BANANE

The elusive straight banana, these are little cylindrical rolls that, in commercial bakeries, have been sent through the molder twice. It is hard to shape them by hand, but not impossible.

Use pieces of dough that weigh about 3 ounces each (they will be the size of a tangerine). First flatten the dough piece and roll it with a rolling pin into a long, thin oval disk.

1. Cut this disk in half.

2. With the fingers of both hands, roll up the dough tightly lengthwise and at a slight angle so that it

continuously overlaps itself. The result will be a solid little roll about 4 inches long and, because the dough is so dense, the seams of the rolled-up dough will still be evident.

3. Hold the roll at a 45-degree angle on the work table in front of you. Roll it

over itself toward you once more. The result will be a tight roll with a spiral overlap of the dough extending up its entire length and one end a little larger than the other.

They will take between 12 and 15 minutes to bake.

This recipe for a very dense dough is used to make rolls in various everyday shapes as well as rolls that look like hands, fingers, and other more private parts of the human anatomy. The dough is slightly easier to work than the genuine *pasta dura,* which is more suitable to commercial production.

MAKES 1 MANO AND 12 SMALL ROLLS

> 1 package (2½ teaspoons; ¼ ounce) active dry yeast
>
> ½ cup warm water
>
> ½ cup hot water
>
> ½ teaspoon honey
>
> 1 tablespoon olive or vegetable oil
>
> 1½ teaspoons salt
>
> 3 cups organic, unbleached white (or all-purpose) flour
>
> Glaze: 1 egg white whisked into ¼ cup cold water, or ⅓ cup olive oil

Proof the yeast in the warm water. In the ½ cup of hot water dissolve the honey, oil, and salt. When this mixture has cooled a little and the yeast is creamy, combine the 2 liquids and then add 2 cups of the flour, mixing vigorously with a spoon or plastic dough scraper for 3 or 4 minutes. Empty the dough out onto the worktable, add the remaining cup of flour, and knead the mass for about 5 minutes until the dough is very firm.

Let the dough rise for 1 hour, covered and in a warm spot. The dough will have nearly doubled.

Divide the dough in 4 equal pieces. Shape one piece into a *mano* (a little, rustic, four-fingered hand) using the instructions on page 139. Place it by itself on a parchment-lined baking sheet. Being larger, the *mano* will take a little longer to bake than will the rolls made from the remainder of the dough.

Divide each of the other pieces in half so that there are 6 pieces the size of tangerines. Flatten each piece and roll it out with a rolling pin into an oval a little wider at the top than at the bottom, measuring about 6 inches in length, about 2 inches wide at the bottom, and 4 inches at the top. With the palms flat to the table, and starting at the wider, top end, roll the dough tightly into a log. Stretch the dough out so that each layer overlaps the previous one. Each roll will measure between 8 and 10 inches long and the layers will overlap visibly, much as they do in a *croissant.* Cut each roll in half.

Place the rolls on another baking sheet lined with parchment paper.

Let the rolls rise, covered and in a warm place, for between 40 and 50 minutes. The lines on the *panini* and *mano* should still be visible.

Whisk the egg white into the cold water and use the mixture (or a little olive oil by itself) to glaze the rolls and *mano*.

Bake the rolls in a preheated 400°F oven. The small rolls will take about 15 minutes; the *mano* about 20 minutes.

PORRIDGE

PANE TOSCANO
TUSCAN BREAD

Among the reasons given for the absence of salt in *pane toscano* is the existence, at one time, of an oppressive tax on the commodity. So you will see many recipes for this classic bread without salt, some with just a pinch. Apparently, however, *pane toscano* was, in ancient times, made from porridge, and the following is such a recipe.

The *bouillie* (mush) process breaks down the gluten in the flour, resulting in a wilder texture; it also brings on a fermentation that produces a more earthy flavor in the bread.

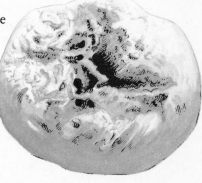

MAKES I ROUND, 2-POUND LOAF

> 6 cups organic, unbleached white (or all-purpose) flour
>
> 1¾ cups boiling water
>
> 1 package (2½ teaspoons; ¼ ounce) active dry yeast
>
> 1½ cups warm water

TO MAKE THE BOUILLIE, place 2 cups of the flour in a bowl or container and pour the boiling water over it. Let the mixture sit for 5 minutes, then mix to incorporate, making sure there are no dry spots. Let the *bouillie* sit overnight covered with a damp towel. The *bouillie* should rest for between 15 and 24 hours. It will not have risen at all, as it will still be a moist porridge.

TO MAKE THE DOUGH, proof the yeast in the warm water. Turn the *bouillie* into a large bowl and add the yeast mixture. Stir until the entire mixture becomes a paste that is somewhat smooth and soupy, enough to be beaten vigorously with a wooden spoon.

Add the remaining 4 cups flour, a handful at a time, working the pasty mixture with a plastic dough scraper until it is smooth and satiny. Eventually it will form a medium-wet dough and you should still have several handfuls of flour left. Using up the rest of the flour, knead the dough for about 8 to 10 minutes on the worktable.

Let the dough rise, covered, for between 1 and 1½ hours, until it has doubled.

Shape the dough into a round, irregular loaf by flattening it and then folding the edges toward the middle and sealing the seams with the heel of the hand.

Let the loaf rise for 30 minutes. Then, with the palms of your hands, flatten

the loaf a few inches so that it is half its original height, and flip it over onto a well-floured surface. This helps give the dough its irregular shape. Cover and let the loaf rise for another 30 minutes.

Then pick the loaf up off the table and, with your hands, stretch it out by a few inches. Bake the loaf on a baking stone in a preheated 400°F oven for between 45 and 50 minutes. Or the loaf can be baked directly on a baking tray. Shut off the oven and let the loaf remain inside for 5 minutes to develop the crust, which should be golden and firm to the touch.

OLD DOUGH

SCHIACCIATA
TUSCAN FLAT BREAD

Schiacciata is what the Florentines call their version of a flat crust of bread dough flavored with an inexpensive topping. Less elaborate than a pizza, it is much like the *focaccia* of Genoa. Because *schiacciate* are made as quick snacks, the dough most likely to be used is whatever is being made for bread, in this case, *pane toscano.* Use any yeasted dough from *pain ordinaire* to *pane all'olio* instead, if that is what is available.

Schiacciate can be crisp or somewhat soft. You can try putting some chopped black or green olives in the dough, mixing them in along with the shortening.

MAKES ONE 9- BY 14-INCH *SCHIACCIATA*

> 2 cups *pane toscano* dough (page 141) or *pain ordinaire* dough (page 69)
>
> 2 tablespoons vegetable shortening or lard
>
> 2 tablespoons extra virgin olive oil
>
> ½ to ¾ teaspoon salt
>
> 2 tablespoons chopped rosemary leaves (optional)

Flatten the dough and spread the shortening on it. Fold the dough over and knead it on the worktable to incorporate the shortening, using a little flour if necessary. Let the dough rise, covered, for between 45 minutes and 1 hour.

With a rolling pin, roll out the dough and make a rectangle measuring 9 by 14 inches and ⅜-inch thick. Place the dough on a cookie tray that has been coated with a teaspoon of oil.

Brush the top of the dough with the olive oil and sprinkle on the salt and the rosemary if you are using it.

Let the *schiacciata* rise for between 20 and 30 minutes.

Dimple the dough with the fingertips and let it rise for another 20 minutes.

Bake the *schiacciata* for between 30 and 35 minutes in a preheated 375°F oven; it should be light in color and crackerlike in its crispness.

Pane Francese

In Milan there is a bread called *pane francese,* that looks like an antique version of French bread, with a dusty, golden, crackling crust and a moist, chewy crumb. Its name means "French bread" and it seems to be an important link in the development of French bread.

What is an Italian bread, made in Italy for Italian tastes, doing with that name? Was this what northern Italians thought French bread tasted like or what they thought it *should* taste like? Was *pane francese* originally a French bread that crossed the border? Or is it a relic from times when the regions were similar in their culture, their food, and their bread?

Pane francese seems to be a link between the bread of the Romans *(casereccio* is an Italian bread with a crisp crust and a fine texture, made from a fairly stiff dough) and the breads of France. The physical appearance of a bread such as *pane francese* may be what the first French bread once looked like. The interior structure of the bread is akin to that of French bread in that it is very moist, like a sourdough, but without a hint of sour flavor. The crust is substantial, like those of French country breads. And there is much more salt in *pane francese* than there is in many Italian breads, a hint, possibly, that it represents a radical departure from traditional Italian baking. Historically bread traveled from Egypt to Israel, from Turkey to Greece, from Italy to France. It seems logical that the passage from Rome through northern Italy (Milan, Como, and Piedmont) had some lasting effect on the nature of the bread we know today in France.

Certainly it came by its name very early. Some recipes, like some of those for *pane toscano* and *pane pugliese,* begin with a mush, or *bouillie,* made by pouring boiling water over flour and left overnight. It is used the next day in the final dough. Recipes that still include a mush provide the link between gruel and bread, and I have come across recipes for Tuscan bread that call for *acqua bollenta* (boiling water) in the first step. (The recipes for *pane toscano* on page 141 and *pane francese* on page 144 are examples.)

Whatever the origin of the name, *pane francese* is a bread made by one of the number of similar baking processes to be found all over the world. In bread making there is a thread of continuity that runs through numerous regions and cultures. The techniques may differ in detail, the names may be unrecognizable, but the flavor and texture will be familiar.

PANE FRANCESE ANTIQUATO
PORRIDGE-METHOD ITALIAN-STYLE FRENCH BREAD

This is an ancient variation of the recipe. Like *pane toscano* and *pain bouillie,* it begins with a mush that is left overnight to ferment.

MAKES TWO 1-POUND LOAVES

- 1 cup whole wheat flour
- 1 cup boiling water
- 3 cups organic, unbleached white (or all-purpose) flour
- 3 packages (2½ tablespoons; ¾ ounce) active dry yeast
- 1½ cups warm water

TO MAKE THE *BOUILLIE,* place the whole wheat flour in a bowl, pour the boiling water over it, and let the mixture sit for 5 or 10 minutes to soak. Stir the mixture together and let it sit, covered, for between 12 and 15 hours or overnight.

TO MAKE THE DOUGH, proof the yeast in ½ cup of warm water. Dilute the mush mixture in a medium-sized bowl with 1 cup of warm water. Then add the yeast, salt, and 2½ cups of flour, gradually, until you have a moist, shaggy dough. Turn the dough out onto the worktable and knead it, using the remaining ½ cup of flour until you have a smooth dough.

Let the dough rise, covered, for 1 hour.

Make up the dough into 2 loaves, each about 10 inches long and 4 inches wide. Cover the loaves and let them rise for 1 hour. Flatten them with the fingertips, flip them over, and let them rise for another 20 minutes.

Bake the loaves in a preheated 350°F oven for between 40 and 45 minutes.

Here is a method using an Italian sponge called *lievito naturale* (natural yeast) or *biga,* made with a small quantity of yeast. The sponge helps give the finished loaves a yeasty, earthy flavor.

MAKES TWO 11-OUNCE *BAGUETTES* OR ONE 1½-POUND OVAL LOAF

THE *BIGA*

> 1 teaspoon active dry yeast
>
> 1⅛ cups warm water
>
> 2 cups organic, unbleached white (or all-purpose) flour

THE DOUGH

> All of the *biga* from the previous step
>
> 1¼ cups organic, unbleached white (or all-purpose) flour
>
> 1½ teaspoons salt
>
> ¼ cup very cold water

TO MAKE THE *BIGA*, proof the yeast in ⅛ cup of the warm water until the mixture is creamy. Add this to the rest of the warm water in a large bowl and start adding the flour, a handful at a time, while mixing with a plastic dough scraper or wooden spoon. When the ingredients have been thoroughly combined, the sponge will be very soupy. It can be left in the same bowl in which it was mixed as long as it is large enough to accommodate the risen sponge, which will triple in bulk.

Let the sponge rise, covered, in a warm spot for between 8 and 10 hours.

TO MAKE THE DOUGH, place the soupy *biga* and the salt into the food processor fitted with the plastic blade. Pulse to combine them. Add the ¼ cup of cold water and process for about 30 seconds. Then add the remaining 1¼ cups flour, ¼ cup at a time, pulsing 3 or 4 times after each addition. The dough will come away from the bowl but will still be quite sticky. Scrape down the sides of the bowl and pulse again 2 or 3 more times.

Dust the dough with a small handful of extra flour and then scrape dough out of the processor bowl onto a floured worktable. The extra flour make it possible to handle the wet dough. Knead the dough for a minute or so to work out any lumps and shape it into a tight, round ball. Do not be afraid to use up to ½ cup of extra flour to prevent the dough from sticking.

Cover the dough with plastic wrap or a damp cloth and let it rise in a warm place for between 2 and 3 hours.

When the dough has doubled in size, sprinkle plenty of flour on the work-

VARIATION

The method for this variation is very similar to the method an Italian village baker would use. The firm biga made with less yeast and a longer rising time, will add a very earthy and much less yeasty flavor to the finished loaf.

Make the biga using only ½ teaspoon yeast, 2 cups flour, and ¾ cup water. Mix to a firm dough (it will not be soupy at all) and let it rise, covered, for 24 hours.

To make the dough add 1 cup flour, 1½ teaspoons salt, and 1¼ cups water to all of the biga.

table, turn out the dough, and divide it in half. Shape the pieces by rolling them roughly but tightly into *baguettes:* logs about 8 inches long. (This recipe will also make a handsome oval loaf to be baked either directly on a baking stone or on a baking tray; it will take between 30 and 35 minutes.)

Cover the 2 logs of dough with a towel and let them rest on the well-floured worktable for 30 minutes.

Carefully pick up each *baguette* and stretch it until it is between 12 and 14 inches and fits neatly into a greased, black *baguette* tray. The *baguettes* may also be baked on a greased or parchment-lined cookie sheet. Let the loaves rise again for between 15 and 20 minutes.

Place the *baguettes* in a preheated 450°F oven (with or without a baking stone) and immediately turn the heat down to 425°F. Bake the loaves for 20 to 25 minutes or until they are golden brown.

PANE FRANCESE NATURALE
SOURDOUGH ITALIAN-STYLE FRENCH BREAD

Bakers in the hills between Milan and the French border would not have had a recipe as we know it today, but this is probably how they were making sourdough bread hundreds of years ago. I learned the method in a bakery in Milan called Due Fratelli, where the baker kept telling me to refresh the dough *"ogni due ore,"* or *"every two hours."* That being similar to a traditional sourdough refreshment schedule, I devised this method. (Here I'm using the French terminology, *chef* and *levain;* if I were to use the Italian term for natural yeast, *lievito naturale,* it might be confusing as that is the term that most modern Italian bakers now use to denote their *biga,* which is a firm yeasted starter.)

I would recommend your using a hard-wheat, white but unbleached bread flour as it will hold up better to the acidity in the sourdough starter. If that is not available, an organic, unbleached or an all-purpose white flour will work.

The process of building a starter into a bread dough occurs in three steps. Starting from scratch, a *chef* is made. (See the Variation if you have been storing your starter in the freezer or if you plan to use a very soupy milk starter.) When the *chef* is between eight and ten hours old, it is refreshed with flour and water and becomes a *levain.* The *levain* is allowed to rise for five or six hours, is itself refreshed (with more flour and water), and set aside to rise again for another three to five hours. Then, with the addition of more flour and water and some salt, the *levain* becomes a bread dough.

A hypothetical timetable (see page 148) might help you visualize the procedure and plan the activities. Keep in mind that bread dough can be made to be flexible within a set timetable: to slow it down, mix it firmer and cooler; to speed it up, mix it wetter and warmer.

(The day after you've made any sourdough bread, you can use a piece of that

dough to start the first refreshment of a new dough. All you need to do is save a one-quarter-cup piece from yesterday's bread, let it rise at room temperature for two or three hours, then wrap it and store it in the refrigerator overnight.)

MAKES TWO 1-POUND *BAGUETTES*

THE *CHEF*

¼ cup starter*

¼ cup warm water

½ cup white, unbleached, hard-wheat bread flour

THE *LEVAIN*

1 cup *levain*† (from the previous step)

½ cup warm water

1½ cups white, unbleached, hard-wheat bread flour

THE DOUGH

2½ cups *levain* (from the previous step)

¾ cup warm water

2 cups white, unbleached, hard-wheat bread flour

2 teaspoons sea salt

TO REFRESH THE *CHEF,* place it in a medium-sized bowl and chop it up roughly with a plastic dough scraper. Add the warm water and then slowly mix in some of the flour, enough to make a paste. Beat the mixture vigorously until it is quite smooth and there are no lumps of *chef* left. Then add the rest of the flour and mix it well. What you will have is a recognizable bread dough, not a soupy starter.

Turn it out onto a floured worktable. Scrape out the bowl and scrape off your hands so that you will be using the entire amount. Knead the dough on the worktable for between 5 and 8 minutes, adding, if necessary, an extra pinch or two of flour. The refreshed *chef,* now called a *levain,* should be moist, but definitely firm.

Place the *levain* in a bowl, cover it with a damp cloth, and set it aside in a warm place to rise. It should nearly double in size, taking between 5 and 6 hours to do so.

TO REFRESH THE *LEVAIN,* chop it into small pieces in a medium-sized bowl, mix in the ½ cup warm water, and ½ cup of the flour, stirring vigorously until you have a smooth mixture. Add the remaining cup of flour gradually, mixing

VARIATION

If you have been keeping the starter in the freezer, leave it out at room temperature for 3 to 4 hours to give it time to become reactivated, then refresh it with the addition of roughly twice its own volume of flour and enough water to make a firm dough. Set that aside to rise for between 6 and 8 hours. At that point, it will be at the same stage of development as a chef that is about 8 hours old and you can proceed with the recipe from that step. In planning your timetable, remember to allow for the extra 9 to 12 hours at the beginning.

---

* For the starter, which should be between 8 and 10 hours old, you can use a *pain de campagne* starter (page 32), the Costa *levain* (page 118), or the milk sour starter (page 33).

† *Levain* is the refreshed and risen *chef.*

each addition in well. When the dough is too stiff to be mixed in the bowl, turn it out onto a floured worktable and knead in the remainder of the flour.

Return the *levain* to the bowl, cover it with a damp cloth, and set it aside in a warm place to rise. In 3 to 5 hours it should have nearly doubled.

TO MAKE THE DOUGH, which will take about 25 minutes, punch down the refreshed and risen *levain*. Chop it into small pieces, return it to a large bowl and add the ¾ cup warm water, stirring until the *levain* starts to dissolve. Add the salt and stir it in. Add the flour gradually, incorporating each addition thoroughly.

When you have added 1½ cups of the flour, turn the dough onto a floured worktable and knead in the remaining ½ cup flour. Continue to knead until the dough is smooth and satiny.

Cover the dough and set it to rise in a warm spot for between 8 and 10 hours.

TIMETABLE FOR *PANE FRANCESE NATURALE*

DAY 1			DAY 2		
NOON 1st refreshment of the 8-hour *chef** *This assumes that your *chef* is already between 6 and 8 hours old. If you are following the variation given on page 147, you would have to start earlier.	**5 P.M.** 2nd refreshment of the 5-hour levain	**10 P.M.** Making the dough	**7 A.M.** Shaping the loaves	**9 A.M.** Stretching the loaves	**9:30 A.M.** Baking

TO SHAPE THE LOAVES, gently punch down the dough and cut it into 2 pieces. Roll each piece into a roughly shaped log about 8 inches long. Leaving the logs covered on the worktable that has been dusted with flour, allow the loaves to rise for between 2 and 3 hours. Then stretch them lengthwise until they will fit snugly into 18-inch-long (greased) *baguette* trays. They can also be placed on a parchment-lined baking tray. Allow the loaves to rise, in the trays and covered, for between 30 and 40 minutes. Do not slash or glaze the loaves before putting them into the oven.

Bake the loaves in a preheated 450°F oven for 30 minutes.

STIRATO
YEASTED ITALIAN-STYLE FRENCH BREAD

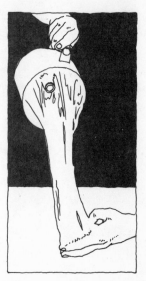

Stirato ("stretched") is a version of *pane francese* made with yeast. Signore Danova of the Panificio Danova in Milan (described on page 154) tells me that his father invented the version and so named it because the dough is rolled into logs and, after a brief rest (for the dough, and perhaps the baker), is stretched out to double its previous length before being baked.

By stretching instead of rolling the bread into shape, the baker helps to elongate the air bubbles that have developed while it rested, creating the characteristic billowy texture. It also produces the long, wispy striations of the flour that is used to handle the very wet dough.

MAKES TWO 10-OUNCE *BAGUETTES* OR ONE 1¼-POUND OVAL LOAF

> 1½ cups water (with 3 or 4 ice cubes)
>
> 1 package (2½ teaspoons; ¼ ounce) active dry yeast
>
> ¼ cup warm water
>
> 3 cups organic, unbleached white (or all-purpose) flour
>
> 1 teaspoon salt
>
> 1 teaspoon sugar

Place the ice cubes in a transparent measuring cup and fill it with cold water to the 1½-cup mark. Set the water aside for 10 minutes or until the ice is close to being completely melted.

Pour the ¼ cup of warm water into a cup and sprinkle in the yeast. After stirring to dissolve the yeast, allow the mixture to sit for 10 minutes until it is creamy.

Place the flour, salt, and sugar into a food processor fitted with the plastic blade and pulse to mix. With the processor running, add the yeast mixture and about ¾ cup of the ice-chilled water. Process for about 1 minute to incorporate the ingredients. With the processor running, slowly add the remaining water. Process the mixture for about 3 to 4 minutes until the dough is satiny and quite wet but still cool. From time to time, use a rubber spatula to scrape up any dry mixture, making sure that all the dry flour is incorporated. When the mixture comes out of the food processor it will be very wet and stretchy. Empty the soupy dough into a large bowl.

Cover the bowl with plastic wrap or a damp cloth, place it in a warm spot, and let the dough rise for between 2 and 3 hours.

When the dough has doubled in size, turn it out onto a well-floured worktable and lightly punch it down. If you plan to make *baguettes,* divide it in half. Shape the pieces of dough into loaves by rolling them roughly into logs about 8 inches long: flatten each piece of dough out and then roll it up toward you. With each roll, seal the join with the heel of the hand. Cover the loaves and let them rise seam-side down on the well-floured worktable for 30 minutes.

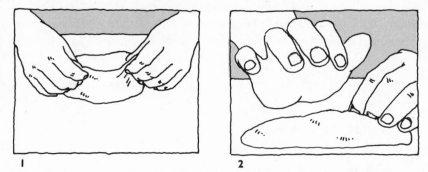

If you plan to make 1 loaf, shape the entire quantity of dough into a rough oval in the same manner. Cover the loaf, set it seam-side down on the worktable, and let it rise for 30 minutes.

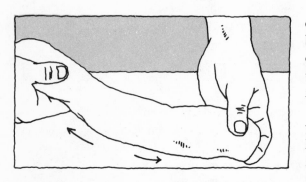

If you are making *baguettes,* carefully pick up each one and stretch it to fit in a greased 18-inch black *baguette* tray. The loaves may also be baked on a parchment-lined or greased baking tray. Let them rise, covered, for between 15 and 20 minutes.

"Stretch" the oval loaf by flattening it with your fingertips about 6 or 8 times, pushing them halfway into the dough. Flip the loaf over, cover it again, and allow it to rise for another 15 or 20 minutes.

Place the *baguettes* into a preheated, 450°F oven and immediately turn the heat down to 400°F. Bake them for 20 minutes or until they are golden brown. For the oval loaf, use a baking stone if you have one, and bake the bread for about 35 minutes, or until it, too, is golden brown and sounds hollow when thumped on the bottom.

With *stirato,* as with any very wet dough, you can leave the loaves in the oven with the heat turned off for another 5 minutes to set the crust.

SPONGE

Ciabatta is an irregular, flat, dusty loaf that was given its name because it looks like a slipper or an old shoe. The breads called *ciabatta, pane francese,* and *pane di Como* are similar in origin, method, and appearance. I learned this variation in the small, picturesque town of Bellagio on Lake Como, from a baker named Nikolas, who told me it was the area's regional bread. His recipe calls for a little bit of milk powder in the dough to soften the crumb.

The bread also contains a starter that is augmented by commercial yeast. The starter will take ten minutes to prepare and fifteen hours to rise; the bread itself about four hours. Be forewarned that *ciabatta* is made with an extremely wet dough, too wet to be kneaded on a worktable. In fact, it is not kneaded so much as stirred. Don't lose heart and don't be tempted to add more flour.

This method is laborious but it is included to show home bakers how a very wet dough can be mixed by hand. The method is, in fact, the hand version of the method used to make *stirato* in a food processor. The only difference is that with a *biga* or firm starter addition you must first chop up the starter and dilute it with half of the chilled water before adding it to the processor.

MAKES FOUR 12-OUNCE LOAVES OR

THREE 10-OUNCE LOAVES AND 24 TO 28 *GRISSINI*

THE STARTER

    1 recipe *lievito naturale,* page 35

THE DOUGH

    2 packages (2½ teaspoons; ½ ounce) active dry yeast

    2 cups warm water

    1 tablespoon powdered milk

    3¼ cups organic, unbleached white (or all-purpose) flour

    1 tablespoon salt

    3 cups *lievito naturale* sponge from the previous step

MAKE UP THE *LIEVITO NATURALE* and let it rise for 15 hours or overnight.

TO MAKE THE DOUGH, proof the yeast in ½ cup of the warm water and let the mixture sit for 10 minutes until it is creamy. Dilute the powdered milk in the rest of the water in a large bowl. Mix the flour and salt together in a small bowl.

To the milk and warm water in the large bowl, start adding small bits of the sponge and, with a plastic dough scraper, break the sponge into small lumps. Now start adding the flour by the handful. After each handful of flour, stir the mixture vigorously 80 times with a wooden spoon. As the lumps of sponge become smaller and the mixture less soupy, mix it even more vigorously. After about 15 minutes, take a break. There will still be 2 or 3 handfuls of flour left.

THE BREADS
OF ITALY

151

Add the dissolved yeast. You will have what is probably the wettest dough you have ever worked and will be asking yourself how this soupy mess will ever make bread dough. Don't worry.

After adding the yeast, add half a handful of the flour and give the dough 100 vigorous strokes with the spoon. To break the monotony, dig the spoon into the soupy dough, pull it out as if it were taffy, and try to make the resulting strand of dough extend itself. This builds elasticity. Continue adding the flour by half-handfuls and stirring vigorously as before until the flour is used. The complete mixing will take between 25 and 30 minutes. The dough will still be very wet and impossible to knead on a table.

Cover the bowl with plastic wrap or a damp cloth and allow the dough to rise for between 1 and 1½ hours, until it has doubled in size and appears blistered and satiny. If the dough is cold (70°F or less), let it rise for the first hour in an oven that has been warmed only by the pilot light.

When the dough has risen sufficiently, turn it out onto a liberally floured worktable or pastry board and sprinkle lots of flour on top. Flatten the dough

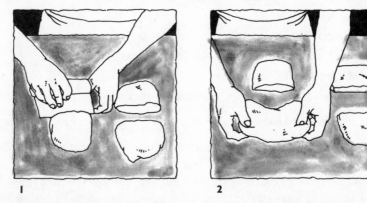

1   2

and cut it into four rectangular pieces, each measuring about 4 inches by 10 inches. These irregular pieces of dough, flattened to about three-quarters of an inch, are the finished, shaped loaves. (At this stage you can save one of the pieces, roughly 2 cups, to make *grissini;* see page 156. Either refrigerate the dough, covered and placed in a bowl, and use it the next day or freeze it. When

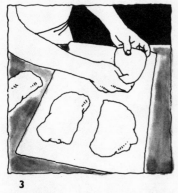

3

you are ready to use the frozen dough, let it thaw at room temperature for 4 or 5 hours before using it.)

Cover the loaves with cloth or plastic wrap and let them rise for 30 minutes on well-floured boards or baking sheets.

Use the fingers to perform the *schiacciare* maneuver: Flatten each loaf with the flat part of the fingers, not the fingertips. Splay the fingers widely so that some areas of the loaf are not even touched. This gives the dough its flat shape, helps give an uneven texture to the crumb, and prevents the loaves from puffing up in the oven. Then flip the loaves over, cover them, and allow them to rise for another 30 minutes.

An hour before baking, preheat the oven and a baking stone to 425°F. Carefully put each loaf on a rimless cookie sheet that has been sprinkled with plenty of flour and, from that, slide it onto the baking stone. Spray the inside of the oven a few times with an atomizer filled with water to create steam and to develop the crispy crust. Bake the loaves for between 25 and 30 minutes or until they are golden brown.

4

Profile: Signore Giuseppe Danova

THE LARGE, BURLY MAN WITH A WIDE SMILE, a big laugh, and a wad of Italian *lire* in his pocket is Signore Danova of the *panificio* on Via Cerva near the intersection with Largo Augusto in Milan. Unlike bakeries almost everywhere else that sell bread to wholesale customers on credit, Danova's transactions are all in cash. That's where the wad of *lire* comes in. You give Danova the *lire* and Danova gives you the bread.

Danova is a man, like many bakers I have met, who worked long hours at his father's side and perhaps alone when his father had retired, eventually to attain a position in which he could hire bakers and, instead, run the business end of the enterprise.

Every morning Danova directs traffic in his bakery, scribbling down orders on a sheet of paper, barking instructions to his seven bakers and two saleswomen, and sending out the orders by way of his delivery man who loads a small Vespa scooter with a bag full of the bread that Danova calls *stirato*—literally, "stretched". (For the recipe, see page 149.)

It is a bread, he says, that his father invented. That final stretching of the loaves after their second rising forces the voluptuous air bubbles in the dough to elongate, creating a wildly uneven texture. The moist, billowy crumb is encased in a flour-dusted, golden, crackling crust. *Pane francese,* the bread that Danova's bakers stretch so roughly to create such an appealing crumb, is the regional bread of Piedmont—the area in and around the cities of Milan, Turin, and the environs of Lake Como—in fact, the entire northwest of Italy, the region closest to France itself, the country that gives this bread its name.

Francese, or *stirato* as Signore Danova calls it, is served at many local Milanese restaurants, among them Da Bice in the fashionable designer district off the Via Monte Napoleone, at 15 Via Borgospesso. That's where we had it. In fact, that's how I learn where to find the good bakers: I eat their bread in some restaurant and then ask the waiter to draw me a map showing its source.

The next day I went to find Signore Danova. He told me that, by coming back at 9 A.M., I could watch the bread being made. My wife and I were astonished that I didn't have to come back in the middle of the night. The Panificio Danova sold so many batches of this popular loaf that the final batch was mixed at 5 A.M. into a very wet dough, allowed to rise for four hours, and made up at nine o'clock. The 10:30 A.M. bake came crackling out of the oven just in time for my wife, Gayle, who had been out shopping, to stop by and sample a slice of salami, a glass of beer, and a hunk of freshly baked *stirato*—the specialty of the neighborhood.

Literacy Resource Center
Renton Technical College
Renton, WA 98056

GRISSINI TORINESE
TURINESE BREADSTICKS

Grissini or breadsticks are usually crisp or crackerlike. At the Danova bakery in Milan they use *pasta normale,* ordinary bread dough. But I would imagine that it would include a little shortening, because fat is the ingredient that helps give *grissini* their crispness.

The following recipe, from the *panificio* in Bellagio, uses shortening, olive oil, and a piece of old *ciabatta* dough.

For breadsticks it is best to use a dough that is two or three hours old and was made with some kind of starter—a sourdough, *biga,* or *poolish.* A piece of six- to eight-hour *pain ordinaire* will also work.

MAKES 24 TO 28 BREADSTICKS

> 1 package (2½ teaspoons; ¼ ounce) active dry yeast
>
> Scant ¼ cup warm (120°F) water
>
> 3 tablespoons extra virgin olive oil
>
> 2 teaspoons vegetable shortening, lard, or margarine
>
> 1 teaspoon salt
>
> ⅛ teaspoon malt extract or ¼ teaspoon honey
>
> 1 pound (2 cups; ¼ recipe on page 151) *ciabatta* dough
>
> Additional olive oil to coat the finished dough
>
> 1 cup poppy seeds, sesame seeds, caraway seeds, or fine rock salt
> for coating (optional)

Proof the yeast in the water. When the mixture is creamy, add the oil, shortening, salt, malt extract, and the *ciabatta* dough. Then slowly add the flour while cutting up the dough with a plastic dough scraper. Knead the dough, which will be medium damp, on the worktable for between 8 and 10 minutes. The dough should be soft and pliable and should spring back at you when touched.

For the first rising, shape the dough into a rectangle measuring 4 inches by 12 inches by 1 inch. Pour about ¼ cup olive oil over and under the dough, cover it with plastic wrap, and let it rise for 1 hour.

Prepare a cookie sheet by brushing it lightly with olive oil. Using a metal dough scraper or knife, cut off a strip of dough, between ¾ and 1 inch wide, from a 4-inch side of the dough rectangle. Take one end of this 1-by-4-inch

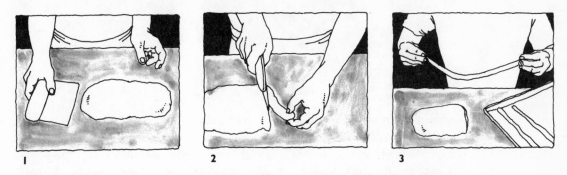

strip between the thumb and forefinger of each hand and, with a shaking motion, stretch it until it is the length of the prepared cookie sheet; 12- to 18-inch *grissini* are long enough. Make sure on your first few attempts that the finished diameter is about ⅜ inch as the *grissini* will rise both before and after they go into the oven. If they are too big at first, cut the strips of dough a little thinner each time until you get the thickness right.

(As a variation you can roll the *grissini* in seeds or salt. Before cutting the breadsticks, pour 1 cup of any of the 3 varieties of seed or of the salt—or ¼ cup of each, separately—onto the worktable. After each breadstick is stretched and before it is placed on the baking sheet, roll it gently through the seeds. Then let the breadsticks rise and bake them according to the recipe.)

Set the *grissini* on the oiled cookie sheet as you shape them and, when all the dough has been shaped, allow the breadsticks to rise, uncovered, for about 30 or 40 minutes.

Bake the *grissini* in a 400°F oven for between 15 and 20 minutes. When they are golden and you think they are ready, pull one breadstick out of the oven and break it open. If it has lost all of its interior softness, it is done.

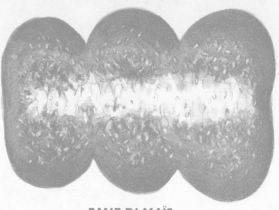

PANE DI MAÏS
POLENTA BREAD

Gruel mixtures vary with the grains that grow in different regions, whether it be in America, France, Germany, or Italy. Corn (which the Italians call *maïs*) was brought over from the New World and grows in the northern plains. Before its advent, the Romans made a porridge called *pulmentum,* out of millet or spelt. Today rough, cracked cornmeal, or *polenta,* is used to make the ever-popular gruel that may be served while it is still warm, garnished with a sprinkling of Parmesan cheese. It was probably leftovers that first went into bread and here it is used as a base for the starter.

MAKES ONE 1-POUND LOAF

THE STARTER

> 1 teaspoon active dry yeast
>
> ¼ cup warm water
>
> ½ teaspoon honey
>
> 1 cup cornmeal porridge (recipe follows)
>
> 1 cup organic, unbleached white (or all-purpose) flour

THE DOUGH

> 1 teaspoon salt
>
> 1 cup organic, unbleached white (or all-purpose) flour
>
> 1 egg for glazing
>
> 2 tablespoons sesame seeds for topping

TO MAKE THE STARTER, proof the yeast in the warm water until it is creamy. Add the honey to the mixture and stir until it is dissolved. After the cornmeal porridge has cooled for at least 10 minutes, combine it with the yeast mixture and the flour.

The mixture will be a very wet batter, but not completely liquid. Let the starter rise in a bowl, covered with a cloth, for between 2 and 4 hours. It will double in size.

TO MAKE THE DOUGH, sprinkle the salt onto the starter and mix it in. Slowly incorporate the flour into the starter. The dough will be very moist but still firm enough to be kneaded on the worktable. Knead it for between 5 and 8 minutes until it is satiny.

Cover the dough and let it rise for 1 hour.

Divide the dough in half. Flatten both pieces and roll each up into a tight log. Braid the 2 pieces together and place the loaf on a parchment-lined baking sheet. Mix the egg with a little water, glaze the top of the loaf, and sprinkle sesame seeds over the glaze.

Let the loaf rise in a warm place for 45 minutes.

Bake the loaf in a preheated 400°F oven for between 30 and 35 minutes.

VARIATION
For a very special bread add ¼ cup toasted pine nuts and ¼ cup raisins to the dough, just after it has been mixed.

A Note for the Advanced Baker

After the dough is mixed, let it rise for 10 to 12 hours or overnight in the refrigerator. The next day let the dough come up to room temperature, which will take about 3 hours. Shape it into a loaf and let it rise according to the recipe, being aware that it may take a little longer to be ready to bake because the dough is cool.

POLENTA
CORNMEAL PORRIDGE

MAKES 3 TO 4 CUPS

1 ½ tablespoons chopped rosemary leaves

1 tablespoon olive oil

4 cups water

¾ teaspoon salt

1 cup *polenta* or coarse cornmeal

In a medium saucepan, sauté the rosemary in the olive oil for a minute or two. Add the water and salt and bring the mixture to a boil. Slowly add the *polenta* in a stream, all the while stirring with a wooden spoon. Cook the *polenta* over medium heat for 35 minutes, stirring it continuously.

PANE INTEGRALE
ITALIAN WHOLE-GRAIN BREAD

Representative of one of the new, healthy breads of Italy, *pane integrale* is dense, chewy, and tangy. This method gives you the chance to use a milk sour starter, but any piece of sourdough or a yeasted starter can be used. The way in which the loaves are shaped allows the bread to break in an irregular and distinctive fashion in the oven.

MAKES TWO 1½-POUND LOAVES

¾ cup milk sour starter (page 33)

½ cup milk

3½ cups organic, unbleached white (or all-purpose) flour

1 cup organic whole wheat flour

1¼ cups organic cracked rye grain (or rye flour)

1 tablespoon salt

THE DAY BEFORE, refresh the milk sour with ½ cup milk and ½ cup flour so it is not overly sour. Let it rise in a large bowl for 12 hours or overnight.

THE NEXT DAY, mix the milk sour in a bowl together with the warm water and salt. Add the rye flour, whole wheat flour, and remaining 3 cups white flour slowly while mixing with a wooden spoon until you have a workable dough. Turn the dough onto the worktable and knead it for 8 to 10 minutes until it is smooth and elastic.

Return dough to the bowl, cover it with a towel, and let it rise for between 6 and 8 hours in a warm place.

Divide the dough in half and shape each piece into a round loaf. For the final folding and sealing, dust the dough with plenty of flour, flatten the outer edges of each loaf, fold the edges into the middle, and seal lightly with the heel of the hand. The extra flour will create an intentionally weakly sealed seam that will burst in the oven later.

Place each loaf, seam-side down, in a small, round basket or *banneton* lined with a dish towel and dusted lightly with flour.

Let the loaves rise, covered, for between 15 and 24 hours in the refrigerator. Then remove them from the refrigerator and set them aside at room temperature to continue to rise for a further 3 or 4 hours. The loaves will have almost doubled in volume.

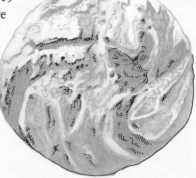

Because they will burst along the lightly sealed seams, the loaves do not need to be cut with a razor.

Preheat the oven, and a baking stone if you are using one, to a temperature of between 425°F and 450°F. Spray the oven with water before placing the loaves in. Turn the loaves out of their baskets onto the stone or a parchment-lined cast-iron baking tray and bake them for 35 minutes.

OLD DOUGH

PANE ALLE OLIVE
OLIVE BREAD

Olive bread can be made out of almost any kind of white bread dough. All you need to do is add some chopped olives to the dough after it has been fully kneaded. At Gayle's we use Capitola Sourdough.

The recipe below can be made with virtually any kind of *levain* and with or without the whole wheat flour. You can even substitute black olives for the green ones used here.

MAKES ONE 1¼-POUND LOAF

½ teaspoon active dry yeast

¾ cup warm water

½ cup whole wheat flour

I cup all-purpose flour

I cup *compagnon levain* (page 34)

I scant teaspoon salt

3 teaspoons olive oil

I cup chopped green olives

Proof the yeast in ¼ cup of the warm water. Mix the whole wheat and all-purpose flours together. Break up the cold *levain* in a large bowl and add the remaining ½ cup of warm water. Start adding the flour, handful by handful, stirring vigorously with a wooden spoon after each addition. Make sure that the *levain* is well broken up in the early stages.

When half of the flour mixture is still left, add the salt and 2 teaspoons of the olive oil. Empty the dough out onto a floured worktable and scrape the bowl and spoon with a plastic dough scraper.

Begin working the wet dough with sweeping motions of one hand, as if it were taffy. Continue for a few minutes until the dough becomes elastic. Do not add any extra flour. Clean off your mixing hand and the worktable with the dough scraper and slowly add a little more flour while kneading the dough.

After all but ¼ cup of the flour has been added, flatten the dough and add the chopped olives. Roll the dough up onto itself and knead it on the workbench for a few more minutes to incorporate the olives, using the remaining flour if the dough becomes sticky.

Cover the dough and let it rise for 1 hour.

Flatten out the dough and fold the edges over into the middle to form a round loaf. Place it on a parchment-lined cast-iron baking sheet, cover it, and let the loaf rise for 2 hours.

Preheat the oven to 400°F.

When it is ready, brush the loaf with the remaining teaspoon of olive oil, slash it 3 times on the top with a razor blade, and bake it for between 30 and 35 minutes until it is golden.

VARIATION

Instead of the levain, 1 cup of pain ordinaire *dough (page 69) may be used. Let it rise covered in a warm place for 6 hours. Then punch it down and let it rise, covered in the refrigerator another 24 to 36 hours.*

PANE PROSCIUTTO
PROSCIUTTO BREAD

MAKES ONE 1½-POUND LOAF

> Half the recipe (3 cups) *pain ordinaire* (page 69)
>
> 5 or 6 thin slices *prosciutto*

Following the recipe, make the *pain ordinaire* and set it aside for the first rising. While the dough is rising, chop up the *prosciutto* into pieces about 1 inch square. You should have about 1 cup, lightly packed.

After the dough has risen for the first time, flatten it on the worktable. Layer the dough with the *prosciutto* and roll up into a tight log. Tuck the ends under and roll the dough on the worktable into a tight, round ball. Set it aside, covered, to rise for 30 minutes.

When it has risen the second time, flatten the dough out again and fold it

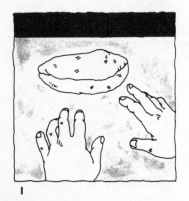

1

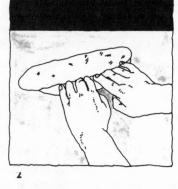

2

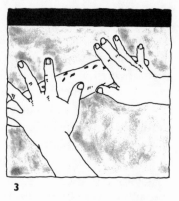

3

over to form a half moon, with the round edge toward you. Fold down the top edge a few inches toward you and seal it. Do this a few more times, until the loaf is in a log shape. Draw the ends of the loaf out into points so that the loaf is fat in the middle and skinny at the ends. Some of the meat should be popping out of the dough. Place the loaf on a parchment-lined baking sheet.

Let the loaf rise, covered and in a warm spot, for 1 hour, until it has doubled.

Preheat the oven to 400°F.

Brush the loaf with olive oil, slash it diagonally with a razor 3 times, and bake it for 20 minutes.

VARIATION
Sauté the prosciutto first. After it has cooled, incorporate it into the dough, oil drippings and all.

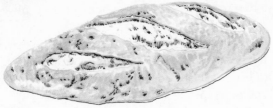

OLD DOUGH

PIZZA

Pizza, being a baking-day snack, was originally fashioned from pieces of whatever dough was being made up into bread on that particular day. So it follows that any starter or old dough, whether sourdough or yeasted, may be used. A variation, at the end of the recipe, gives instructions for making a yeasted dough by the direct method, instead of starting with an old dough.

The quantities are generous, yielding too much dough to be worked in a food processor at one time; instructions are give for mixing this pizza dough in two batches.

MAKES TEN 5-OUNCE PIZZAS, EACH MEASURING

6 INCHES IN DIAMETER

2½ cups water

1 teaspoon active dry yeast

¾ cup old dough*

6 cups organic, unbleached white (or all-purpose) flour

1 teaspoon malt extract or ½ teaspoon honey

4 teaspoons fine sea salt†

1½ tablespoons olive oil

Warm 1 cup of the water and proof the yeast in it until it bubbles.

In a small bowl, mix the old dough with 1 cup of cool water and 4 or 5 handfuls of flour, stirring until you have a pasty mixture. Dissolve the honey or malt extract in the yeast mixture and add this to the old dough mixture.

---

* Dough that has been kept at room temperature should be between 6 and 8 hours old. If kept in the refrigerator, it should be 24 hours old.

† If the old dough contains salt, use only 1 tablespoon salt in this recipe.

VARIATION

To make a pizza dough directly, with yeast instead of using an old dough, replace the ¾ cup old dough called for in the recipe with ½ cup flour and add 1 package (2½ teaspoons; ¼ ounce) active dry yeast. (The extra flour will make a drier dough, but it will be easier to work.) Use only 1 tablespoon of salt, instead of the 4 teaspoons called for in the recipe.

The method is identical up to the point of the second rising: Then the direct, yeast dough should be covered and put into the refrigerator to rise slowly and acquire some nice air

Place half of the rest of the flour and half of the salt in a food processor and pulse to mix. Add half of the old dough, yeast, and malt extract mixture. Pulse the processor to combine the ingredients, then slowly add half of the remaining water (¼ cup) through the feed tube while the processor is running. Process the mixture for between 30 seconds and 1 minute. The dough should be wet and sticky. In the last 10 seconds of processing, pour half of the olive oil through the feed tube.

Empty the dough into a large bowl and combine the remainder of the ingredients in the food processor to make a dough in the same way.

Combine both batches in the bowl by mixing them together with a wooden spoon or plastic dough scraper.

Let the dough rise, covered, in a warm place for 1 hour.

The dough will still be very wet, so sprinkle plenty of flour over it and remove it from the bowl, turning it out onto a well-floured worktable.

Divide into 10 pieces about the size of tangerines (each will weigh about 4 to 5 ounces) for individual pizzas or *calzone*. Round the dough up into tight little balls. Cover the balls with plastic wrap and let them rise a second time for between 3 and 5 hours. When ready the dough balls will be very puffy but, because they are so moist, will be somewhat flat.

Flatten each piece of dough with the palm of your hand. With your finger-

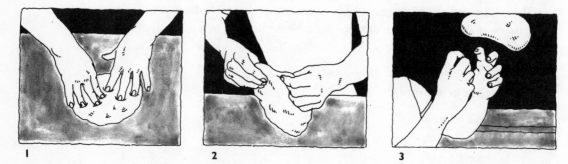

1   2   3

bubbles and sour flavor. This can take as little as 3 hours or as long as 5 hours, until the balls of dough are the size of small oranges.

Take the dough out of the refrigerator to warm up for at least 1 hour and up to 2 hours. They can then be shaped and baked immediately.

tips, poke the dough in the middle, leaving a ½-inch strip around the edge untouched, and making sure you do not poke through the dough. Lift the piece up, place it on the curled-up knuckles of both hands and gently stretch, while rotating the piece. The result will be a flat disk that measures ⅛ inch thick and 6 or 7 inches in diameter.

Cover with your favorite sauce and toppings and bake on a preheated baking stone at between 450°F and 500°F for 5 to 8 minutes or until the bottom crust is crisp and the top is bubbling.

OLD DOUGH

FOCACCIA
GENOAN FLAT BREAD

MAKES TWO 12-INCH-BY-18-INCH *FOCACCE*

- 1 recipe pizza dough (page 163)
- 2 cups extra virgin olive oil
- 2 teaspoons salt
- 8 cloves garlic, chopped
- 24 whole leaves fresh sage

Make the dough according to the recipe for pizza, up to the point at which the first rising is complete.

While the dough is rising, combine the olive oil, salt, chopped garlic, and sage leaves. Place equal amounts in 2 medium-sized bowls and set them aside.

Turn out the risen dough onto a well-floured worktable and divide the dough in half. The pieces will be wet and sticky, but use a little extra flour and round them up into tight balls. Place each piece in a separate bowl. Roll the dough balls around in the oil mixture and set them aside, still in the oil, to rise for between 3 and 4 hours. The dough will have almost tripled in size and be very soft and airy.

Remove the balls of dough from the oil and transfer them onto large cookie sheets that have a rim at least ½ inch high. With the palms of the hands and with your fingers open wide, spread the dough out to about 12 inches by 18 inches, and about ⅜ inch thick. The dough may spring back. If so, let it relax for a few minutes, then repeat the stretching process. Pour the remaining oil, along with the sage, garlic, and salt over the top of the dough.

Set the *focacce* aside, covered, to rise for 1 hour. When they have risen, poke the dough with the fingertips several times and bake in a 400°F oven for between 15 and 17 minutes, or until they are golden brown.

CHAPTER 6

The Breads of Germany

THE FRENCH MAY BOAST of a hundred or so regional breads; the Germans have several thousands. German village bakers not only use different varieties of flour milled to different degrees, but also they use seeds, spices, and herbs in numerous combinations to create breads of different textures and flavors. The emphasis is on sturdy, unrefined grains that have not had all of the nourishment milled out, to leave only the starch.

According to Kurt König, a baker in the Bavarian village of Miesbach, there are more than twenty-six hundred kinds of breads in Germany. In France, the village bakers usually specialize in their own regional varieties of breads; in Germany, bakers will make many assorted varieties in one shop and will use all three basic methods of breadmaking—direct, sponge, and sourdough—in different combinations to create unique breads. There are also 156 legally permissible chemical additives for bread in Germany. König himself uses none. He does use only organically grown grains, and his standards are so strict that, after the nuclear accident at Chernobyl in 1986, he started importing some of his organic grains from the United States.

German bakers such as König are very aware that, in order to make an organic bread that tastes good and has an interesting texture without using chemical additives, one must be willing to take the time demanded by the sourdough process. Sourdough, called *Sauerteig,* is seen as much in Germany as it is in France.

With all-purpose flour being just that—useful, easily available, and reliable—we have perhaps forgotten that there are other grains, other possibilities. If you have your own grain mill, you can use fresh organic grains such as barley and rye as well as wheat to make your own variations on grain breads. Grains can be milled to a coarse, medium, or fine consistency depending on the texture desired for the bread. This is basically what is done for *Vollkornbrot* (see page 176), which derives much of its tasty chewiness from rough cracked rye seeds that have barely been milled at all.

The German chemical additives are so far beyond the scope of this book that they will be ignored entirely. But we can certainly emulate the village bakers in their use of grains, seeds, nuts, fruits, herbs, and spices to give breads a multitude of flavors and textures. The caraway flavoring (used in the recipe for *pain bouillie* on page 106) and the sesame seed and soy sauce mixture (page 170) are classic examples. Other workable ingredients in any combination are sunflower seeds, millet, poppy seeds, boiled potatoes, sage, rosemary, pine nuts, hazelnuts, prunes, raisins, candied orange peel, and ground cumin, cinnamon, and cloves. Just remember that any ingredients added to a bread dough may prolong its rising times by at least half again as much.

Profile: Kurt König

WE ATE BREAD AND DRANK BEER that night for dinner. But first Kurt König gave us a mad tour of his bakery, cluttered to the ceiling with boxes, ingredients, and orders for the Christmas season. He showed us his grain bins and he taught us how to make a pumpkin seed and sesame seed mixture for rye bread.

We sampled his organic fruit bars, his whole wheat breadsticks, whole wheat cookies, whole wheat *Stollen.* He told us that millet and poppy seeds when eaten together make it easier to digest protein. König is a maniac about nutrition. In a recent postcard he described himself as "your organic grain madman."

His product list includes hundreds of interesting sounding breads—all of which are made with some kind of healthful grain—among them *Mischbrot hell, Mischbrot dunkel, Landbrot hell, Buttermilchbrot, Frankenlaib, Bergsteiger Weckerl, Zwiebelbrot, Vintschgauer Fladen, Weißbrot,* and *Bauernwecken.*

His bakery is the oldest one on the plaza of the small Bavarian village of Miesbach; it has been there since 1650. Upstairs in one of his storage areas—before he showed us the grinder he uses to make a paste of nuts and raisins mixed with liqueur—he reached into a bag and pulled out a handful of Spanish almonds. So full of nourishment are these almonds, according to König, that, when ground up, as little as ten grams a day would be enough food to survive on if and when the world runs out of food.

"People are testing me and my products all the time," König says. "After Chernobyl many local people bought their own food radiation detecting devices and a week doesn't go by that someone doesn't come in and tell me that my baked goods are completely free of any contamination."

We ate our dinner in the local pub right next to his bakery, our conversation translated by the friend of an American friend who lives there. König darted back and forth between tidbits of interesting, obscure information about his obsession, grains, and Bavarian stories, folk tales, and jokes.

"When you come back," he said to me, "You study here and in eight days you can learn everything."

When I told him, through the translator, that I didn't understand a word of Bavarian, he said it didn't matter. "You can learn by watching."

The whole experience made me realize that healthy breads could also taste good. And every time I think of Kurt König I imagine myself returning to uncover, not only the meaning of the names, but also the secrets behind the breads: *Mishbrot hell, Mishbrot dunkel, Bergsteiger Weckerl.* . . .

Kurt König taught me how to make the seed mixture for this bread. The light, tangy rye sourdough provides the perfect background for the combination of soy sauce and seeds.

MAKES I OVAL, 2-POUND LOAF

SEED MIXTURE

½ cup sesame seeds

2 teaspoons soy sauce

I cup pumpkin seeds

THE RYE SOUR

I package (2½ teaspoons; ¼ ounce) active dry yeast

2½ cups warm water

1½ cups organic rye flour

I cup organic, unbleached white (or all-purpose) flour

THE DOUGH

All of the rye sour from the previous step

2½ cups organic unbleached white (or all-purpose) flour

2¼ teaspoons sea salt

All of the reserved seed mixture

Glaze: I whole egg whisked together with I tablespoon milk

TO PREPARE THE SEED MIXTURE, mix the sesame seeds and soy sauce together in a bowl, place them on a cookie sheet, and toast them for between 15 and 20 minutes in a 350°F oven. Toss the seeds 2 or 3 times while they are roasting to ensure that they crisp evenly.

Roast the pumpkin seeds on a separate cookie sheet for between 10 and 15 minutes until they are just browned. (Some will be a little darker than others.)

Take half of the sesame seed mixture and one-third of the pumpkin seeds and grind them together in a mortar with a pestle (or in a food processor, pulsing 4 or 5 times) until they have been reduced to a medium fine powder. Combine the remaining half of the sesame seed and soy mixture and the remaining two-thirds of the whole pumpkin seeds with the seed powder and set the mixture aside.

TO MAKE THE RYE SOUR (SPONGE), proof the yeast in half a cup of the warm water. When the mixture is creamy, mix in the rest of the warm water and slowly add all of the rye flour and the white flour by handfuls, stirring the mixture with a wooden spoon. Set the batter aside in a large bowl, covered with a dish towel in a warm place, for between 10 and 12 hours or overnight.

TO MAKE THE DOUGH, transfer the rye sour to a medium bowl, start adding the remaining 2½ cups white flour, a handful at a time, and stir vigorously with a wooden spoon. After each addition of flour, mix the dough with the spoon for a minute or so before adding the next. After all but 1 cup of the flour has been added (this will take about 10 minutes), sprinkle the salt over the dough and knead it on your worktable for another 2 or 3 minutes while you add the rest of the flour. The dough should be moist and sticky.

Flatten the dough out on the worktable. Set aside ¼ cup of the seed mixture and sprinkle the rest over the dough. Incorporate the seed mixture by kneading and folding it into the dough.

Set the dough aside, covered, to rise for 1 hour. If it is a cold day or the dough itself is cold (70°F or below when measured with a dough thermometer), let it rise in a very warm place.

When it has doubled in volume, flatten the dough and shape into an oval loaf by folding it over onto itself several times and sealing the join each time with the heel of the hand.

The loaf is best proofed in a *banneton* and then baked on a stone in the oven. But it can also be placed on a parchment-lined baking sheet. However you choose to let it rise the second time, give the loaf between 1 and 1½ hours in a warm place. It will be sufficiently risen when the indentation made by the touch of a finger fails to bounce back.

Slash the loaf diagonally 3 or 4 times with a razor. Glaze the top and then sprinkle the glaze with the reserved ¼ cup of seed mixture. Bake the loaf in a preheated 350°F oven for 45 minutes.

This is the actual recipe used at Gayle's. It produces a moister, sourdough texture and a very tangy flavor.

MAKES I OVAL, 2½-POUND LOAF

I recipe (1½ cups) seed mixture (page 170)

THE RYE SOUR (SPONGE)

1 cup 8-hour-old *pain de campagne* starter (page 32)

2 cups warm water

1 cup organic rye flour

1 cup organic, unbleached white (or all-purpose) flour

THE DOUGH

All of the sponge from the previous step

3½ cups organic, unbleached white (or all-purpose) flour

2½ teaspoons (scant) sea salt

PREPARE THE SEED MIXTURE according to the directions on page 170 and set it aside. (The mixture is best made fresh each time.)

To make the sourdough sponge, which should be mixed cool (between 70°F and 75°F), chop up the *levain,* place it in a large bowl, and incorporate the water. Add the rye flour and 1 cup of the white flour and stir it until you have a smooth batter. Set the sponge aside in the large bowl in which it was mixed, covered with a tea towel, to rise for between 7 and 8 hours. In a few hours it will become quite frothy. When it has risen sufficiently, it will have doubled its original size and dropped a little.

Once the sponge has risen sufficiently, the dough is mixed, shaped, and proofed according to the methods given for the main recipe. The final rising time may have to be extended to as long as 3 hours.

Korni means corn or grain. This is an example of a bread Gayle and I first tasted in Heidelberg. It is made from a combination of grains that go well together for flavor, crunchiness, and good nutrition.

MAKES 1 ROUND, 3½-POUND LOAF

SOY BEAN MIXTURE
- ½ cup organic soy beans
- 1 cup boiling water

THE *POOLISH*
- 1 package (2½ teaspoons; ¼ oz) active dry yeast
- 2½ cups warm water
- 1 cup organic rye flour
- 1 cup organic whole wheat flour
- 1½ cups organic unbleached white (or all-purpose) flour

THE DOUGH
- 1 teaspoon active dry yeast
- ¼ cup warm water
- All of the starter from the previous step
- 3 cups organic, unbleached white (or all-purpose) flour
- 1 tablespoon sea salt
- 1 tablespoon ground caraway seeds*
- ¼ cup organic flax seeds
- ½ cup organic millet
- All of the soy mixture
- Glaze: 1 whole egg whisked with 1 tablespoon milk

TO PREPARE THE SOY BEANS, place them in a small bowl, cover them with the boiling water, and let them soak for 10 minutes. Drain the beans and let them cool. Process the beans in a food processor fitted with the metal blade until they are roughly chopped.

Place the beans on a cookie sheet and roast them in a preheated 350°F oven for between 15 and 20 minutes, until they are completely dried out. Set them aside.

---

* To make your own, grind a few tablespoons of whole caraway seed in a mortar with a pestle until you have a fine powder. If your powder still contains large chunks of seed, sift the mixture and use 1 tablespoon of the sifted powder.

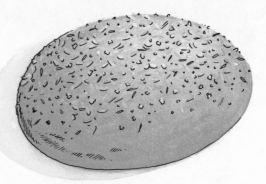

TO MIX THE SPONGE OR *POOLISH,* first proof the yeast, in a large bowl, in 1 cup of the warm water. When it is creamy, mix in 1¼ cups warm water and slowly add the rye flour, whole wheat flour, and 1½ cups of white flour by handfuls while stirring the mixture with a wooden spoon. Set the batter aside, in a large bowl, covered with a dish towel, for between 8 and 10 hours or overnight.

TO MAKE THE DOUGH, proof the yeast in the warm water, add it to the risen sponge, and mix the two together. Start adding the flour, handful by handful, stirring vigorously with a wooden spoon. After all but 1 cup of the flour has been added (this will take about 10 minutes), turn the dough out onto your work-table, sprinkle the salt and the ground caraway over the dough, and incorporate them by kneading the dough for about 5 minutes while adding the last of the flour. The dough should be very moist.

Add the flax seeds, millet, and roasted soy beans and knead the dough to incorporate them.

Set the dough aside, covered, to rise for 1 hour, until it has doubled in size.

Flatten out the dough again and then shape it into a round loaf. This loaf is best proofed in a canvas-lined basket and then baked on a baking stone in the oven. It can also be placed on a parchment-lined baking sheet. Let the loaf rise for about 1½ hours.

Glaze the loaf with the egg and milk mixture and bake it in a preheated 425°F oven for between 30 and 35 minutes.

To make an entirely sourdough bread, substitute a piece of whole wheat sourdough starter that is between 8 and 10 hours old for the yeast in the sponge.

MAKES ONE 3-POUND ROUND LOAF

THE SOY BEAN MIXTURE

    I recipe chopped and roasted soybeans (page 173)

THE STARTER

    I cup *pain de campagne* starter (see page 32) 8 to 10 hours old

    2 cups warm water

    I cup organic rye flour

    I cup organic whole wheat flour

THE DOUGH

    ½ cup organic millet

    ¼ cup organic flax seed

    I tablespoon ground caraway seeds (see note on page 173)

    I tablespoon sea salt

    3 cups organic, unbleached white (or all-purpose) flour

    Any extra water needed to make a moist dough

    All of the soy mixture

    Glaze: I whole egg whisked with I tablespoon milk

TO MAKE THE SPONGE, chop up the starter and dilute it with the water, stirring vigorously until you have a smooth batter. Add the rye and whole wheat flours, mix thoroughly, and allow the batter to rise, covered, for between 10 and 12 hours.

TO MAKE THE DOUGH, follow the directions given in the main recipe for incorporating the rest of the ingredients when the sponge is sufficiently risen. An additional 1 teaspoon of yeast that has been proofed in ¼ cup warm water may be used in the sourdough method in exactly the same way as it is used in the original recipe, but is not necessary.

Sourdough *Korni* will take about twice as long for the second rising, that is, between 3½ and 4 hours before it is ready to be baked.

VOLLKORNBROT
WHOLE-GRAIN BREAD

One of the breads commonly found all over Germany, *Vollkornbrot* is a tangy, sourdough loaf made entirely of rye. Many village bakers make it with industrially produced lactic and acidic sours, but some still make it the old-fashioned way, with pure sourdough as the base and a little yeast in the final dough. It is made with an assortment of differently milled rye grains.

MAKES ONE 2-POUND LOAF OR ONE 1¼-POUND LOAF AND 3 ROLLS

THE MUSH

> 1 cup rough cracked, organic rye seeds or coarse rye meal
>
> 1 cup very hot tap water

THE STARTER

> ¼ cup firm *levain* (see page 32), 8 to 10 hours old
>
> 2 cups warm water
>
> ¾ cup organic rye flour

THE DOUGH

> 1½ teaspoons active dry yeast
>
> ¼ cup warm water
>
> All of the starter (about 2 cups) from the previous step
>
> All of the mush from the first step
>
> 2 teaspoons sea salt
>
> 2 teaspoons ground caraway seeds (optional) (see note on page 173)
>
> 2½ cups organic rye flour
>
> Crushed rye grain, rye meal, or cracked rye cereal and
> rolled oats for topping
>
> Glaze: 1 whole egg whisked with 1 tablespoon milk

TO MAKE THE MUSH, place the rye grain in a bowl, pour the hot water over it, and mix together. Soak this mush for between 12 and 15 hours.

TO MAKE THE STARTER, chop up the *levain* and dilute it in the warm water. Slowly add ¾ cup of the rye flour and mix the ingredients into a soupy sponge, making sure that all of the *levain* is completely broken up. Let the sponge rise for between 12 and 15 hours.

TO MAKE THE DOUGH, proof the yeast in the warm water in a small bowl. When it is creamy (this will take about 10 minutes), mix it together with the starter and mush in a medium-sized bowl. Add the salt and ground caraway to the mixture and combine everything.

Start adding the flour by handfuls while mixing with a spoon. Continue adding the flour until you have several handfuls left and the dough is still quite wet (this will take about 10 minutes).

Whip the dough up with a plastic dough scraper (see page 40), slowly adding the rest of the flour.

When all the flour has been incorporated, the dough will be soft, sticky and moist. With the aid of the plastic dough scraper, shape it roughly into a ball and let it rise, in a large container or bowl and covered with a damp towel, for 1 hour. The dough will expand noticeably but certainly not double.

When it has finished rising, shape the dough into a log by flattening and folding it over onto itself, squaring the ends, and then rolling it up toward you several times. The dough will still be very sticky, so use white or rye flour to help shape it.

One recipe of this dough will fit into a 9-by-5-by-2½-inch pan, which should be well greased. To make a smaller loaf and 3 rolls, cut off one-third of the dough, dividing the smaller piece in thirds and rolling each piece into small logs measuring about 1 inch by 4 inches. Roll these logs in a mixture of crushed rye grain and rolled oats and place them on a parchment-lined baking sheet. Shape the larger piece into a loaf and place it in a well-oiled loaf pan measuring 7⅜ inches by 3⅝ inches by 2¼ inches.

The loaves of whatever size should come up to within about half an inch of the top of the pan.

Let the loaves and rolls, covered with a moist towel, rise for between 1¼ and 1½ hours, until the indentation made by a finger in the dough does not spring back quickly. By that time the dough should be approximately ¼ inch above top edge of the pan.

Glaze the loaf and sprinkle the top with rye meal or cracked rye cereal mixed with a little rolled oats. Pat the grains in so they stick.

Bake the bread in a preheated 425°F oven for 25 minutes, then turn the heat down to 400°F and bake the large loaf for another 40 minutes and the small loaf for 30 minutes. Bake the rolls for between 25 and 30 minutes at 400°F.

VARIATION
Vollkornbrot may also be made with a very soupy refrigerator starter that takes 2 days to prepare. On the first day, instead of using an 8-hour levain, mix ½ teaspoon milk sour (page 33) with ¼ cup rye flour and ¼ cup warm water. Let the mixture rise for between 12 and 15 hours.

On the following day, add ¾ cup warm water and ½ cup rye flour to the starter. Mix well and set the batter aside to rise for 24 hours.

On the third day, make up the dough following the directions in the main recipe.

SPONGE

ONION WHEAT BREAD

I saw this bread in Vienna, in Salzburg, and throughout Germany. The Italians also have a version, which is made in the shape of a ring.

MAKES 1 LARGE, HORSESHOE-SHAPED LOAF OR
6 SMALL, HORSESHOE-SHAPED ROLLS

THE ONION FLAVORING

3 medium yellow onions

3 tablespoons light cooking oil

¾ teaspoon salt

THE SPONGE

1 package (2½ teaspoons; ¼ ounce) active dry yeast

1 cup warm water

1 tablespoon honey

3 tablespoons milk

2 tablespoons soy or corn oil

1 cup whole wheat flour

THE DOUGH

All of the sponge from the previous step

1½ teaspoons salt

¼ cup cool water

2 cups organic, unbleached white (or all-purpose) flour

The onion mixture from the first step

TO PREPARE THE ONION FLAVORING, slice the onions thinly. Heat the oil in a skillet and when it is warm, put in the onion slices and salt. Sauté the onions for 15 to 20 minutes over medium-low heat, stirring occasionally. Remove the onions from the heat when they are medium to dark brown in color; allow them to cool. You should have between ¾ and 1 cup cooked onions.

TO MAKE THE SPONGE, proof the yeast, in a large bowl, in ¼ cup of the warm water. When it is creamy (this will take about 10 minutes), add to it the rest of the water, the honey, milk, and oil. Start adding the whole wheat flour to the liquid in handfuls while mixing with a wooden spoon. Mix the liquid starter for 2 to 3 minutes until all the ingredients are well incorporated.

Let the sponge rise, in a large container or bowl and covered, until it triples in size. This will take about 2 hours.

TO MAKE THE DOUGH, stir down the sponge and sprinkle the salt over the top of it. Incorporate the water and salt into the sponge. (If the sponge is very warm, add cool water; if it is cool, use warm water.) Add the flour by handfuls while mixing the dough with a plastic dough scraper or a wooden spoon. As the dough comes together and when you still have a few handfuls of flour left, empty the dough out onto your worktable and clean off your hands and the bowl with the plastic dough scraper. Knead the dough on the worktable for between 5 and 8 minutes longer, using up the rest of the flour to prevent the dough from sticking to the bench. The dough should be moist and somewhat sticky.

Set aside 3 or 4 tablespoons of the onions. Flatten the dough out and coat it with the remainder of the onion mixture. Fold and knead the dough for a few minutes longer to mix in the onions. Use a little more white flour on the worktable if necessary.

Let the dough rise on the bench or in the bowl, covered, for between 35 and 40 minutes, until it doubles in size.

To make onion rolls, divide the dough into 6 equal pieces. Flatten each piece and then, by rolling the ends under the palms, roll the dough up into little torpedo shapes that measure about 8 inches long. Curve the rolls into horseshoe shapes and place them on a parchment-lined baking tray.

To make 1 large loaf, roll and shape the entire batch of dough into a large horseshoe.

Brush the rolls or loaf with a little water and then distribute the reserved onion mixture on top.

Let rolls and loaf rise for between 35 and 40 minutes.

Bake in a preheated 400°F oven, the rolls for between 10 and 15 minutes and the large loaf for 35 minutes. The loaf will be a deep golden brown and sound hollow when thumped on the bottom.

Viennese bakers, who first made use of the *poolish* method, know how to handle yeast. In a bread bakery in Vienna run by the Mugitch family I came across an original technique for handling yeast. The day before it is needed, yeast is dissolved in water in a big vat. The following day it is ready to use and the bakers can reduce the quantity of yeast normally called for in a recipe by 20 percent. The method described in the following recipe is an approximation of that technique. I call it a "flourless sponge." It helps to give a spongy, more flavorful texture.

You see pretzels in many sizes in the outdoor *Christkindlesmarkts* at Christmastime throughout Germany and Austria. They are also found in bakeries all year long.

MAKES FOUR 5-INCH PRETZELS OR TWO 8-INCH PRETZELS

YEAST MIXTURE

    1 ½ teaspoons active dry yeast

    ¼ cup cool water

THE DOUGH

    1 teaspoon active dry yeast

    ¼ cup warm water

    ½ cup hot water

    ½ teaspoon honey

    1 tablespoon corn or vegetable oil

    1 ½ teaspoons salt

    3 cups organic, unbleached white (or all-purpose) flour

    Glaze: 1 egg yolk whisked into 1 tablespoon milk

    Rock salt or caraway seeds for topping

FOR THE FLOURLESS SPONGE, dissolve the yeast in ¼ cup of the water in a cup and let the mixture stand for 2 to 3 hours.

TO MAKE THE DOUGH, proof the yeast in the warm water until it is creamy. Dissolve the honey and mix in the oil and salt in the ½ cup hot water. When cool, combine it with the sponge and the yeast mixture. Then add 2 cups of the flour, incorporating them with a spoon or plastic dough scraper and mixing vigorously for 3 or 4 minutes. Turn the mixture out onto the worktable and, using the remaining cup of flour, knead the mass into a medium-firm dough.

Let the dough rise, covered and in a warm spot, for 30 minutes. It will almost double in bulk.

Punch the dough down and form it into a tight ball. Coat with a little corn or vegetable oil and place it back in the bowl. Cover the dough with plastic wrap and let it rise in the refrigerator for between 2 and 4 hours.

When it is sufficiently risen, take the dough out of refrigerator and shape it immediately. Divide the dough in 4 equal pieces and roll each piece into a log

VARIATION
To make large pretzels, divide the dough in half and make 2 pretzels.

about 24 inches long. The strands of dough should be about ¾ inch in diameter in the middle and taper down to ¼ inch at each end. Then bend each strand into a pretzel (see illustration) and place it on a parchment-lined baking sheet.

Brush the pretzels with the egg and milk mixture, sprinkle them with rock salt or caraway seeds, and set them aside, covered, for a final rising—about 30 to 45 minutes.

Bake the pretzels in a preheated 375°F oven for about 30 to 35 minutes or until they are a deep golden brown.

KAISERSEMMEL
THE EMPEROR'S ROLLS

Kaisersemmels are called Kaiser rolls in New York. They are very light in texture with a crisp crust. In Austrian bakeries the shaping by hand is usually done by a baker who sits on a stool and can pump out hundreds of them each hour.

MAKES SIX 3-OUNCE ROLLS

THE SPONGE

    1½ teaspoons active dry yeast

    ¼ cup warm water

    2 teaspoons sugar

    ½ teaspoon malt extract or honey

    ½ cup milk, scalded and allowed to cool slightly

    1½ cups all-purpose flour

    ½ cup cool water

THE DOUGH

    1½ teaspoons salt

    1 cup organic, unbleached white (or all-purpose) flour

    All of the sponge from the previous step

    Poppy seeds for topping

TO MAKE THE SPONGE, proof the yeast in the warm water until it is creamy. Dissolve the sugar and malt extract in the milk after it has cooled a bit. Pour the yeast mixture into a medium bowl, add the flour, milk, and water to the mixture, and mix everything together with a wooden spoon. Let this sponge rise, covered and in a warm place, for 2 hours.

TO MAKE THE DOUGH, mix the salt in with the flour and then start adding this dry mixture to the risen sponge by handfuls, mixing it in with a spoon. When you have ¼ cup of flour left and the dough has come together somewhat (this will take about 10 minutes), turn the dough out onto your worktable, clean off your hands and the bowl with a plastic dough scraper and knead the dough for another 5 to 8 minutes while incorporating the rest of the flour. (If you need a little extra flour to make a medium-firm dough, add up to ½ cup.)

When the dough is soft and satiny, round it into a ball and let it rise in a large container or bowl, covered with a damp towel, until it doubles in size (this will take about 1 to 1¼ hours).

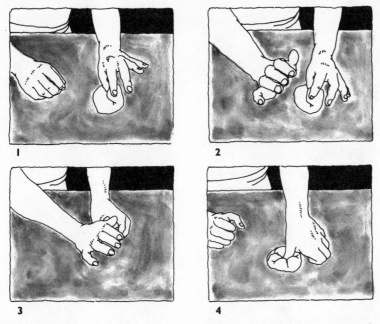

Divide the dough into 6 equal pieces. Round each piece into a tight ball and let the dough rest on the worktable, covered with a damp towel, for 15 minutes.

Then flatten each ball with the palm of the hand. The next step, shaping the rolls, is probably easier done than described. Place the thumb of the left hand in the middle of the flattened disk of dough and pick up a section of the edge of the disk with the index finger, folding it over toward the middle. Seal the fold with the heel of the right hand. Rotate the dough a quarter turn counterclockwise and continue the folding and sealing until you have made 4 or 5 little tucks meeting in the middle of the dough. Fold any excess dough that still hangs out of the roll into the middle by making 1 final tuck and pressing it down firmly with the thumb. Shape the rest of the dough into rolls in this way.

Place the rolls on a cookie sheet lined with parchment paper. Brush them lightly with vegetable oil and cover them with another piece of parchment paper, a cookie sheet, and then a cast-iron skillet.

Let the rolls rise for between 35 and 40 minutes. They will have almost doubled in size, although they will be flat from the weight of the tray on top.

Remove the skillet, cookie sheet, and parchment from the top of the rolls. Brush them lightly with water and then sprinkle them with poppy seeds.

Just before placing the rolls in a preheated 450°F oven, use an atomizer to spray water inside the oven 5 or 6 times and spray again at 5-minute intervals while the rolls are baking. The rolls will be a light golden color and baked through in 20 minutes. The crust should be very crisp.

MUESLI PORRIDGE CAKES

This recipe was devised after I discovered that the first breads were made from porridge. The rich, healthy taste of the gruel is the dominant flavor. The dough can also be made up into a loaf or 2 *baguettes*, allowed to rise for between one and two hours, and baked in the oven.

MAKES 6 FLAT, 3-OUNCE CAKES

THE STARTER

> ½ cup muesli porridge (recipe follows)
>
> ½ cup (scant) all-purpose flour

DOUGH

> 1 teaspoon yeast
>
> 1 cup warm water
>
> All of the starter from the previous step
>
> 2½ cups all-purpose flour
>
> 1½ teaspoons salt
>
> Topping: A mixture of pumpkin and sesame seeds

TO MAKE THE STARTER, mix the porridge and flour together into a firm dough and let rise, covered and in a warm place, for between 24 and 36 hours.

TO MAKE THE DOUGH, proof the yeast in a little of the warm water, then mix all the ingredients (except the topping) together into a medium-wet dough. Knead the dough for about 8 or 10 minutes.

Let the dough rise for 2 hours.

Divide the dough into 6 pieces. Flatten each piece into a flat, round cake or *galette* about 4 inches across. Pat the cakes down onto the mixture of pumpkin seeds and sesame seeds to coat the top and set them aside to rise for 20 minutes. (Or shape the dough into 1 oval loaf or into 2 *baguettes* and let the bread rise for 1 to 2 hours, covered to avoid crusting.)

Bake the cakes on a preheated, hot griddle for 20 minutes. (Bake the loaf or *baguettes* in a preheated, 425°F oven for 30 to 35 minutes or 18 to 20 minutes, respectively.)

A Note for the Advanced Baker

If the first starter ferments vigorously and produces large bubbles, try making the cakes or bread without yeast. Use 1 cup water, 1¼ cups all-purpose flour, and a few pinches of salt. Proceed according to the recipe and allow the dough to rise overnight before shaping the cakes.

MUESLI PORRIDGE

Like all gruels, this can be used as a base for breads. This recipe makes a nourishing breakfast food and is often found in Germany and Switzerland.

MAKES ABOUT 3 CUPS

¼ cup rolled wheat

¼ cup rolled oats

¼ cup whole barley

¼ cup sunflower seeds

¼ cup rolled rye

1¼ cups water

¼ teaspoon salt

⅛ cup sesame seeds

⅛ cup pumpkin seeds

⅛ cup chopped almonds

½ cup raisins

1 to 1½ teaspoons honey

Mix the wheat, oats, barley, sunflower seeds, and rye with the water and allow the mixture to soak overnight.

The next morning, add the salt and cook the soaked mixture until the water evaporates. While it is cooking, combine the sesame and pumpkin seeds, the almonds, and raisins and set this topping aside.

When the soaked mixture is cooked, stir in the honey.

To serve as a breakfast cereal, garnish each bowlful with some of the topping mixture, a pat of butter, and a little milk. To use in a muesli bread, combine the soaked and cooked grains, the honey, and the topping mixture with flour, to make a starter; the recipe is on page 184.

CHAPTER 7

Village Baking in the United States

VILLAGE BAKERIES, MAKING LOCAL BREADS, are again appearing all over America. At the turn of the century, when immigrants from Europe started to enter the United States, they surely established in the cities new, specialized bakeries that were just a carryover of their European traditions transplanted to a new land. Then the supermarket and the availability of mass-produced, inexpensive bread that stayed fresh longer made it harder for the neighborhood bakery to survive. Perhaps as proof that our civilization is not in irretrievable decay, we can cite the fairly recent willingness of Americans to seek out good bread; their willingness to make a trip to the neighborhood bakery to buy fresh-baked bread and not expect the stuff to have a shelf life that is measured in months.

Many of the breads in this chapter are American variations of European breads; others are ethnic variations made with natural improvers that give the loaves a distinct flavor and character. We do have one authentically native American bread, San Francisco sourdough, that owes its existence to the presence in San Francisco of a natural culture, a bacterium, that feeds on the flour and water mixture of a beginning bread dough.

Many people believe the myth that the best American sourdough bread can be made only in San Francisco. To an extent, that is true. But the answer to the question, "Why can't we recreate in our area a bread that tastes like the one we had in Provence or San Francisco?" should not be entirely discouraging. The reason is that certain areas foster their own very distinct cultures in the air. The local flour and water, climate, and atmosphere induce each natural, regional sourdough culture to create flavors and textures unique to that area.

The climate of San Francisco, with all its fog and moisture, is conducive to sourdough baking. And the particular *Lactobacillus* culture that gives the bread its flavor is unique to that area.

Of that myth, Gratienne Guerra, the former owner of a bakery in Sonoma, north of San Francisco, once said: "It's baloney!" What he meant was that one can, indeed, make good sourdough bread anywhere. It will not be *San Francisco* sourdough, but the question we should be asking is, "How can we capture a natural sourdough culture unique to our own area and make a bread that complements our local food?"

✧✧✧✧✧✧ *Village Bakeries in the United States* ✧✧✧✧✧✧

ACME BREAD COMPANY, 1601 San Pablo Avenue, Berkeley, California.
  Telephone: (510) 524-1021.
Specialties: *levain* bread, sourdough *baguettes, fougasse*
  Steve Sullivan, once the baker for Chez Panisse, and his partners now supply bread for the best restaurants and markets in San Francisco and Berkeley. Get there early; breads are often sold out by noon.

BAKERS OF PARIS, 3989 24th Street, San Francisco, California.
  Telephone: (415) 871-9400.
Specialties: seeded *baguettes,* sourdough, and French bread
  Won the Best of Show award at the 1992 International Bread Tasting put on by *Bay Food* magazine; several shops throughout the Bay Area. They also sell *croissants* and other pastries.

THE BREAD GARDEN, 2912 Domingo Avenue, Berkeley, California.
  Telephone: (510) 548-3122.
Specialties: *baguettes* and malted barley bread
  A friendly neighborhood shop near the Claremont Hotel. (Back in 1977, David Morris was good enough to give my wife, Gayle, his recipe for *pain ordinaire.*)

BROTHER JUNIPER'S, 463 Sebastopol Avenue, Forestville, California.
  Telephone: (707) 542-6546.
Specialties: Struan (a Celtic five-grain bread), wild rice and onion, Cajun three-pepper bread, oreganato (a French bread with oregano), garlic, parsley, and black pepper bread, polenta bread, and roasted three-seed bread
  Won an honorable mention at the 1992 *Bay Food* magazine's International Bread Tasting. The owner, Peter Reinhart, has written an interesting book, *Brother Juniper's Bread Book: Slow Rise as Method and Metaphor.*

THE CHEESEBOARD, 1504 Shattuck Avenue, Berkeley, California.
  Telephone: (510) 549-3183.
Specialties: sourdough *baguettes,* different daily cheese breads, including Cheddar and provolone with olives, pizza
  The chewiest *baguettes* around.

THE DOWNTOWN BAKERY AND CREAMERY, 308A Center Street, Healdsburg, California. Telephone: (707) 431-2719.
Specialties: sourdough *baguettes,* Como bread (another name for *pane francese*), *focaccia*
  A small, provincial bakery that also makes the best ice cream and cookies to be found anywhere.

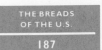

DRAEGER'S, 1010 University Drive, Menlo Park, California.
Telephone: (415) 688-0690.
Specialties: *pain Beaucaire,* Richard's rye, sun-dried tomato
The *pain Beaucaire* won first place in the sweet-wheat category at the 1992 *Bay Food* magazine's International Bread Tasting.

ELI ZABAR'S EATS, Madison Avenue at 81st Street, New York, New York.
Telephone: (212) 787-2000.
Specialties: sourdough *baguettes,* onion *baguettes,* rye raisin-nut
In many people's opinion the best bread in Manhattan.

FRAN GAGE PÂTISSERIE, 40690 18th Street, San Francisco, California.
Telephone: (415) 864-8428.
Specialties: *pain au levain,* pumpernickel-rye, *pain au noix*
Small neighborhood bakery that won a first-place award for sourdough in the *Bay Food* magazine's 1992 International Bread Tasting.

THE MODEL BAKERY, 1357 Main Street, St. Helena, California.
Telephone: (707) 963-8192.
Specialties: country bread, sourdough *baguettes*
A cozy little village bakery in the wine country.

ORWASHER'S, 308 East 78th Street (between 1st and 2nd Avenue), New York, New York. Telephone: (212) 288-6569.
Specialties: Jewish rye, challah, challah rolls with cinnamon and raisins, raisin pumpernickel
One of the best ethnic bakeries anywhere.

ROCK HILL BAKEHOUSE, Box 70, Spraguetown Road, Greenwich, New York.
Telephone: (518) 692-2943.
Specialties: *pane bello* (a rustic Italian bread), whole wheat farm bread, and San Francisco–style sourdough, all baked in a brick oven
The bread, made by Michael London, the owner and head baker, has been featured in *Gourmet* magazine.

SANITARY BAKERY OF A. ZITO, 259 Bleeker Street, New York, New York.
Telephone: (212) 929-6139.
Specialties: Italian-style wheat and white breads with sesame seeds baked in a coal-fired brick oven
Frank Sinatra used to get his bread here.

SEMIFREDDI'S, 372 Colusa Avenue, Kensington, California.
Telephone: (510) 596-9935; and 4242 Hollis Street, Emeryville, California.
Telephone: (510) 596-9930.
Specialties: sourdough *baguettes,* challah, *Pugliese, pan bigio,* Odessa rye
An award-winner in the 1992 *Bay Food* magazine's International Bread Tasting.

SONOMA FRENCH BAKERY, 470 1st Street East, Sonoma, California.
Telephone: (707) 996-2691.
Specialties: French-style sourdough baked in a brick oven
It is said that the former owner, Gratienne Guerra, brought his sourdough starter from his native town in the Basque mountains.

SUZANNE'S BAKERY, 118 Main Street, Northampton, Massachusetts.
Telephone: (413) 586-2312.
Specialties: a whole-wheat country bread called Fanny Bread

TASSAJARA, 1000 Cole Street, San Francisco, California.
Telephone: (415) 664-8947.
Specialties: potato bread, sourdough *bâtard,* Viennese five-grain

This bakery used to be a part of the San Francisco Zen Center but was recently sold to Just Desserts. It still has the same good bread and pastries. With the publication of a book on bread back in the 1960s, Tassajara Bakery helped fuel the development of small neighborhood shops. The bakery won numerous awards at the *Bay Food* magazine's International Bread Tastings in 1992 and 1990.

THE WOOD-FIRE BAKERY, 958 San Leandro Avenue, Mountain View, California.
Telephone: (415) 966-1022.
Specialties: old-world-styled country breads baked in a wood-fired brick oven

Most people try to make what they hope will be authentic San Francisco–style sourdough bread from a soupy sourdough starter that's been in the refrigerator for a few hundred years. That may be how the "sourdough" settlers in California first did it. But better results can be had by refreshing the starter (mixing it with more flour and water) several times, as is done in commercial sourdough bakeries. This recipe does just that. To make a basic sourdough starter from scratch, see page 31. For this recipe, use the starter when the *levain* has been refreshed once and allowed to rise in a warm place for between eight and ten hours or in the refrigerator for between fifteen and twenty-four hours.

MAKES 2 ROUND, 1½-POUND LOAVES

THE FIRST REFRESHMENT

¼ cup sourdough starter (page 31), after
it has been refreshed at least once

¼ cup very warm water

½ cup plus 2 to 3 tablespoons organic,
unbleached white (or all-purpose) flour

THE SECOND REFRESHMENT

All of the starter (about 1 cup) from the previous step

¾ cup cool water

1¾ to 2 cups organic, unbleached white (or all-purpose) flour

THE DOUGH

All of the sourdough starter (3½ cups) from the previous step

2⅛ cups warm water

5 cups organic, unbleached white bread (or all-purpose) flour

1 tablespoon plus 1 teaspoon salt

Glaze: 1 egg white whisked with 1 tablespoon cold water

FOR THE FIRST REFRESHMENT, dilute the starter as much as possible in the water, then gradually add the flour, pinch by pinch, while stirring the mixture with a plastic dough scraper. When the piece of dough comes together quite firmly, clean the hands and the bowl and make sure that every bit of dough goes into the mixture. Knead the dough on the worktable for between 6 and 8 minutes. The dough will be very firm but not dry. Let it rise in the small bowl, covered with a moist towel and in a warm place, for between 5 and 6 hours.

When the first refreshment is about twice its original size, smells slightly acidic, and does not seem to bounce back at you when touched with the fingertip, it is ready to be taken to the next stage.

FOR THE SECOND REFRESHMENT, again dilute the starter in the water (use very warm water in winter when the ambient temperature is low enough to keep the culture inert), stir the flour in gradually, and then knead the dough for between 6 and 8 minutes on the worktable. Set it aside, again covered and in a warm place, to rise for another 5 or 6 hours.

TO MIX THE DOUGH, dissolve the starter as much as possible in the water and add 4 cups of the flour, gradually. This will take about 10 minutes. Sprinkle the salt over the dough and incorporate it by kneading the dough for a few minutes.

Empty the dough out onto the worktable and continue kneading it for 5 more minutes while adding the remaining cup of flour. The dough will be shiny and more elastic and stretchy than that of a regular yeasted dough. The consistency will be medium firm.

The dough needs to rise twice, and there are 2 ways of treating it, depending on your time schedule and expertise. You can allow 1 hour for the first rising and between 8 and 10 hours for the final rising or between 6 and 8 hours for the first rising and between 4 and 6 hours for the final rising. However you divide it, the total time should add up to around 10 hours. (When professionals make this bread, the dough is so active that the first rising takes only 1 hour and the final rising only 6.)

For the first rising, set the dough aside in a warm place and covered with a dish towel for whatever length of time you have chosen. At the end of that time, cut off a small piece of dough about the size of a large olive, round it into a tight ball, and place it in a Mason jar of water that is at room temperature. When this piece of dough rises to the surface, the loaves will have risen sufficiently and be ready to bake.

To shape the loaves, divide the dough in half and make 2 round loaves by flattening and tucking 4 or 5 of the outer edges of the dough in toward the middle and sealing them. Turn the dough over and drag it across the worktable with some friction so that it is shaped into a tight, round loaf. Place it in a flour-dusted *banneton* or a basket lined with a piece of canvas or with a dish towel that has been well dusted with flour.

Let the loaves rise, covered and in a warm place, for between 4 and 8 hours (depending on the length of the first rising) or until the little ball of dough in the Mason jar has risen to the top of the water.

Empty the loaves onto a flour-dusted, rimless baking tray if you are using a baking stone, or onto a parchment-lined baking sheet, dust off any excess flour on the loaves, and glaze the tops. With a straight razor cut loaves in a criss-cross pattern 5 or 6 times in each direction.

Spray the oven 4 or 5 times with water from an atomizer before the loaves go into the oven. Bake the loaves, either on a baking stone or directly on a tray, in a preheated 425°F oven for between 40 and 45 minutes.

When we first came up with our own version of white sourdough bread at Gayle's, we knew it would be unique to our region. So the only logical name to give it was Capitola Sourdough.

This is just one variation of the classic San Francisco sourdough method. The refreshment dough is softer, the fermentation shorter, the final dough wetter, and the final rising shorter.

MAKES TWO 1¼-POUND LOAVES

THE FIRST REFRESHMENT

¼ cup basic sourdough starter (page 31 and recipe
  introduction on page 190)

¼ cup plus 2 teaspoons very warm water

½ cup plus 2 to 3 tablespoons organic, unbleached white bread
  (or all-purpose) flour

THE SECOND REFRESHMENT

All of the starter (about 1 cup) from the previous step

¾ cup plus 2 tablespoons cool water

1¾ to 2 cups organic, unbleached white bread (or all-purpose) flour

THE DOUGH

Most of the sourdough starter (3 cups) from the previous step

1¼ cups warm water

3 cups organic, unbleached white bread (or all-purpose) flour

1 tablespoon salt

Glaze: 1 egg whisked with 1 tablespoon cold water

FOR THE FIRST REFRESHMENT, dilute the starter completely in the water and then add the flour, pinch by pinch, while stirring the mixture with a plastic dough scraper. When the dough comes together quite firmly, clean your hands and the bowl and make sure that every bit of dough goes into the mixture. Knead the dough on the worktable for between 6 and 8 minutes. The dough will be medium firm and a little sticky. Set it aside to rise, covered and in a warm place, for between 2½ and 3 hours.

When the first refreshment is about twice its original size, smells slightly acidic, and does not seem to bounce back when touched with the fingertip, it is ready to be mixed again.

FOR THE SECOND REFRESHMENT, dilute the starter in the water (use very warm water in winter when the ambient temperature is low enough to keep the culture inert), stir the flour in gradually, and then knead the dough for between 6 and 8 minutes on the worktable. Set it aside, again covered and in a warm place, to rise for 3 hours.

TO MIX THE DOUGH, dissolve the starter thoroughly in the water and add 2 cups of the flour, gradually. This will take about 10 minutes. Sprinkle on the salt and incorporate it by kneading the dough for a few minutes. This dough will be very moist.

Empty the dough out onto the worktable and continue kneading it for 5 minutes longer while adding the remaining cup of flour. The dough will be shiny and elastic and of a rather soft consistency.

For the first rising, set the dough aside, in a warm place and covered with a dish towel, for 1 hour. At the end of that time, cut off a small piece of dough about the size of an olive, round it into a tight ball, and place it in a Mason jar of water that is at room temperature. When this piece of dough rises to the surface, the loaves will have risen sufficiently and will be ready to be baked.

To shape the dough into loaves, divide it in half and make each into a round loaf by flattening and tucking 4 or 5 of the outer edges in toward the middle and sealing them. Turn the ball over and drag it across the worktable with some friction so that it is shaped into a tight round loaf. Place it in a flour-dusted *banneton* or a basket that has been lined with canvas or a well-floured dish towel.

Let the loaves rise, covered and in a warm place, for between 3 and 4 hours, depending on the activity level of the starter, or until the little ball of dough in the Mason jar has risen to the surface of the water.

Empty the loaves onto a flour-dusted, rimless baking tray if you are using a baking stone or onto a parchment-lined baking tray, dust off any excess flour from the loaves, and glaze the tops. With a straight razor cut the loaves in a criss-cross pattern 5 or 6 times in each direction.

Spray the oven 4 or 5 times with water from an atomizer before putting the bread in the oven. Bake the loaves, either on a baking stone or directly on a tray, in a preheated, 450°F oven for between 35 and 40 minutes.

CAPITOLA SOURDOUGH SANDWICH LOAF

At Gayle's we wanted to make a light, fluffy sourdough bread in a loaf-pan shape that, when sliced, would be good for making sandwiches. The inclusion of a little yeast, milk powder, and oil add to the softness of the crumb.

Use a *levain* or sourdough starter that is between four and eight hours old. Or you can use an old dough—a piece pulled from a previous batch of bread—in which case your starter will have salt in it; reduce the salt in this recipe by one-half teaspoon. Even if you are using the recipe for the basic starter on page 31 and only come up with 1½ cups of *levain,* this recipe will still work fine. (You can always augment a *levain* in its final refreshment by adding a little more flour and water and letting it rise for a little longer.)

MAKES ONE 2-POUND LOAF

I teaspoon active dry yeast

1¼ cups water

1 tablespoon soy or corn oil

3 cups organic, unbleached white (or all-purpose) flour

2 teaspoons salt

1 tablespoon powdered milk

2 cups *levain* (page 31)

Glaze: 1 egg white whisked with ½ cup cool water

Proof the yeast in ¼ cup of the warm water. Add the soy oil to the remaining cup of warm water. Combine all the dry ingredients and set them aside.

In a large bowl break up the *levain* and pour in the water and oil, mixing the ingredients for several minutes to dilute the *levain.* Then start adding the flour mixture by handfuls and stirring with a wooden spoon until you have a soupy paste; this will take about 5 minutes. Add the yeast mixture and a little more flour and continue mixing. When 1 cup of the flour mixture is left and the

dough starts to come together, empty it out on the worktable and knead it for 5 more minutes until it becomes a firm, satiny bread dough.

Let the dough rise, covered and in a warm spot, for 1 hour. Punch down the dough and flatten it out on the worktable. Fold it in half, over itself and away from you. Square the edges, pushing the dough an inch or so toward the middle of the piece. Then roll the dough into a tight log (that will fit into a 9-by-5-by-2½-inch loaf pan), sealing it at each turn with the heel of your hand.

Grease the loaf pan before placing the dough in it and set the loaf aside, covered with a damp towel, for between 4 and 6 hours, until it doubles in size.

With a razor blade slash the loaf on top making 1 long cut. Then glaze the loaf. Before placing the loaf in the oven, spray the oven 4 or 5 times with water from an atomizer. Bake the loaf in a preheated 425°F oven for between 40 and 45 minutes.

BERKELEY SOURDOUGH

Bob Wacks of the Cheeseboard in Berkeley, California, invented this method. Now other bakeries in the area also use it. What makes the recipe interesting is the soupy sourdough starter and the dough that is refrigerated overnight.

Any piece of sourdough can be used to make the starter as long as it is very active.

MAKES TWO 10-OUNCE *BAGUETTES*

THE STARTER

> 1 piece of *levain* the size of a tangerine (kept out at room temperature
>   for 6 to 8 hours or in the refrigerator for a few days)
> 2 cups warm water
> 2 cups organic, unbleached white (or all-purpose) flour

THE DOUGH

> 2½ cups organic, unbleached white (or all-purpose) flour
> 1½ teaspoons salt
> ¾ cup starter from the previous step
> ¾ cup cool water

TO MAKE THE STARTER, break up the *levain,* dilute it in the water, then add the flour and mix until it is incorporated. The starter will be soupy. Set the mixture aside, loosely covered and in a warm spot, for between 18 and 24 hours or until it is quite bubbly.

TO MAKE THE DOUGH, mix the flour and salt together in a food processor fitted with the plastic dough blade. Pour the soupy starter in the bowl and pulse the machine several times to mix the ingredients. Then, with the machine running,

slowly add the water through the feed tube until it is all incorporated. Process for a few minutes. The dough will be wet and shiny. Turn the mixture out of the bowl and onto a well-floured bench where it can be roughly rounded up into a ball.

Let the dough rise in a well-oiled bowl, covered, in the refrigerator for between 12 and 15 hours. Remove the dough from the refrigerator and allow it to sit out at room temperature for 2 hours to warm up.

To shape the loaves, divide the dough into 2 pieces, stretch them into tight, but irregular *baguette* shapes, and place each in a *baguette* tray that has been well oiled. (They can also be placed on a parchment-lined baking tray.)

Let the *baguettes* rise for between 6 and 7 hours, covered and in a warm place, until they have doubled in size.

Preheat the oven to 450°F.

With a sharp razor blade, cut the loaves 3 or 4 times diagonally and then spray them with a fine mist of water from a spray bottle.

Place the *baguette* trays in the oven and immediately spray the loaves again and spray the walls and floor of the oven to generate some steam.

After about 5 minutes open the door and quickly spray another 5 or 6 squirts of water into the oven.

Bake the loaves for between 25 and 30 minutes, until they are entirely golden and the crust is crisp and blistered.

BERKELEY SOURDOUGH WITH YEAST

For this recipe use two cups of the Berkeley Sourdough starter. The addition of the yeast speeds up the process, enabling the dough to rise faster.

MAKES TWO 14-OUNCE *BAGUETTES*

> ¼ cup warm water
>
> 1½ teaspoons active dry yeast
>
> 2 teaspoons salt
>
> 3 cups organic, unbleached white (or all-purpose) flour
>
> 2 cups 18- to 24-hour-old soupy sourdough starter (page 195)
>
> ½ cup cold water

Proof the yeast in ¼ cup warm water, setting the mixture aside until it is bubbly. Make up the dough according to the method given for Berkeley Sourdough (page 195), adding the yeast mixture and the salt right at the beginning.

For the first rising, place the dough in the refrigerator for 8 hours and, before continuing with the recipe, take it out of the refrigerator and allow it to sit out, at room temperature, for 1½ hours, until it has warmed up.

Following the recipe for Berkeley Sourdough, shape the loaves and let them rise for 4 hours, before baking them as directed above.

This is one of the first breads we ever made at Gayle's Bakery back in 1978.

MAKES I SMALL, I-POUND LOAF AND 6 TO 8 ROLLS OR
I LARGE 2-POUND LOAF

THE SPONGE

> 3 packages (2 tablespoons plus 1 ½ teaspoons; ¾ ounce) active dry yeast
>
> 2 cups warm water
>
> ½ cup honey
>
> ⅓ cup soy or corn oil
>
> I tablespoon powdered milk
>
> 2 cups whole wheat flour

THE DOUGH

> All of the sponge from the previous step
>
> I tablespoon salt
>
> I cup water
>
> 4 cups whole wheat flour
>
> Glaze: I whole egg whisked with 3 tablespoons cold milk (optional)

TO MAKE THE SPONGE, proof the yeast in 1 cup of the warm water. When it is creamy (this will take about 10 minutes), add to it the rest of the water, the honey, and the oil. Combine the powdered milk with the flour and then start adding the dry mixture to the liquid in handfuls while mixing with a wooden spoon. Mix this liquid starter for a few minutes until the ingredients are well incorporated.

Let the sponge rise, covered, in a large container or bowl until it triples in size; this will take about 2 hours.

TO MAKE THE DOUGH, stir down the starter and sprinkle the salt over the top of it. Stir the water into the sponge, using cool water if the sponge is very warm; in winter, when the sponge is cool, use warm water. Add the flour by handfuls while mixing with a plastic dough scraper or a wooden spoon. As the dough comes together and when you still have a few handfuls of flour left, empty the dough out onto the worktable and clean off the bowl and your hands with the plastic dough scraper. Knead the dough on the worktable for 5 to 8 minutes more, using the rest of the flour to prevent the dough from sticking to the table. The dough should be moist and somewhat sticky.

Let the dough rise, covered, on the bench or in the bowl for between 35 and 40 minutes, until it doubles in size.

Cut off about one-third of the dough, divide it into 6 or 8 equal pieces, and make them into rolls by rounding them on the table and placing them on a parchment-lined baking tray. (This piece of dough, which will weigh about 1 pound, can also be made into a walnut or raisin loaf as described in the recipes on pages 99 and 100.)

Punch back the remaining two-thirds piece of dough and flatten it. Fold it over onto itself and away from you. Square the edges by pushing the dough an inch or so in toward the middle. Then roll the loaf up into a tight log, sealing the dough on each turn with the heel of the hand.

Place the loaf in a greased 9-by-5-by-2½-inch loaf pan and let it rise for another 35 to 40 minutes.

The rolls and the loaf may be baked glazed or unglazed.

Bake the bread in a preheated 425°F oven. The loaf will take between 45 and 50 minutes and will be baked when it sounds hollow when thumped on the bottom. The rolls will take around 15 minutes; a nut or raisin loaf between 35 and 40 minutes.

WHOLE-GRAIN BREAD

This is the first bread I ever created for Gayle's; all my other recipes at that time came from other sources. My marketing slogan was, and always will be, "It turns to cake in eight days."

MAKES 4 SMALL 10-OUNCE LOAVES

I cup boiling water

¾ cup cracked wheat

3 packages (2 tablespoons plus 1½ teaspoons; ¾ ounce) active dry yeast

I cup warm water

I tablespoon soy oil

I tablespoon molasses

½ cup honey

I tablespoon salt

½ cup rye meal

I cup medium rye flour

½ cup bran flakes

4 cups whole wheat flour

Glaze: I whole egg whisked with I tablespoon milk

Stir the boiling water into the cracked wheat and allow the mixture to soak for between 1 and 2 hours.

Proof the yeast in all of the warm water in a very large bowl. When it is creamy (this will take about 10 minutes) add to it the cracked wheat mixture with the oil, molasses, and honey.

Mix the salt in with the rye meal, rye flour, bran flakes, and wheat flour. Then start adding the dry mixture to the liquid mixture by handfuls while stirring with a spoon. Continue adding the flour until you have only a few handfuls left and the dough has come together somewhat (a process that will take about 10 minutes). Empty the dough out onto a worktable, clean off your hands and the bowl with a plastic dough scraper, and knead the dough for another 5 to 8 minutes while incorporating the rest of the flour.

The dough will be soft, sticky, and moist. Round it into a ball and let it rise in a large container or bowl covered with a damp towel until it doubles in size, about 1½ to 2 hours.

Cut the dough into 4 pieces. Flatten each piece and shape it into a small loaf by folding it in half over onto itself and away from you. Square the outer edges and fold the dough in about 1 inch on either side toward the middle. Roll the loaf up into a tight log, sealing the dough with the heel of the hand on every turn.

Place each loaf on a cookie sheet lined with parchment paper or in small, well-greased bread pans that measure approximately 7 inches by 3 inches by 2 inches. The loaves should come up at least 1½ inches inside the pans.

Let the bread rise, covered with a moist towel, for between 45 and 60 minutes, until the indentation of a finger made in the dough does not spring back quickly when touched. The dough should be between ¼ and ½ inch above the top edge of the pan.

Glaze each loaf and then sprinkle the top with bran flakes.

Bake the loaves in a 400°F preheated oven for between 35 and 40 minutes or until they sound hollow when thumped on the bottom.

This recipe is from a book called *The Gold Medal Rye Dictionary* (see bibliography) that the General Mills Company put out in the 1940s. It is the closest thing I could find to a tangy rye loaf similar to those I remember from bakeries in New York and Los Angeles.

The goat's milk is not kosher but it adds a nice tangy flavor.

MAKES ONE 2½-POUND LOAF

THE MILK SOUR

1½ cups raw goat's milk or high-fat buttermilk

¾ cup medium rye flour

THE RYE SPONGE

1 package (2½ teaspoons; ¼ ounce)
   active dry yeast

1 cup warm water

All of the milk sour from the
   previous step

¼ cup medium rye flour

2 cups organic, unbleached white
   (or all-purpose) flour

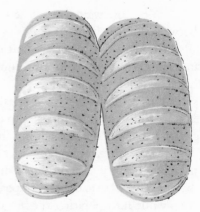

THE DOUGH

All of the sponge from the previous step

1 tablespoon salt

¼ ounce (½ teaspoon) malt extract or 1 teaspoon honey

½ cup warm water

3 cups organic, unbleached white (or all-purpose) flour

4 to 6 tablespoons caraway seeds

Glaze: 1 egg whisked with 2 tablespoons cold milk

TO MAKE THE MILK SOUR, let the milk sit out overnight in a warm place, uncovered. The next morning slowly pour the rye flour into the milk and stir with a wooden spoon. Make sure that there are no lumps of flour left. Cover the mixture and let it sit at room temperature overnight.

FOR THE SPONGE, proof the yeast in the warm water. When it is creamy—after about 10 minutes—pour it and the milk sour into a large bowl. Mix in the flours, stirring until you have a batter like that used for *crêpes*. Let the sponge sit, covered and at room temperature, for 4 hours, until it has tripled in size and dropped.

TO MAKE THE DOUGH, stir down the starter and sprinkle the salt over the top of it. Dissolve the malt extract or honey in the warm water and add it to the sponge. Add the flour by handfuls while mixing with a plastic dough scraper or a wooden spoon. As the dough comes together and when you still have a few handfuls of flour left, add the caraway seeds and mix them in.

Empty the dough out onto the worktable and clean off the bowl and your hands with the plastic dough scraper. Knead the dough for between 4 and 6 minutes longer, using the rest of the flour to prevent the dough from sticking to the table. The dough should be moist and very sticky, but avoid the temptation to incorporate any more flour.

Let the dough rise, covered, on the bench or in the bowl for between 50 and 60 minutes, until it doubles in size. Punch the dough back and flatten it out. Fold the piece of dough over onto itself away from you. Square the edges and push them an inch or so in toward the middle. Then roll the loaf up into a tight log, sealing the dough at each turn with the heel of the hand. Then use the pinkie edge of each hand to give the ends of the loaf a sharp judo chop, squaring them off.

Sprinkle a rimless baking sheet with cornmeal and place the loaf on the sheet, seam-side down.

Preheat the oven, with a baking stone inside, to 450°F.

Let the loaf rise for between 30 and 40 minutes. When the loaf fails to spring back quickly when touched with a fingertip, the bread is ready. To give the loaf a nice healthy bloom, it is better to bake it a few minutes early than a few minutes late.

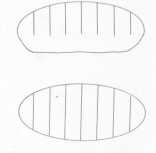

1   2

When the loaf is ready, slash it 6 or 7 times with a razor blade across the top of the loaf, starting from about halfway up one side and ending halfway down the other side. Glaze the top.

Spray the oven a few times, using an atomizer filled with water, and then bake the loaf for between 35 and 40 minutes or until it sounds hollow when thumped on the bottom.

This bread is a denizen of New York, to be found from Brooklyn to Manhattan. Mr. Orwasher himself, of Orwasher's Bakery on Seventy-Eighth Street near Second Avenue, claims to have invented it. When I tried flattery to get information, a trick that usually works on French bakers, by saying, "It's amazing how all of the raisins are so full and moist—how do you do it?" Mr. Orwasher merely said, "That took years to figure out and I don't tell anyone how we do it; it's a secret." Realizing that the venerable Mr. Orwasher would not give me any hints on how to make the bread, I came up with a recipe of my own.

All three sponges are made up on one day, they rise overnight, and all go into the dough on the next day. The dough is then refrigerated overnight and baked on the third day. Medium rye flour and cracked rye grain may be substituted for the rye meal. If you can obtain some caramel color from your local baker, use it in place of the molasses in the recipe.

MAKES I OVAL 3-POUND LOAF

THE RYE SPONGE

- I package (2½ teaspoons; ¼ ounce) active dry yeast
- ¾ cup warm water
- I cup rye meal

THE RAISIN SPONGE

- 2½ cups raisins
- I cup rye meal
- I ¼ cups very hot water

THE OLD-DOUGH ADDITION

- I cup *pain ordinaire* dough (page 69)

THE DOUGH

- I cup old *pain ordinaire* dough from the third step
- All of the rye sour from the first step
- I ¼ teaspoons active dry yeast
- ¼ cup very warm water (115°F)
- I tablespoon sugar
- I tablespoon corn or soy oil
- I tablespoon natural black molasses
- 2½ cups organic unbleached white (or all-purpose) flour
- 2½ teaspoons salt
- All of the raisin sponge from the second step

Glazes: 1 egg yolk beaten up with 3 tablespoons milk
1 egg white whisked with 3 tablespoons cold water

TO MAKE THE RYE SPONGE, proof the yeast in the warm water until it is creamy; this will take about 10 minutes. Place the rye meal in a small bowl and pour the yeast mixture over it, stirring with a wooden spoon or with the hand to incorporate the ingredients. The mixture will be somewhat dry, but it should come together and look like a thick paste. Mix it for 2 or 3 minutes, then cover it with a damp cloth and let it rise overnight or for at least 10 to 12 hours.

TO MAKE THE RAISIN SPONGE, mix the raisins and the rye meal together in a large bowl and pour the hot water over them, mixing the ingredients together with the hands. Let the sponge sit, covered, overnight.

TO PREPARE THE OLD-DOUGH ADDITION, thaw a piece of frozen *pain ordinaire* dough for 3 or 4 hours, then let it rise overnight in the refrigerator. (For remarks on the use of old dough (*pâte fermentée*), see page 68 and the recipe on page 73.)

Or make a *pain ordinaire* dough with 2 cups all-purpose flour, ¾ cup water, 1 teaspoon active dry yeast, and 2 teaspoons salt. See the recipe on page 69 for the method. Let it rise for 3 hours at room temperature. Then cut off 1 cup for this recipe, wrap it loosely in plastic wrap, and let rise overnight in the refrigerator. Flatten the remaining piece of *pain ordinaire* dough into a 3-inch-by-8-inch strip, cover it with plastic wrap, and freeze it. This piece will be used for decoration on top of the finished loaf.

BEFORE MAKING UP THE PUMPERNICKEL DOUGH, take the *pain ordinaire* dough out of the refrigerator and set it aside at room temperature for a few hours to warm up. Then chop it into little pieces and mix it with the rye sour in a very large bowl.

Proof the yeast in the very warm water. When it becomes creamy add the sugar, oil, and molasses. Mix the salt into the flour.

Pour the yeast liquid over the old-dough and rye-sour mixture and stir with a wooden spoon for 3 or 4 minutes until all the lumps of *pain ordinaire* begin to break down. Gradually start adding the flour by handfuls, while continuing to mix with the wooden spoon or a plastic dough scraper.

After all but ½ cup of the flour has been added and the dough is still quite moist, empty it out onto your work surface and knead it for 4 or 5 minutes. Return the mixture to the bowl, add the raisin sponge, and mix until all the ingredients are incorporated.

Clean off your hands, the bowl, and the worktable with the plastic dough scraper. Then knead the dough on the worktable for a few more minutes, using the remaining flour to keep it from sticking to the table.

Return the dough to the cleaned bowl, cover it with plastic wrap, and let it rise for 1 hour in a warm place and then for between 4 and 6 hours or even overnight in the refrigerator.

When the dough comes out of the refrigerator after its first rising, take the extra piece of *pain ordinaire* dough that was reserved for the decoration out of the freezer and let it thaw. The raisin pumpernickel dough should be set aside in a warm place to rise for an hour or so before being shaped into a loaf.

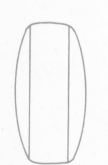

Shape the loaf by flattening the dough and rolling it over onto itself several times, each time sealing the dough with the heel of the hand. The loaf will measure about 4 inches by 10 inches, and be 2 inches high. Then take the thawed *pain ordinaire* dough and roll it out into a long, thin strip about 14 inches long by 3 inches wide.

Liberally coat a rimless baking sheet with cornmeal and place the pumpernickel loaf on it. Take the strip of *pain ordinaire* dough and lay it lengthwise over the loaf, tucking it under at each end. Let the loaf, covered with a towel, rise in a warm place for between 2 and 3 hours.

One hour before baking, preheat the oven and a baking stone (if it is large enough to accommodate the loaf; otherwise just bake the loaf on the rimless baking sheet) to 450°F. The loaf is ready to be baked when it barely springs back when touched with the finger.

Glaze the pumpernickel sections of the top of the loaf with the egg yolk glaze and the *pain ordinaire* decoration with the egg white glaze.

Slide the loaf onto the baking stone or leave it on the baking tray and immediately turn the oven temperature down to 375°F. Bake the loaf for between 1½ and 1¾ hours.

This is a very simple recipe for a light and flavorful bread.

MAKES 2 BRAIDED, 1¼-POUND LOAVES

2 packages (1 tablespoon plus 2 teaspoons; ½ ounce) active dry yeast

2 cups warm water

2 whole eggs or 4 egg yolks, beaten

3 tablespoons corn or soy oil

3 tablespoons sugar

1 tablespoon salt

6 cups organic, unbleached white (or all-purpose) flour

Glaze: 1 egg beaten with 1 tablespoon cold milk

Poppy seeds or sesame seeds for topping

Proof the yeast in a little of the warm water and, when it is creamy (in about 10 minutes), add to it the rest of the water, the eggs, oil, and sugar. Mix the salt in with the flour and then start adding the dry mixture to the liquid mixture by handfuls while mixing with a spoon. Continue adding the flour until you have only a few handfuls left and the dough has come together somewhat; this will take 10 minutes.

Empty the dough out onto a worktable, clean off your hands and the bowl with a plastic dough scraper, and knead the dough for another 5 to 8 minutes while incorporating the rest of the flour.

When the dough is soft and satiny, round into a ball and let it rise in a large container or bowl, covered with a damp towel, until it doubles in size (about 1 to 1¼ hours).

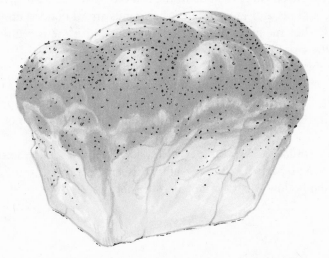

Punch the dough back and flatten it out. Fold the piece of dough in half, over onto itself and away from you. Square the outer edges and push the dough in on either side about 1 inch toward the center. Then roll the loaf up into a tight log, sealing the dough with the heel of the hand at each turn. Let this loaf, covered with a moist towel, rest on the flour-dusted worktable for between 10 and 15 minutes.

To shape the challah, cut the loaf in half, then cut each half into three equal parts. Shape each of these pieces into small loaves in the same way as the first loaf was shaped, each measuring about 2 inches by 4 inches. Then roll out each log until it is 8 inches long.

Use 3 strands for each loaf; connect them at the top and start braiding by putting the left one over the one in the middle, then the right strand over the one in the middle, and so forth until the strands are all braided up. Seal the end with the heel of the hand. Repeat the procedure with the remaining 3 strands to shape the second loaf.

Place the loaves either on a cookie sheet lined with parchment paper or in a well-greased bread pan that measures 9 inches by 5 inches by 2½ inches.

Let the loaves rise, covered with a moist towel, for between 35 and 40 minutes, until the indentation of a finger made in the dough does not spring back quickly.

Glaze each loaf and sprinkle it with poppy seeds or sesame seeds.

Bake in a preheated, 400°F oven for between 25 and 30 minutes or until the loaves sound hollow when thumped on the bottom.

GAYLE'S HERB AND CHEESE ROLLS

These are very tasty rolls by themselves or they can be used to make little sand-wiches with ham, turkey, or tuna fish.

MAKES TWENTY 2-OUNCE ROLLS

½ recipe challah (page 205)

2 cups finely diced sharp Cheddar cheese

½ cup minced green onion

3 tablespoons chopped fresh chervil, thyme, or oregano, or a
  combination of all three

Glaze: 1 whole egg, beaten

Follow the recipe for challah until the dough has doubled in size in the first rising. Flatten it on the worktable and sprinkle it with the diced cheese, chopped green onion, and chopped herbs. Push the ingredients gently into the dough, then start folding the dough over onto itself, incorporating the embel-lishments. With both hands drag this ball of dough around on the table until the cheese and onion almost seem to pierce the outer surface of the dough. Then leave the dough on the bench or in a bowl to rest, covered, for between 15 and 20 minutes.

Preheat the oven to 375°F.

Divide the dough into quarters, then divide each quarter into 5 equal pieces (20 in all). Round each into a small roll. Do not be alarmed if the cheese seems to break out of the dough; when baked those little cheese bits form a crusty coat-ing on the rolls. Place the rolls on a parchment-lined baking sheet and let them rise, covered and in a warm place, for between 20 and 30 minutes.

Glaze the rolls and bake them for between 12 and 15 minutes until they are golden brown. If a thin, crispy, waferlike crust has pooled underneath some of the rolls, be careful not to break it off when removing them from the tray; it is part of their crunchy appeal.

PART III

The Professional Village Baker

Most of the recipes that follow are versions of those given for the home baker, although that section actually contains a few more incidental recipes. With the use of a calculator, the professional can easily adapt those recipes. These recipes do not include explanations of technique because, by using the index, one can find any technical elaboration in the home baker section. Village bakers, restaurant bakers, and caterers can make batches of any size, from twelve loaves to twelve hundred; it all depends on the size of the oven. A batch of any size can even be mixed by hand if you have a large enough table (or dough trough) and a strong enough back.

CHAPTER 8

The Professional Recipes

THREE HUNDRED YEARS AGO there were very few village bakers. Back then most families baked their own bread. On certain days the communal oven was fired, and the rustic loaves were mixed, shaped, and set to rise at home. Later they were taken to the oven to be baked. Eventually the trade of a village baker evolved. He took with him to his shop the techniques, methods, and recipes of the home bakers who, even before the advent of the communal oven, had developed the art of bread baking over hundreds of years of practice.

The invention of the mechanical mixer in the early 1900s was the major force that took bread baking from its humble home beginnings to what it is today—a refined and controllable craft. But the domestic origins show us that the nature of bread baking is simpler and more organic than it might appear.

Bread baking has always been a natural process—as rustic and organic as the making of wine or cheese. When bread was made at home, almost everyone knew the simple, natural time patterns that made up the method. Bread making was just another domestic task, like sewing, milking the goats, or tending the garden. As an ongoing process, it took on a life of its own; the dough had to be watched, guarded, and responded to. This is still true—as today's creative commercial bakers would agree—because bread baking must be tempered by human care, observation, and judgment if we are to create flavorful, nourishing loaves. Because village baking was perfected in the home, an awareness of the artisans' point of view will help professional bakers to understand the natural requirements of bread baking, requirements that have developed out of its natural origins.

I like to think of bread in process as a puppet and the baker as the puppeteer. Fermentation (the dough's activity) is the body and the individual ingredients, the water, flour, salt, and yeast are the arms and legs of the puppet. The controls of fermentation—such elements as the weather, the temperature of the bake shop, and the wetness of the dough—and all the possible variations in the four ingredients that will turn one bread recipe into another are the strings of the puppet. The analogy reflects a viewpoint common to village bakers and used every day: Simply by tugging on one of the puppet strings, a baker can create a different style of bread.

This is what *The Village Baker* is all about. It explains how, after baking professionally for fifteen years, teaching both home and village bakers, and studying myself with bakers in the United States and in Europe, I look at bread. It demonstrates the ways in which a baker can manipulate a recipe to achieve different varieties of crust, texture, and flavor much as a puppeteer regulates the strings of a puppet, by varying the proportions of the four basic ingredients, mixing fractions of the ingredients, then remixing the rest according to different time patterns, and by using various combinations of flours in various proportions. *The Village Baker* shows how every method of making bread is interrelated because each variation grew out of one basic recipe. The emphasis on the basic four ingredients reinforces the notion that bread can be made without any chemical additives. After bakers learn to work the "puppet strings" that control the dough's activity, they can write their own recipes. Or they can use the book simply as a handbook and recipe guide for each and every one of the recipe variations.

I have to admit that baking great bread requires an attitude of faith and a willingness to let nature take its course. It has to do with knowing that the process, once set in motion, has a way of determining its own destiny. All the baker does is to become a guide, leading the fermentation of the bread through its natural cycles. In this point of view, the puppet is seen to have its own life.

The recipes for professional bakers have been culled from fifteen years of commercial baking in a village bakery in California, from many books on professional baking written in Italian, French, German, and English, and from conversations with scores of village bakers in Europe and America. The sources have been given for each method, whether it comes from a book, from a particular village bakery, or from my own work at Gayle's.

The recipe format is a combination of the best of several recognized presentations that professional bakers are used to encountering. The recipes are given without elaboration because most village bakers—whether they have learned their craft from experience, in an apprenticeship to an expert baker, or by going to school—understand the methods and techniques of professional baking so well that all they need is the barest outline of a formula. Any explanation of technique, method, theory, even philosophy that may be necessary—whether it is for a novice village baker or an experienced baker who knows that something happens in a certain process, but wants to know why—can be found in the first three sections of the book. Explanations of, for example, "knocking back," *contre-frasage,* or *extensibility* may be found in the first part of the book by referring to the index; definitions may be found in the glossary.

Nearly all of the recipes have been tested at least once; those from my own bakery have been used in daily production for over a decade. A recipe must be attempted several times before it can yield consistent results. (There are so many things a professional can do to adjust or modify a fermentation—cooler water, cooler or warmer proofing, extra or less mixing—that a recipe must be made every day for a few weeks to create a consistent product.) Furthermore, the baker might find that the methods described can be used with slight variations or by borrowing steps or usages from other variations in order to achieve a desired loaf.

The recipes follow as closely as possible the order of the recipes presented for the home baker in the first part of the book. Also, I have attempted to keep the home recipe consistent in method (direct, sponge, or sourdough) with that of its village baker equivalent. For some recipes, the methods for the professional's and the home baker's versions are different, the variations supplied for the home baker to make the bread more accessible. Recipes such as those for pumpkin seed bread, *korni,* and *pain bouillie* fall into this category; each is made with true natural sourdoughs in the professional version and with a yeast starter in the home version.

❖❖❖❖❖❖❖❖❖❖❖❖ *Some Notes on the Recipes* ❖❖❖❖❖❖❖❖❖❖❖❖

- I have rarely seen notes on elapsed time given in professional recipes, but I have included them here to make it easy for a village baker, restaurant baker, or caterer to adjust an established production schedule. It denotes the time from the beginning of mixing through the bake-off. Only exceptions are noted. Sourdough and sponge rising times are given separately.

- Dough temperatures are given in degrees Fahrenheit. The *température de base* is the sum of the temperatures of the water, flour, and air from which the optimum water temperature may be calculated.

- Metric equivalents are given only in recipes that were derived from European methods.

- Traditionally American village bakers use quarts to measure water volume in bread recipes. Because European village bakers use weight, making it easier to calculate the total weight of a batch and giving the bakers an immediate sense of the percentage of water used in a batch of dough, it is done so here. To calculate the equivalent in quarts, bakers can divide the given pound weight of water by two.

- All of the mixing times are given for spiral-type mixers. Bakers using Hobart, Artofex, or the French-style *pétrin* (wishbone arm) mixers must make adjustments in the mixing times.

PAIN ORDINAIRE—LA MÉTHODE CLASSIQUE
CLASSIC YEASTED FRENCH BREAD

METHOD: Classic method.
SOURCE: *La boulangerie moderne,* by Raymond Calvel, page 121.
ELAPSED TIME: 7 to 8½ hours, mixing through bake-off.
DOUGH TEMPERATURE: 75°F. *TEMPÉRATURE DE BASE:* 225°F.

INGREDIENTS	MEASURES				
	METRIC	PERCENTAGES	U.S.		
flour*	1,000 g	100%	100 lb	50 lb	25 lb
water	600 g	60%	60 lb	30 lb	15 lb
salt	20 g	2%	2 lb	1 lb	8 oz
yeast	10 g	1%	1 lb	8 oz	4 oz
total	1,600 g		160 lb	80 lb	40 lb

* To emulate a true classic method texture, use half bread flour and half all-purpose white flour.

MIXING: Add all the ingredients to the mixer at once. Mix for 6 to 8 minutes on first speed.

FIRST RISING: 2 to 2½ hours.

PUNCH BACK: Let the dough rest for 1 more hour.

SCALING: *Baguettes:* 11 to 12 ounces; *bâtard* or French loaf: 1 pound, 3 ounces; *petit pain:* 3 to 4 ounces.

When one person hand scales a batch of more than 80 pounds, each piece must be hand squared and allowed to rest before being run through a molder or being hand molded. (This is called an intermediate proof, or in French, *la détente.*) If the batch being scaled is less than 80 pounds, each scaled piece may be left on the bench for 15 to 20 minutes and then hand shaped or passed through the molder. This step will take between 30 minutes and 1 hour.

INTERMEDIATE PROOF: (optional) 1 hour.

SHAPING: Fifteen minutes to 1 hour.

FINAL RISING: 1½ to 2 hours; total proofing time is 7 hours.

Let the loaves rise on perforated trays for rack or convection ovens, or in *couches* for deck ovens, in a 75°F, draft-free area. Loaves may have to be covered to prevent them from crusting over.

BAKE-OFF: 400°F, with low-pressure steam for the first few minutes. *Baguettes:* 20 to 30 minutes; 1-pound loaves: 40 minutes; *petit pain:* 12 to 15 minutes.

Traditionally steam was not used in the classic method, so each loaf may be glazed with a wash of 1 or 2 egg whites mixed in cold water to give a shiny, crackling crust. Or the light flouring from the *couches* and no glazing will give a rustic look.

METHOD: Direct, with modern accentuated mixing.
SOURCE: Boulangerie-Pâtisserie le Feyeux, 56 rue de Clichy, Paris.
ELAPSED TIME: 5½ hours, including bake-off.
DOUGH TEMPERATURE: 75°F. *TEMPÉRATURE DE BASE:* 225°F.

Technically speaking, this is a combination of the French methods of *pétrissage accentué* and *pétrissage amélioré.* For the accentuated method, the baker would use a very weak flour (organic, unbleached white or all-purpose) and a 20-minute mixing on second speed. In this modified method, the stronger American bread flour, which contains 12% gluten, can be fully developed in about 10 minutes. It saves time for the baker, saves wear and tear on the mixer, and requires less ice to cool down the mixing water.

INGREDIENTS	MEASURES				
	METRIC	PERCENTAGES		U.S.	
flour	1,000 g	100%	100 lb	50 lb	25 lb
water	600 g	60%	60 lb	30 lb	15 lb
salt	20 g	2%	2 lb	1 lb	8 oz
yeast	10 g	1%	1 lb	8 oz	4 oz
vitamin C			½ tsp	¼ tsp	⅛ tsp
total	1,600 g		160 lb	80 lb	40 lb

MIXING: 10 to 12 minutes on second speed. Add the vitamin C to the water, then add the flour and mix on first speed to incorporate. Crumble the yeast on top of the dough and mix for 10 to 12 minutes on second speed. Add the salt 5 minutes before the end of mixing.

FIRST RISING: 20 minutes to 1 hour.

SCALING: *Baguettes:* 12 ounces; *bâtard* or French loaf: 1 pound, 3 ounces; *petit pain:* 3 to 4 ounces.

By machine: Scale the pieces to the size that will fit in the divider (large *pâtons*) and then round them. Let the rounds rest on the bench for 15 to 20 minutes. Divide them and let the individual pieces rest for 30 to 40 minutes on floured boards or on the bench, covered, until they have relaxed enough to go through the molder.

By hand: If one baker hand scales a batch of more than 80 pounds, all the pieces of dough should be hand squared and allowed to rest before being run through the molder or being hand molded. If the batch being scaled is less than 80 pounds, each scaled piece may be left on the bench for 15 to 20 minutes and then hand shaped or passed through the molder.

SHAPING: 20 minutes by machine; 40 to 50 minutes by hand.

FINAL RISING: For loaves shaped by hand, the first rising takes 30 minutes, scaling takes 60 minutes, hand shaping 60 minutes, and the final rising should take be-

tween 2½ and 3 hours. For loaves shaped by machine, the first rising takes 15 minutes, scaling into *pâtons* for the divider takes 15 minutes, resting takes 30 minutes, dividing 15 minutes, the second resting 30 minutes, machine shaping 30 minutes, and the final rising should take between 2 and 2½ hours. The total proofing time is 5 hours.

Let the loaves rise on perforated trays for rack or convection ovens or in *couches* for deck ovens in a 75°F, draft-free area. The loaves may have to be covered or placed in a covered cabinet to avoid their crusting over.

BAKE-OFF: 400°F with low-pressure steam for the first few minutes. *Baguettes:* 20 to 30 minutes; 1-pound loaves: 40 minutes; *petit pain:* 12 to 15 minutes.

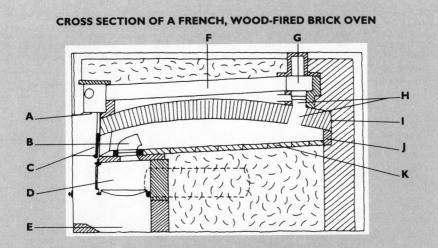

CROSS SECTION OF A FRENCH, WOOD-FIRED BRICK OVEN

A. *Soupape* (vent)

B. *Gueulard* (flame director)

C. *Bouche* (door)

D. *Foyer à bois* (fire box)

E. *Cendrier* (ash pan)

F. *Conduit de soupape* (vent pipe)

G. *Coffre* (vent box)

H. *Ouras* (damper)

I. *Chapelle* (arched oven roof)

J. *Pied droit* (straight footing)

K. *Carrelage* (tiled oven floor)

METHOD: *Pâte fermentée* (old-dough addition).
SOURCE: Boulangerie-Pâtisserie le Feyeux, 56 rue de Clichy, Paris.
ELAPSED TIME: 5½ to 7 hours, mixing through bake-off.
DOUGH TEMPERATURE: 73°F. *TEMPÉRATURE DE BASE:* 219°F.

INGREDIENTS			MEASURES		
	METRIC	PERCENTAGES		U.S.	
old dough*	100 g	10%	10 lb	5 lb	2½ lb
flour†	1,000 g	100%	100 lb	50 lb	25 lb
water‡	600 g	60%	60 lb	30 lb	15 lb
salt	20 g	2%	2 lb	1 lb	8 oz
yeast	8 g	.8%	12 oz	6 oz	3 oz
vitamin C	—	—	½ tsp	¼ tsp	⅛ tsp
total	1,700 g		170 lb	85 lb	42½ lb

* Use a piece of *pain ordinaire* that is 4 or 5 hours old, or one that has been in the retarder for between 6 and 8 hours. Anything older and the results become unpredictable.

Because there is salt in the old dough, no additional salt is necessary in the formula. The yeast is reduced from the 1 percent used in the direct method to .8 percent and the proofing times are prolonged slightly to take advantage of the slower, more natural effects of the fermentation of the old dough.

† The strength of American bread flour may be cut by using 50 percent all-purpose flour.

‡ To make a medium-wet dough, add about 5 to 7 percent extra water toward the end of mixing.

MIXING: Around 12 minutes on second speed. Chop up the old dough into small pieces. Add the vitamin C to the water, then add the flour and mix on first speed to incorporate. Crumble the yeast on top of the dough and mix on second speed. Add the salt 5 minutes before the end of mixing.

FIRST RISING: 20 minutes to 1 hour.

KNOCKING BACK: Punch back the dough, then let it rise for 30 minutes more.

SCALING: *Baguettes:* 14 ounces; *bâtard* or French loaf: 1 pound, 3 ounces; large *baguettes:* 2 pounds, 6 ounces.

By machine: Scale pieces to a size that will fit in the divider (large *pâtons*) and then round them. Let the rounds rest on the bench for 15 to 20 minutes. Divide the rounds and let the individual pieces rest for 30 to 40 minutes on floured boards or on the bench, covered, until they have relaxed enough to go through the molder.

By hand: If one person is hand scaling a batch of more than 80 pounds, hand square each piece of dough and allow it to rest before running it through the molder or hand shaping it. If a batch of less than 80 pounds is being hand scaled, each scaled piece may be left on the bench for 15 to 20 minutes and then hand shaped or passed through the molder.

INTERMEDIATE PROOF: (advisable) 30 to 45 minutes.

FINAL RISING: 2½ to 3 hours. Let the loaves rise on perforated trays for rack or convection ovens; or in *couches* for deck ovens in a 75°F, draft-free area. The loaves may have to be covered to avoid their crusting over. Total proofing time from mixer to bake-off: 6 hours.

BAKE-OFF: 425°F to 450°F, with low-pressure steam for the first few minutes. *Baguettes:* 18 to 20 minutes; 1-pound *bâtards:* 25 to 30 minutes; 2-pound *baguettes:* around 35 minutes.

LA COURONNE DE FIGEAC
FIGEAC CROWN LOAF

METHOD: *Levain.*
SOURCE: Boulangerie Haettel, Figeac, France.
ELAPSED TIME: 22 hours including sourdough; 4 hours for dough only.
DOUGH TEMPERATURE: 75°F. *TEMPÉRATURE DE BASE:* 225°F.

INGREDIENTS	U.S. MEASURES	
*levain**	4½ lb	9 lb
bread flour	1½ lb	3 lb
salt	½ oz	1 oz
cold water	½ lb	1 lb
total	6½ lb	13 lb

* The 16- to 18-hour *levain* must be kept very cold to avoid its overrising. If this is impossible, allow a 2½-pound piece off yesterday's batch to rise for a few hours, then refresh it with 2 pounds of flour and enough water to make a firm dough. Use this piece, after a 10- to 12- hour rising, in the final dough.

MIXING: Dilute the levain as best as you can with the water. Add the flour and mix on first speed for 8 to 10 minutes, adding the salt in the last 5 minutes of mixing.

FIRST RISING AND KNOCKING BACK: Let the dough rise for 30 minutes and then give it one turn.

SECOND RISING: 30 minutes.

SCALING: Round the 6-pound loaves into *boules* and let them rest for a few minutes.

SHAPING: Use the elbow to press a hole into the middle of each *boule;* then stretch the loaves to fit crown-shaped *bannetons* or allow them to rest on floured boards or canvas.

FINAL RISING: 1 hour.

BAKE-OFF: 425°F for between 50 minutes and 1 hour.

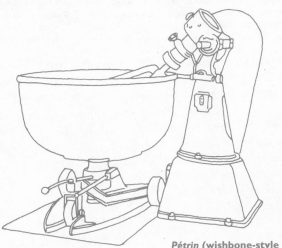

Pétrin (wishbone-style mixer)

METHOD: *Poolish* (sponge method).
SOURCE: *Le pain retrouvé,* by J. Y. Guinard and P. Lesjean, page 66.
ELAPSED TIME: 8½ hours between mixing the sponge and the end
    of the bake.
DOUGH TEMPERATURE: 68°F. *TEMPÉRATURE DE BASE:* 60°C (140°F).

INGREDIENTS	MEASURES			
	METRIC		U.S.	
THE POOLISH				
flour	2,000 g	4 lb	8 lb	16 lb
water	2,000 g (2 ltr)	4 lb	8 lb	16 lb
yeast	25 g	¾ oz	1½ oz	3 oz
total	4,025 g	8 lb	16 lb	32 lb
THE DOUGH				
poolish	4,025 g	8 lb	16 lb	32 lb
flour*	4,600 g	9½ lb	19 lb	38 lb
water†	2,000 g (2 ltr)	4 lb	8 lb	16 lb
salt	150 g	5¼ oz	10½ oz	21 oz
yeast	25–40 g	1 oz	2 oz	4 oz
vitamin C	—	⅛ tsp	¼ tsp	½ tsp
total	10,815 g	26¾ lb	44 lb	88 lb

* As with many French recipes for bread that is to be made with American ingredients, it is often advisable to cut our standard bread flour with 50 percent all-purpose or organic, unbleached white flour.

† To accommodate strong American flours, it is often necessary to add extra water to this dough after about 8 minutes of mixing (see *bassinage*).

MAKING THE *POOLISH*: Dilute the yeast in the warm water, then add the flour and mix to incorporate. The mixture is very liquid so it can be made by hand. The *poolish* can be set to ferment in a bowl or wooden trough for at least 3½ to 4 hours. When the *poolish* has risen and then fallen in the middle, it is ready to use (in American baker's terms this is called a "full drop").

MIXING THE DOUGH: 12 to 14 minutes on first speed. The dough is wetter than that of a normal *pain ordinaire.*

FIRST RISING: 2 hours. If after 30 minutes the dough seems to lack a good, active "force," knock it back.

SCALING: 12-ounce; 1-pound, 3-ounce; or 2-pound, 6-ounce loaves.

MOLDING: As *baguettes, bâtards,* or as *baguettes deux livres* (2-pound *baguettes* that are 30 inches long).

FINAL RISING OR MAKEUP *(L'APPRÊT):* 1½ to 2 hours. The loaves should be made up, placed in *couches,* and baked in a deck oven to give them a full, rich bloom. But they can be placed on perforated trays and baked in a rack oven. Total rising time: 4 hours from mixer to bake-off.

BAKE-OFF: 475°F to 500°F, with low-pressure steam for the first few minutes. *Baguettes:* 17 to 20 minutes; 1-pound loaves: 30 to 35 minutes; *petit pain:* 10 to 14 minutes; 2-pound *baguettes:* 40 to 45 minutes.

PAIN DE CAMPAGNE—TROIS LEVAINS
COUNTRY-STYLE BREAD

METHOD: *Levain.*
SOURCE: Gayle's Bakery, Capitola, California.
ELAPSED TIME: 24 hours.
DOUGH TEMPERATURE: 75°F. *TEMPÉRATURE DE BASE:* 225°F.

A refreshment schedule for the quantities of *levain* used in this formula is provided at the end of the recipe. *Levain* breads can be made with numerous different schedules (see for example the recipes for Capitola sourdough on page 262 and San Francisco sourdough on page 261 and the notes on building a sourdough on page 278).

The amount of *levain* necessary in a *levain* bread ranges from 30 percent to 60 percent, according to the season. In very cold weather a larger *levain* is needed to attain the required acidity. In summer, when *levains* go wild from the heat, a smaller *levain* is adequate to achieve a similar product.

It is hard to figure the exact percentage of water for a *levain* bread because one ingredient—the *levain* —is already hydrated. In any formula the percentage of *levain* is generally estimated in terms of the entire batch of dough.

The normal amount of salt in a *levain* bread is 2.2 percent. The amount used here is for health and flavor reasons.

INGREDIENTS	U.S. MEASURES		
levain	15 lb	23 lb	30 lb
flour	17½ lb	26¼ lb	35 lb
water	12 lb	18 lb	24 lb
salt	8 oz	12 oz	1 lb
yeast	½ oz	¾ oz	1 oz
vitamin C	1 tsp	1½ tsp	2 tsp
total	45 lb	68 lb	90 lb

MIXING: Break up the *levain* completely in one-third of the water. Add the vitamin C, the rest of the water, and all of the flour. Mix for a few minutes on first speed to incorporate the ingredients, then mix for 10 minutes on second speed. Add the salt 5 minutes before the end of mixing. This technique will accommodate the addition of extra water toward the end of the mixing in order to achieve a moister crumb. Add more water according to the dough consistency you desire.

FIRST RISING: 1 hour in the mixer or covered on the bench.

PULL-BACK *(PRÉLÈVE)*: A piece of dough is always pulled back from the rest after the first rising. (Some bakers pull back the dough for the next day's batch before the salt goes in; others feel that the salt in the starter helps to control the acidity for the

8-hour rise that this *chef*—or chief leavening agent—must undergo.) The amount of *chef* pulled back depends on the size of the batch planned for the following day, and may be anything from 8 ounces to 1½ pounds.

SCALING: Hand scale at 2 pounds, 6 ounces for 2-pound round loaves; at 4 pounds, 12 ounces for 4-pound round loaves.

SHAPING: Hand shaping is preferred. Shaping takes 30 to 45 minutes, depending on the size of the batch.

FINAL RISING: 8 to 10 hours in flour-dusted *bannetons* or in *couches,* uncovered but out of drafts. The loaves may have to be covered to avoid their crusting over.

BAKE-OFF: 400°F, right on the hearth of a deck oven with low-pressure steam for the first few minutes. 1 hour for 2-pound round loaves; 1½ hours for 4-pound round loaves.

Refreshment Schedule

A starter, *levain,* or *chef* is usually doubled or tripled in volume each time it is refreshed or "built" into another stage of development. Refreshments are mixed firm, at around 50 percent hydration, to control their activity. Because *levains* get wetter as they ferment, it is impossible to forecast water requirements exactly, so the village baker has to use good sense and judgment. The quantities given for the first three refreshments will yield enough *levain* for the batch sizes given in the recipe.

The *levain* may be given a fourth refreshment, which will double the size of the final batch.

INGREDIENTS		U.S. MEASURES	
PULL-BACK (PRÉLÈVE)—8 HOURS			
bread dough	½ lb	¾ lb	I lb
FIRST REFRESHMENT—8 HOURS			
chef	½ lb	¾ lb	I lb
whole wheat flour	I lb, 10 oz	2½ lb	3¼ lb
water	I lb	I½ lb	2 lb
SECOND REFRESHMENT—2½ HOURS*			
levain	3 lb, 2 oz	4 lb, 10 oz	6¼ lb
whole wheat flour	2 lb	3 lb	4 lb
water	I½ lb	2¼ lb	3 lb
THIRD REFRESHMENT—2 HOURS			
levain	6 lb, 10 oz	10 lb	13¼ lb
whole wheat flour	6 lb	9 lb	12 lb
water	3 lb	4½ lb	6 lb
final *levain* available for the dough	15 lb, 10 oz	23½ lb	31¼ lb
FOURTH REFRESHMENT			
levain	15 lb, 10 oz	23½ lb	31¼ lb
whole wheat flour	10 lb	15 lb	20 lb
white flour	10 lb	15 lb	20 lb
water	10 lb	15 lb	20 lb
total	46 lb	67½ lb	91 lb

* The second refreshment, because it lasts for only 2½ hours, is mixed wetter to allow the fermentation to proceed more actively as it goes into the final stages.

The fourth refreshment is mixed and two-thirds of it is left in the bowl of the mixer for the first batch of bread and one-third is set aside on the bench or placed in a tub to develop acidity for 2 hours, after which the second batch of bread is mixed. This doubling method (*dédoubler*, literally, "to divide into two") enables the baker to accommodate the production of bread to the size of the oven. Six or seven batches are possible, each batch becoming lighter and lighter in texture as the *levain* becomes progressively fresher and lighter in color because white flour is used from the fourth refreshment on and in the dough.

Dédoubler

In the simplest *dédoublé* procedure, when the fourth refreshment is mixed two-thirds of the resulting dough is used immediately for the *dédoublé* recipe and the first batch. Two hours later the one-third of *levain* left over from the fourth refreshment is used for the standard *pain de campagne* recipe. If, however, the baker wants to continue the procedure (up to seven batches, so Calvel says), the one-third *levain* that would have been used for the second batch of dough to make *pain de campagne* is instead given *another* refreshment (the fifth, if you will). Two-thirds of that is left in the bowl for another (the second batch) and one-third is set aside for a third batch to be made 2 hours hence or to be refreshed again to give 2 more batches.

Using the two-thirds of the fourth refreshment *levain* that is still in the mixer, make up your first batch of bread according to the following formula.

INGREDIENTS		U.S. MEASURES	
levain	30 lb	45 lb	60 lb
white bread flour	8 lb	12 lb	16 lb
water	9 lb	13½ lb	18 lb
salt	8 oz	12 oz	1 lb
yeast	½ oz	¾ oz	1 oz
vitamin C	1 tsp	1½ tsp	2 tsp
total	48 lb	71 lb	95 lb

This formula is mixed firmer than the original *pain de campagne* batch (now the second batch); because it contains a larger, fresher *levain,* it will be more active.

For the one-third of the fourth refreshment *levain* thrown on the bench or in a tub to proof for an extra two hours, use the original formula at the top of page 220. (Or refresh it for what might be called a fifth refreshment, use two-thirds immediately and one-third 2 hours later for a third batch.)

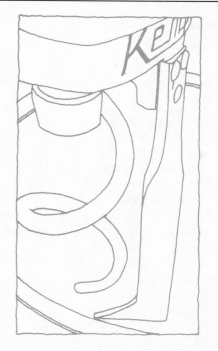

Spiral mixer (*spirale* in Italian)

PAIN DE CAMPAGNE SUR POOLISH
COUNTRY-STYLE SPONGE BREAD

METHOD: *Poolish.*
SOURCE: *Le compagnon boulanger,* by J.-M. Viard, page 269.
ELAPSED TIME: 5 hours.
DOUGH TEMPERATURE: 75°F. *TEMPÉRATURE DE BASE:* 225°F.

INGREDIENTS	MEASURES		
	METRIC	U.S.	
THE *POOLISH*—AROUND 2 HOURS			
rye flour	1 kg	2 lb, 3 oz	4 lb, 6 oz
white bread flour	1 kg	2 lb, 3 oz	4 lb, 6 oz
water	2 ltr	4 lb, 6 oz	8¾ lb
yeast	120 g	4¼ oz	8½ oz
total	**4,120 g**	**9 lb**	**18 lb**
THE DOUGH			
all of the *poolish*	4,120 g	9 lb	18 lb
white flour	6 kg	13¼ lb	26½ lb
water	3 ltr	6 lb, 5 oz	12 lb, 10 oz
yeast	30 g	1 oz	2 oz
salt	160 g	5½ oz	11 oz
total	**13.3 kg**	**29 lb**	**58 lb**

MIXING THE *POOLISH*: Combine all the ingredients and set the sponge aside to rise. When it has fallen, it will be ready to use; this will take about 2 hours.

MIXING THE DOUGH: 4 minutes on first speed, 8 minutes on second speed.

FIRST RISING: 40 minutes.

SCALING: 2 pounds, 6 ounces or 4 pounds, 12 ounces in round loaves.

SHAPING: 15 minutes; place in *bannetons* or on floured boards.

FINAL RISING: 1½ hours.

BAKE-OFF: 425°F to 460°F in a deck oven; 40 minutes for 2-pound loaves, 50 minutes for 4-pounders. Open the door of the oven at the end of baking to dry the loaves.

VARIATIONS

Reduce the yeast in the poolish by half and let it rise for 4 to 5 hours.

Add a pinch of vitamin C, more water, and less yeast to the final dough. Extend the final rising time to 2 or 3 hours.

PAIN DE CAMPAGNE—PÂTE FERMENTÉE
COUNTRY-STYLE BREAD WITH OLD-DOUGH ADDITION

METHOD: *Pâte fermentée* (old-dough addition).
SOURCE: *Le compagnon boulanger,* by J.-M. Viard, page 268.
ELAPSED TIME: 4 to 6 hours for the old dough and 5 hours for the bread.
DOUGH TEMPERATURE: 22°C (72°F).   *TEMPÉRATURE DE BASE:* 62°C (144°F).

INGREDIENTS	MEASURES		
	METRIC	U.S.	
*pâte fermentée**	1.5 kg	2 lb, 3 oz	4 lb, 6 oz
bread flour	6 kg	13¼ lb	26½ lb
rye flour	I kg	2 lb, 3 oz	4 lb, 6 oz
water	4.5 ltr	10 lb (scant)	20 lb
yeast	100 g	3½ oz	7 oz
salt	140 g	5 oz (scant)	10 oz
total	13.25 kg	28 lb	56 lb

* Old dough, after 4 to 6 hours fermentation.

MIXING: 4 minutes on first speed, 8 minutes on second speed.

FIRST RISING: 45 to 50 minutes.

SCALING: Scale at 2 pounds, 6 ounces or 4 pounds, 12 ounces.

SHAPING: 15 minutes; shape into round or oval loaves and proof on boards or on baking trays.

FINAL RISING: 1½ to 1¾ hours.

BAKE-OFF: 465°F in a deck oven, 35 to 40 minutes for 2-pound loaves; 50 to 60 minutes for 4-pound loaves. Open the door of the oven at the end of baking to dry the loaves.

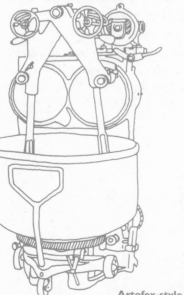

Artofex-style mixer

METHOD: Direct method.
SOURCE: Fédération des Pâtissiers et Boulangers de l'Ile-de-France.
ELAPSED TIME: 4 hours, mixing through bake-off.
DOUGH TEMPERATURE: 73°F to 74°F. *TEMPÉRATURE DE BASE:* 220°F.

INGREDIENTS	MEASURES				
	METRIC	PERCENTAGES		U.S.	
flour*	1,000 g	100%	100 lb	50 lb	25 lb
water	660 g	66%	66 lb	33 lb	16½ lb
salt	20 g	2%	2 lb	1 lb	8 oz
yeast	30 g	3%	3 lb	1½ lb	12 oz
total	1,710 g		171 lb	85 lb	43 lb

* Use all-purpose flour or 50 percent all-purpose flour and 50 percent bread flour. Add the salt to the flour
before mixing the dough.

MIXING: In a spiral mixer: 2 minutes on the first speed, and 16 to 18 minutes on the second speed; in a vertical mixer: 2 minutes on the first speed (with the paddle) and 12 to 15 minutes on the second speed. The dough is much wetter than that for an ordinary French bread.

FIRST RISING: 20 minutes if the scaling is to be done by machine. Then weigh out the dough in sizes that the divider can accommodate and round lightly. Let the dough rest for 15 minutes before dividing it and 25 minutes after dividing; 40 minutes if scaling is to be done by hand. Then scale the pieces one by one and let them rest, without rounding them, for another 20 minutes. The total time of the first rising plus the intermediate proofing should be 60 minutes.

SCALING: 11 ounces or 1 pound, 3 ounces.

SHAPING: Shape in ovals 10 inches long for 1-pound loaves, and 8 inches long for ½-pound loaves.

FINAL RISING: Make up in *couches* and allow the loaves to rise for between 1½ and 2 hours in an ambient temperature of 75°F.

CUTTING: The *coup de lame* in this ancient loaf is distinctive. Two cuts are made, each down the middle of the loaf about 1 inch apart. Both are about 1 inch deep and angled toward the outer edge of the loaf. See illustrations on pages 93 and 226.

BAKE-OFF: Bake on the deck at 425°F to 450°F with lots of steam at the beginning of the bake-off; 25 minutes for ½-pound loaves, 35 minutes for 1-pound loaves.

METHOD: One *levain,* retarded; yeast added.
SOURCE: Boulangerie-Pâtisserie le Feyeux, 56 rue de Clichy, Paris.
ELAPSED TIME: 20 hours.
DOUGH TEMPERATURE: 75°F. *TEMPÉRATURE DE BASE: 225°F.*

For the original starter see the recipe for the yeast starter (*compagnon*) on page 34. Use about 7 pounds flour, 3 pounds water, 1 ounce salt, and ½ ounce yeast. Let the dough rise for 6 to 8 hours at room temperature and then put it in the retarder to rise again for between 24 and 36 hours before using it in this recipe.

INGREDIENTS	MEASURES			
	METRIC		U.S.	
levain	300–400 g	9 lb	11¼ lb	18 lb
flour	1 kg	22 lb	27½ lb	44 lb
water	550 g	12 lb	15 lb	24 lb
salt	25 g	6 oz	7½ oz	12 oz
yeast	5 g	1 oz	1¼ oz	2 oz
vitamin C	1 g	2 tsp	2½ tsp	4 tsp
total	1,981 g	43 lb	52 lb	86 lb

MIXING: Dilute the *levain* in half of the water, then add half of the flour and mix for 2 or 3 minutes to break up the *levain.* Add the rest of the flour and water (and, after a few minutes, the yeast) and mix for 8 to 10 minutes on second speed. Add the salt 5 minutes before the end of mixing.

FIRST RISING: 1 hour, 15 minutes, with a turn (punch back) after 30 minutes.

PULL-BACK (*PRÉLÈVE*): Cut off a piece of dough (between 9 and 18 pounds, depending on the size of the batch) for the next day's batch and set it aside, covered and in the retarder, for between 12 and 15 hours.

SCALING: Large loaves: 1 pound, 3 ounces; small loaves: 9½ ounces; rolls: 2 ounces.

SHAPING: Hand or machine shape large loaves in ovals 10 inches long; round small loaves into *boules.*

FINAL RISING: Proof in a covered rack at ambient temperature for about 4 hours.

CUTTING (*COUP DE LAME*): Cut the oval loaves twice with blade.

Cut the round loaves and rolls 4 times, straight across the top.

BAKE-OFF: Bake at 400°F in either a convection or, preferably, a deck oven, with steam for the first 10 minutes.

PAIN BLANC AU LEVAIN
WHITE SOURDOUGH BREAD

METHOD: One *levain*.

SOURCE: Boulangerie Maurice Duquerroy, 2 rue Thiers,
   Brantôme, France.

ELAPSED TIME: 22 to 24 hours.

DOUGH TEMPERATURE: 75°F. *TEMPÉRATURE DE BASE*: 225°F.

This method is often used in the provinces of France. It works well for a single-family village baker whose *boulangerie* is not manned throughout the night, so repeated refreshments cannot be made to control the acidity of the dough. The greatest problem with this method is that, because the *chef* and the refreshment are subject to long proofing times, an excess exaggeration of acidity can give undue force to the dough, resulting in a badly developed, overly sour bread.

The *prélèvement,* or dough pulled back from the previous batch, is left to rise right in the mixer. Traditionally, it comes off the last batch and is allowed to rise for between eight and ten hours. The first and only refreshment is made with twice as much water and four times as much flour as the size of the original *chef* that was pulled back. It is mixed firm so it can withstand a five-hour to seven-hour rising.

Then the dough is mixed with this *levain de tout point* or final starter, which usually makes up anywhere from 15 percent to 20 percent of the batch size. Quite often village bakers will mix a triple batch of the refreshment so that it can be used for three different batches of bread to be baked in three successive oven loads. In each successive batch of dough a smaller and smaller piece of *levain* is used to make up for its increased acidity.

In the recipe below the metric and U.S. ingredients are not equivalent; the latter yield a considerably smaller quantity of dough.

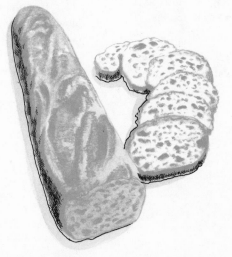

INGREDIENTS	MEASURES		
	METRIC	PERCENTAGES	U.S.
PULL-BACK (*PRÉLEVÈMENT*) FROM PREVIOUS NIGHT'S BATCH—8 TO 10 HOURS			
dough	2 kg		1 lb
REFRESHMENT—5 TO 7 HOURS			
levain	2 kg		1 lb
water	4 ltr		2 lb
flour	8.5 kg		4½ lb
total	14 kg		7½ lb
DOUGH			
*levain**	14 kg	18–20%	7½ lb
bread flour	80 kg	100%	40 lb
water	50 ltr†	63–65%	26 lb
salt	1.5 kg	2.2%	15 oz
yeast	60–70 g	0.3–0.5%	2¼ oz
vitamin C	—	—	⅛ tsp
total	146 kg		75 lb

* One-fifth (of the flour weight) in winter and one-sixth in summer.

† According to one village baker I spoke to in Beaune, 250 to 300 grams of *levain* is used for each liter of water. His method did not include a refreshment of the *chef*. He used a little more yeast and only a 4-hour to 5-hour final rising time.

VARIATIONS

Add 2 to 3 percent more water to the final dough.

Add half again as much yeast, eliminate the vitamin C, and reduce the final proofing to 5 or 6 hours.

Cut the bread flour with all-purpose or organic, unbleached white flour.

MIXING: 10 to 12 minutes on second speed. Break up the *levain* in the water. Add the vitamin C to the water, then add the flour and mix on first speed to incorporate. Crumble the yeast on top of the dough and mix on second speed. Add the salt 5 minutes before the end of mixing.

FIRST RISING: 1 hour.

SCALING: *Baguettes:* 12 ounces; *bâtard* or French loaf: 1 pound, 3 ounces; large *baguettes:* 2 pounds, 6 ounces; *petit pain:* 3 to 4 ounces.

FINAL RISING: 8 to 10 hours in *couches* or *bannetons,* or on curved, perforated *baguette* trays for deck or convection ovens.

BAKE-OFF: 450°F to 460°F, with low-pressure steam for the first few minutes. *Baguettes:* 20 to 30 minutes; 1-pound loaves: 40 minutes; *petit pain:* 12 to 15 minutes.

PAIN COMPLET
WHOLE WHEAT BREAD

METHOD: Direct method.

SOURCE: *Le compagnon boulanger,* by J.-M. Viard, page 290.

ELAPSED TIME: 3½ hours, mixing through bake-off.

DOUGH TEMPERATURE: 75°F. *TEMPÉRATURE DE BASE:* 225°F.

INGREDIENTS	MEASURES		
	METRIC	PERCENTAGES	U.S.
whole wheat flour	4 kg	100%	10 lb
water*	2.8 ltr	70%	7 lb
yeast	90 g	2.25%	3¾ oz
salt	80 g	2%	3¼ oz
powdered milk	100 g	2.5%	4 oz
total	7.07 kg		24 lb

* Whole milk can be used to replace the water and powdered milk. Use the milk straight from the refrigerator.

MIXING: Dilute the yeast and the milk powder in the water. Then add the flour and salt, and mix 4 minutes on first speed, 8 minutes on second speed of a spiral mixer. The dough will be firm.

FIRST RISING: 1 hour.

ROUNDING AND INTERMEDIATE PROOFING: (optional) 15 to 20 minutes.

SCALING: *Baguette:* 12 ounces; oval loaf, *boule,* or pan loaf: 1 pound, 3 ounces (for a 1½-pound loaf pan, scale at 1 pound, 12 ounces); *petit pain:* 3 to 4 ounces.

Deck oven

MAKEUP: Best made up in loaf pans, *boules,* or oval hearth loaves: 15 to 20 minutes.

FINAL RISING: 1½ hours. Total proofing time is around 3 hours.

Let the loaves rise on perforated trays for rack or convection ovens, or in *couches* for deck ovens in a 75°F, draft-free area. The loaves may have to be covered to prevent their crusting over. It is best to bake *pain complet* 5 minutes before it is fully risen rather than 5 minutes after; an early bake-off will create a full, rich expansion of the loaf. Glaze the loaves with a wash of 1 or 2 whole eggs mixed with a tablespoon of milk to give them a shiny, crackling crust. (Glaze them after they are taken out of the oven with a mixture of ¾ ounce cornstarch diluted and boiled for 30 seconds with 4 cups water.)

BAKE-OFF: 450°F, with low-pressure steam for the first few minutes. Then evacuate the steam if possible. 1-pound loaves: 35 minutes; *baguettes:* 15 to 17 minutes; pan loaves: 40 minutes; *petit pain:* 12 to 15 minutes.

METHOD: *Pâte fermentée* (old-dough addition).
SOURCE: Boulangerie-Pâtisserie le Feyeux, 56 rue de Clichy, Paris.
ELAPSED TIME: 3 hours, mixing to bake-off.
DOUGH TEMPERATURE: 78°F. *TEMPÉRATURE DE BASE:* 234°F.

INGREDIENTS	METRIC	MEASURES	
		U.S.	
old dough*	20 kg	11 lb	22 lb
bread flour	3 kg	1 lb, 10 oz	3¼ lb
bran	3 kg	1 lb, 10 oz	3¼ lb
warm water	4 ltr	2 lb, 2 oz	4¼ lb
salt	120 g	1 oz	2 oz
yeast	150 g	1¼ oz	2½ oz
total	3.37 kg	16½ lb	33 lb

* Use a piece of *pain ordinaire* dough that is 4 hours old or one that has been in the retarder for between 6 and 8 hours.

MIXING: 8 minutes on second speed. Place all the ingredients in the bowl and mix on first speed until they are incorporated. Complete the mixing on second speed. The dough is a little drier than that of regular *pain ordinaire.*

FIRST RISING: 1 hour.

SCALING: 1 pound for small, ¾-pound loaves.

SHAPING: Shape by flattening each loaf and folding it over onto itself. Square the side edges, then roll the dough over itself twice, each time sealing with the heel of the hand. The loaf will be a small cylinder about 3 inches in diameter by 5 inches long. The last seal with the heel of the hand should be done lightly so the dough only just holds together. The loaf when baked will burst along this seam without being cut (see the home baker's version, page 101). Let rise in *couches,* seam-side up.

FINAL RISING: 30 to 40 minutes.

TOTAL RISING TIME: From mixer to bake-off, 2 hours.

BAKE-OFF: 400°F, with low-pressure steam for the first few minutes; 25 to 30 minutes until the loaves are a golden brown.

PAIN DE RÉGIME
WHOLE-GRAIN BREAD

METHOD: *Levain-levure.*
SOURCE: Gayle's Bakery, Capitola, California.
ELAPSED TIME: 24 hours.
DOUGH TEMPERATURE: 75°F to 76°F. *TEMPÉRATURE DE BASE*: 225°F.

To make the *levain* for *pain de régime,* use the ingredients and refreshment schedule given on pages 220–221 for *pain de campagne.* When the *levain* has been given its third refreshment, let it rise for between two and three hours before using it in this recipe.

INGREDIENTS	U.S. MEASURES		
THE DOUGH			
levain	10 lb	30 lb	60 lb
rye meal	1 lb	3 lb	6 lb
bran flakes	8 oz	1½ lb	3 lb
dark rye	1 lb	3 lb	6 lb
water	3½ lb	10½ lb	21 lb
salt	3 oz	9 oz	1 lb 2 oz
total	16 lb	48½ lb	97 lb

MIXING: Mix 10 minutes on second speed; the dough will be moist.

FIRST RISING: 1 to 1½ hours.

SCALING: 1 pound, 3 ounces or 2 pounds, 6 ounces.

SHAPING: The loaves should be shaped by hand, not machine.

FINAL RISING: Between 10 and 12 hours; in floured *bannetons.*

BAKE-OFF: 400°F; 1 hour for 2-pound loaves; 40 to 45 minutes for 1-pound loaves.

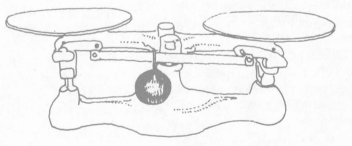

Balance scale

PAIN BOUILLIE
PORRIDGE BREAD

METHOD: *Bouillie* (boiled mush).
SOURCE: Fable.
ELAPSED TIME: 21 hours.
DOUGH TEMPERATURE: 78°F to 80°F.
TEMPÉRATURE DE BASE: 234°F to 240°F.

INGREDIENTS	U.S. MEASURES
THE BOUILLIE	
medium rye flour	**6 lb**
boiling water	**7½ lb**
malt extract	**1½ oz**
total	12½ lb
THE DOUGH	
bouillie	12½ lb
rye meal	**3 lb**
dark or medium rye flour	**1 lb**
salt (2%)	**3¼ oz**
water (variable)	**1 lb**
total	18 lb

Ideally these small loaves should be proofed in wooden frames with the oiled sides touching one another. The frames should measure 7 inches wide by 9 inches long, by 4 inches high. Place the wooden frame on top of a flat, wooden proofing board and sprinkle the inside of the frame liberally with cornmeal. After cutting the loaves into flat rectangles, oil them on all sides with light vegetable oil. Place 4 loaves in each frame. When the loaves are ready to be baked, slide them, frame and all, right onto the hearth of the oven.

MIXING THE *BOUILLIE:* Measure the flour into a large ceramic bowl or plastic tub. Mix the malt extract into the boiling water and pour it over the flour and, *without* stirring, allow the ingredients to sit for 5 minutes. Then use a wooden spoon to mix the gruel. Let the *bouillie* sit out, covered lightly with a towel and in a warm spot, for 7 hours.

MIXING THE DOUGH: Combine the rye meal, flour, and the *bouillie* on first speed to incorporate them, then add the salt on top. Mix on second speed for 5 to 6 minutes. Do not overmix.

FIRST RISING: Proof the dough on an 18-inch-by-24-inch bun tray lined with parchment paper. Try to shape the wet mass into a tidy rectangle about 2½ inches high by about 12 inches wide by 24 inches long. Cover it with plastic wrap and let the dough rise in a warm spot for 7 hours.

SHAPING: Cut the dough into rectangles 3 inches wide by 4 inches long and 2½ inches high. Oil the sides of the loaves where they will touch in the pan so they can be pulled apart later, and place 4 in each greased "pillow"-loaf pan (wider than a normal loaf pan) that measures 7 inches by 9 inches.

BAKE-OFF: Bake at 200°F to 225°F for 7 hours.

PAIN DE SEIGLE—PÂTE FERMENTÉE
RYE BREAD WITH OLD-DOUGH ADDITION

METHOD: *Pâte fermentée* (old-dough addition).

SOURCE: Boulangerie-Pâtisserie le Feyeux, 56 rue de Clichy, Paris.

ELAPSED TIME: 10 hours for the old dough; 5 hours from the start of the mixing to end of the bake.

DOUGH TEMPERATURE: 76°F to 78°F. *TEMPÉRATURE DE BASE:* 234°F.

INGREDIENTS	MEASURES	
	METRIC	U.S.
old dough*	10 g	4½ lb
rye flour †	12–15 kg	9 lb
bread flour	—	4 lb
water	10 ltr	9–9½ lb
salt ‡	250 g	4¼ oz
yeast	200 g	3 oz
total	35.5 kg	30 lb

* Use a piece of *pain ordinaire* dough that is between 8 and 10 hours old, or one that has been in the retarder for between 12 and 15 hours. (If the old dough is only 4 or 5 hours old, double the quantity.)

† The rye flour can be cut with up to 30 or 40 percent bread flour.

‡ Because there is salt in the old-dough addition, no extra salt, over and above the quantities that would normally be used, is necessary in the formula.

MIXING: 4 minutes on first speed, 4 to 5 minutes on second speed. Add the yeast and the old dough to the water with half of the flour. Mix on first speed to break up the old dough. When it is broken up, add the rest of the flour and the salt, and finish mixing. The dough should be moist.

FIRST RISING: 20 minutes to 1 hour.

SCALING: For 1-pound loaves, scale at 1 pound, 3 ounces; for 2-pound loaves, at 2 pounds, 6 ounces.

SHAPING: Oval or round loaves are traditional.

FINAL RISING: 2½ to 3 hours. Let the loaves rise on perforated trays for rack or convection ovens or in *couches* or *bannetons* for deck ovens in a 75°F, draft-free area. The loaves may have to be covered to avoid their crusting over. The total rising time from mixer to bake-off is 4 hours.

BAKE-OFF: 400°F to 425°F, with low-pressure steam for the first few minutes. 1-pound loaves: 35 to 40 minutes; 2-pound loaves: 50 to 55 minutes. Rye bread should be baked for a little longer than white or wheat varieties are.

METHOD: *Poolish* (sponge method).
SOURCE: *Le compagnon boulanger,* by J.-M. Viard, page 274.
ELAPSED TIME: 2 to 3 hours for the *poolish,* 3 hours for the dough.
DOUGH TEMPERATURE: 78°F to 79°F. *TEMPÉRATURE DE BASE: 236°F.*

INGREDIENTS	MEASURES	
	METRIC	U.S.
THE POOLISH		
rye flour	3 kg	6 lb, 10 oz
water	3.3 ltr	7 lb, 8 oz
yeast	150 g	5¼ oz
total	6,450 g	14½ lb
THE DOUGH		
poolish	6,450 g	14½ lb
rye flour	2.5 kg	5½ lb
bread flour	2.5 kg	5½ lb
water	2 ltr	4½ lb
salt	160 g	5¾ oz
yeast	—	2 oz
total	13.61 kg	30 lb

MIXING THE *POOLISH:* Dilute the yeast in the warm water, then add the flour. The sponge is very liquid so it can be mixed by hand. The *poolish* can be set to ferment in a bowl or a plastic bucket for at least 2 or 3 hours. When the *poolish* has risen and fallen in the middle, it is ready to use (in American baker's terms this is called a "full drop").

MIXING THE DOUGH: 4 minutes on first speed, 5 minutes on second speed.

FIRST RISING: 40 minutes.

SCALING AND SHAPING: For 2-pound loaves, at 2 pounds, 6 ounces. 15 minutes.

FINAL RISING OR MAKEUP *(L'APPRÊT):* Around 1 hour. The loaves should be made up, placed in *couches,* and baked on the deck of the oven to achieve full, rich bloom. But they can be placed on perforated trays and baked in a rack oven. The total rising time from the mixer to the bake-off is 1½ to 2 hours.

BAKE-OFF: 425°F to 435°F, with low-pressure steam for the first few minutes; 2-pound loaves, 45 to 50 minutes. It is better to bake rye breads a little early rather than a little late.

PAIN DE SEIGLE DE THIÉZAC
THIÉZAC RYE BREAD

METHOD: *Levain.*
SOURCE: Boulangerie Thiézac.
ELAPSED TIME: 1 to 2 days for the *chef,* 10 to 11 hours for the dough.
DOUGH TEMPERATURE: 78°F. *TEMPÉRATURE DE BASE:* 234°F.

The texture of this bread is like that of a dense but moist cake, with a spongy grain. The flavor is piquant and almost bitingly sour, with a heavy salted flavor. But most of the flavor is provided by the starter rather than the salt that is added. My choice for this bread is a medium rye flour, preferably organic. The medium milling gives a tangy, rich flavor.

With this, as with other advanced methods, it is advisable to try a small batch using the home baker's recipe in order to get the feel of the dough: the wetness of each refreshment, its capacity for rising, and its final appearance.

When first starting this method you will need to make a *chef,* directions for which appear at the end of this recipe. For each successive batch thereafter, a piece is pulled back (*le prélèvement du chef*) from each day's batch of dough for the starter.

Note that the metric and U.S. measures are not equivalent.

INGREDIENTS	MEASURES	
	METRIC	U.S.
PULL-BACK (*PRÉLÈVEMENT*) FROM A PREVIOUS BATCH—1–2 DAYS		
dough	3 kg	1 lb
FIRST REFRESHMENT—5–10 HOURS		
levain	3 kg	1 lb
water	8 ltr	3–3¼ lb
rye flour	16 kg	5 lb
total	27 kg	9 lb
THE DOUGH		
levain	27 kg	9 lb
rye flour	80 kg	22–23 lb
water	40 ltr	15 lb
salt	2,160 g	11–11½ oz
total	147 kg	48 lb

FERMENTING THE *PRÉLÈVEMENT*: Set the piece of dough aside to ferment for 1 or 2 days.

MIXING THE FIRST REFRESHMENT: Mix the ingredients together to a medium-wet dough and set aside to rise for between 5 and 10 hours.

MIXING THE DOUGH: 5 to 8 minutes on first speed. Dilute the *levain* in the water and add only as much flour as necessary to make a very moist dough. The dough will be wetter than the dough made for *pain ordinaire*. A rye dough should not be overmixed.

FIRST RISING: 2 to 2½ hours.

SCALING: Hand scale at 4½ pounds for 4-pound loaves; at around 9 pounds for 8-pound loaves.

PULL-BACK *(PRÉLÈVEMENT)* FOR A SUBSEQUENT BATCH: Pull back 1 pound of dough (for a 48-pound batch) and set it aside to rise for 1 to 2 days.

SHAPING: 20 to 50 minutes, depending on the size of the batch. Because the dough is very moist and sticky, the loaves must be shaped by hand.

FINAL RISING: 1 hour. When the hand shaping of a large batch takes between 45 and 50 minutes, the first loaves shaped can often go in the oven by the time the last ones are being made up. The loaves are best set to rise in *bannetons* or *couches*, uncovered but out of drafts. With such a short rising time, these loaves can be placed on floured boards to proof, then later transferred to a peel to be loaded into the oven. They can also be placed on trays lined with parchment paper.

BAKE-OFF: 400°F, with low-pressure steam for the first few minutes. Give rye breads a good long bake because there is so much moisture in the dough. One hour and 20 minutes for 4-pound round loaves; 1¾ hours for 8-pound rounds.

THIÉZAC CHEF

1½ pounds rye flour

2 teaspoons honey

3 cups warm water

Mix the ingredients into a pasty mass and let the mixture rise for between 2 or 3 days until it is bubbly and smells very sour. Use all 2¾ pounds of this *chef* in the first batch of bread. For subsequent batches, use 1 pound pulled off the previous day's batch and allowed to rise for 1 to 2 days. (The initial *chef* will not be nearly as acidic as a piece pulled back from a dough batch.)

PAIN DE SEIGLE DE COSTA
MONSIEUR COSTA'S RYE BREAD

METHOD: *Levain*.
SOURCE: Boulangerie Costa, 19 rue Paul-Bert,
    Aix-en-Provence, France.
ELAPSED TIME: 20 to 24 hours.
DOUGH TEMPERATURE: 76°F to 78°F.
TEMPÉRATURE DE BASE: 228°F to 234°F.

Monsieur Costa's *levain* is a separate entity, that is, the *levain* for the next day never comes off the previous day's dough. Instead the *levain* is kept going by itself through a single refreshment each day and it is used for each of his sourdough breads, *pain complet au levain, pain seigle au levain,* and *pain blanc au levain.* Because the *levain* is not built like other starters, but is a very active and very "old" starter, only small percentages of it are used in the final doughs. Also, he uses between twenty and thirty grams of salt per four kilos of flour, which is about one-half to two-thirds of that used for a normal bread dough; these qualities enable him to control the starter in its long, twenty-four-hour rising.

INGREDIENTS	MEASURES		
	METRIC	U.S.	
THE *LEVAIN DE TOUT POINT*			
levain	200 g	2 oz	7 oz
white flour	4 kg	2¼ lb	9 lb
salt	20–30 g	I tsp	I oz
water*	2 ltr	2¼ cups	4 lb
total	6,230 g	3½ lb	13½ lb
THE DOUGH			
levain de tout point	6 kg	12 lb	3 lb
white bread flour	22 kg	44 lb	11 lb
rye flour	8 kg	16 lb	4 lb
salt †	900 g	I lb, 9 oz	6¼ oz
water ‡	16 ltr	32 lb	8 lb
total	53 kg	105½ lb	26 lb

---
* At 60°F.
† 30 g *au kilo* (when Costa makes *pain blanc* he uses only 20 g *au kilo*).
‡ If you use, say, 45°F water for *pain ordinaire,* use 56°F water for *seigle.*

THE *CHEF*: Follow the directions for the honey starter on page 33. After the *levain* has been brought to a strong, healthy state (after at least 4 or 5 refreshments) refresh it once more to make the *levain de tout point* (the final starter).

MIXING THE *LEVAIN DE TOUT POINT*: Combine the ingredients, mix on second speed for 6 to 8 minutes, and set aside to rise for 24 hours before using it in the dough.

MIXING THE DOUGH: Mix for 6 to 8 minutes; the dough will be firm.

FIRST RISING: 1½ hours.

SCALING: 2 pounds, 6 ounces for 2-pound loaves.

ROUNDING UP: Round each loaf and let it rest on the bench or on flour-dusted boards, covered.

LA DÉTENTE (INTERMEDIATE PROOFING): 3 hours.

SHAPING: Shape the dough into oval loaves by hand and place them in *couches*.

FINAL RISING: 15 to 20 hours.

BAKE-OFF: 400°F, with lots of low-pressure steam at the beginning; 50 minutes to 1 hour for 2-pound loaves.

PAIN DE SEIGLE AUX RAISINS
RYE BREAD WITH RAISINS

In France, little rolls made out of this dough are called *les benoîtons*. The tang of the sourdough rye and the sweetness of the raisins create an irresistible flavor.

INGREDIENTS	MEASURES	
	METRIC	U.S.
pain de seigle dough*	1 kg	2 lb
raisins†	250 g	4–12 oz
total	1.25 kg	2¼–2¾ lb

* Use a piece of dough from a batch of *seigle* made according to the recipes on pages 233 or 234.

† Soak the raisins in hot water for between 2 and 8 hours to give them some moisture and to remove some of their acidity (optional). Drain them before using.

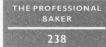

MIXING: After the first rising period, mix the raisins and dough together. Make sure, when incorporating the raisins into the dough, that you work gently so that the fruit is not broken up.

RISING: Let the dough rise for another 30 minutes.

SHAPING: Scale it into 12-ounce or 1-pound pieces, round them into *boules,* and continue according to the directions given for the original dough. For rolls, scale at 2 or 3 ounces.

METHOD: *Levain.*

SOURCE: Gayle's Bakery, Capitola, California.

ELAPSED TIME: 3 hours.

DOUGH TEMPERATURE: 78°F. *TEMPÉRATURE DE BASE:* 234°F.

INGREDIENTS	U.S. MEASURES
bread flour	25 lb
compagnon levain (page 34)	2 lb
olive oil	4 oz
yeast	4 oz
salt	4 oz
fresh sage leaves (weighed after stems are removed)	4 oz
or	
anchovy fillets (soaked in milk, drained and chopped)	10 oz
water	16 lb
total	28½ lb

MIXING: Mix as a *baguette* dough, but wetter (you may need extra water). Add the sage or anchovy fillets at the end of mixing and incorporate them gently on first speed for about 1 or 2 minutes.

FIRST RISING: 1½ to 2 hours.

SCALING: 1 pound, 3 ounces.

INTERMEDIATE PROOF: Round the dough and let it rise on the bench or on floured boards for 50 to 60 minutes.

SHAPING: Flatten into rectangles or triangles. Cut with scissors into ladder or tree shapes.

FINAL RISING: Let the *fougasse* rise on parchment-lined trays, or on boards coated with cornmeal or flour.

BAKE-OFF: 400°F for 20 minutes with steam for the first 5 minutes. *Fougasse* may be baked right on the oven floor or they may be taken off the trays and placed on the oven floor for the last 5 minutes of baking.

Loaf duster

PAIN AUX POMMES
SOURDOUGH APPLE BREAD

METHOD: *Levain.*

SOURCE: *Le pain retrouvé,* by J. Y. Guinard and P. Lesjean, page 87.

ELAPSED TIME: 8 to 10 days for the apple starter and 2 days for the refreshments; 6 hours for the bread.

DOUGH TEMPERATURE: 75°F to 76°F. *TEMPÉRATURE DE BASE:* 225°F.

INGREDIENTS	MEASURES	
	METRIC	U.S.
LEVAIN DE POMMES (APPLE STARTER)—8 TO 10 DAYS		
apple	1 medium-sized	
sugar	50 g	1½ oz
water	a few tablespoons	
total	200 g	8 oz
FIRST REFRESHMENT—10 HOURS		
fermented apple mixture	200 g	8 oz
flour	500 g	1 lb (3½ cups)
malt extract	20 g	¾ oz (4 tsp)
water	200 dltr	1 cup
total	940 g	2 lb
SECOND REFRESHMENT—8 TO 10 HOURS*		
levain	940 g	2 lb
flour	enough to make a firm dough	
malt extract	20 g	¾ oz (4 tsp)
salt	10 g	⅓ oz (2 tsp)
water	1 ltr	2 lb (4 cups)
total	4 kg	8 lb
THIRD REFRESHMENT—2½ TO 3 HOURS†		
levain	4 kg	8 lb
flour	enough to make a firm dough	
malt extract	20 g	¾ oz (4 tsp)
salt	10 g	⅓ oz (2 tsp)
water	4.4 ltr	8 lb (1 gal)
total	16 kg	32 lb

INGREDIENTS	MEASURES		
	METRIC	U.S.	
DOUGH			
levain de pommes	1,000 g	2 lb	4 lb
bread flour	1,000 g	2 lb	4 lb
rye flour	300 g	12 oz	1½ lb
warm water			
(variable)	850 g	2¼ lb	4½ lb
salt	40 g	1¼ oz	2½ oz
malt extract	10 g	¼ oz	½ oz
yeast‡	5–10 g	½ oz	1 oz
tart apples (Granny			
Smith, *Pommes*			
reinettes)§	1,000 g	2 lb	4 lb
total	4,210 g	8½ lb	17 lb

* If you do not want to end up with 32 pounds of *levain*, you may use half or even a quarter of the quantities given for the second and third refreshments.

† If, after the second refreshment, the *levain* rises in 3 or 4 hours and appears to be strong and active, there will be no need for a third refreshment.

‡ The yeast helps to support the *levain*.

§ The apples are cut up and then sautéed in butter for a few minutes.

PREPARING THE SPONGE: Chop the apple into pieces and mix it with the sugar and water. Set this aside in a warm place. After about 8 or 10 days, carbonic gas will start to develop.

For the first refreshment, mash up the fermented apple, mix in the refreshment ingredients, continue mixing for 5 or 6 minutes, to make a firm dough, and then set the container aside for 10 hours in a very warm and humid place to rise.

For the second refreshment, add the refreshment ingredients to the risen *levain,* again making a firm dough, and set it aside to rise again, for 8 to 10 hours.

If a third refreshment is necessary, make it as for the second and set the refreshed *levain* aside for between 2½ to 3 hours before mixing it into the dough.

MIXING THE DOUGH: 10 minutes on first speed, 5 minutes on second speed. Put all the ingredients except the apples, in the mixer. After mixing for 15 minutes, add the apples. It is easier to do this by hand by making a series of folds.

FIRST RISING: 2½ to 3 hours, with a turn (punching back) done after 1 hour.

SCALING: Scale at 14 ounces or at 2 pounds, 6 ounces.

SHAPING: *Bâtard* shapes; about 8 inches long for 14-ounce loaves; 12 to 14 inches long for 2-pound loaves. Place the loaves to rise in *couches* or *bannetons*. It is all right if the pieces of apple break through the skin of the loaf slightly during shaping.

FINAL RISING: 1½ to 2 hours.

BAKE-OFF: 465°F; 35 to 40 minutes for 2-pound loaves; 20 to 25 minutes for 14-ounce loaves.

VARIATION

A piece of pain ordinaire that has undergone a fermentation of 8 to 10 hours may replace the levain de pomme. The quantities of salt and yeast and the time of fermentation should be modified.

METHOD: Direct.

SOURCE: Moule à Gateau, rue Mouffetard, Paris.

ELAPSED TIME: 12 to 15 hours.

DOUGH TEMPERATURE: 78°F to 80°F.

TEMPÉRATURE DE BASE: 234°F to 240°F.

Three distinct recipes are given below.

INGREDIENTS	MEASURES		
	METRIC		U.S.
	RECIPE 1	RECIPE 2	RECIPE 3
bread flour	1,000 g	1,000 g	4 lb
yeast	30 g	30 g	3 oz
salt	20 g	25 g	2 oz
sugar	50 g	100 g	8 oz
malt extract	20 g	—	—
unsalted butter	300–500 g	500 g	3 lb
eggs	8–14	12	25
water or milk	(if needed)	(if needed)	(if needed)
total	2,120 g	2,160 g	9 lb

MIXING: For recipe 1, place all the ingredients, except the butter, in the mixer. For recipes 2 and 3, place all the ingredients except for half of the eggs into the mixing bowl (a vertical mixer with the dough hook can be used). Mix first to incorporate, then on second speed for 8 or 9 minutes. Mix on third speed for 2 to 3 minutes while, for recipe 1, adding the butter, or for recipes 2 and 3, slowly pouring in the balance of the eggs, 1 or 2 at a time. The resulting dough will be soft, moist, and satiny. If the dough does not come away from the vertical mixer bowl because it is still a little dry, ½ to 1 cup of cold water or milk may be added slowly down the side of the bowl. Total mixing time, 15 minutes.

FIRST RISING: 1 to 1½ hours in a warm spot; the dough should double in volume.

SECOND RISING: Punch back the dough. Let it rise for 8 to 12 hours, covered, in the refrigerator. The dough can also be scaled into daily batch-sized pieces and frozen for future use (but not more than 8 days). Wrap 1 piece of dough for the next day and the others for consecutive days. (To thaw, move the wrapped piece of dough from the freezer to the retarder at least 1 day before it is needed.)

SCALING: Large *brioche à tête,* 12 ounces; *brioche mousseline,* 14 ounces; *petite brioche à tête,* 2 ounces.

SHAPING: See shaping instructions on page 129.

FINAL RISING: 1 to 1½ hours depending on proofing temperature. Best done in a cabinet with heat and a little steam.

BAKING: 375°F to 385°F; 20 minutes for large and 12 to 15 minutes for small. Glaze with whole egg and milk glaze.

Spécialité
d'Alsace
STREUSSEL
pur beurre
amandes
cannelle

Kougelhopf
Pur Beurre
25 frs

PAIN AU LAIT
MILK BREAD

METHOD: Direct.

SOURCE: Boulangerie-Pâtisserie le Feyeux, 56 rue de Clichy, Paris.

ELAPSED TIME: 2½ hours.

DOUGH TEMPERATURE: 78°F. *TEMPÉRATURE DE BASE:* 234°F.

INGREDIENTS	MEASURES	
	METRIC	U.S.
bread flour	1 kg	2 lb, 3 oz
water	400 g	14 oz
yeast	30 g	1 oz
salt	25 g	¾–1 oz
sugar	100 g	3½ oz
powdered milk	50 g	1¾ oz
butter (at room temperature)	200 g	7 oz
eggs	6	6
total	1,900 g	4 lb

MIXING: 10 to 15 minutes. Place all the ingredients in the bowl except for 25 percent of the water and all of the butter. Mix to incorporate, then mix on second speed. (A small batch can be done in a vertical mixer.) After 10 to 12 minutes the dough will be of a medium consistency. Soften the butter with your hands and then add it in lumps. Add the remainder of the water. The dough will be very wet.

FIRST RISING: 1 hour.

RETARDING: Place the dough, covered, in the refrigerator overnight.

SHAPING: This dough is used to make enriched sweet rolls with fruits and fillings. See the home baker's recipe on page 130 for shapes and sizes.

FINAL RISING: 45 minutes to 1 hour, depending on the proofing temperature; the rolls may be proofed in a cabinet with heat and a little steam.

BAKE-OFF: 400°F for 15 to 20 minutes (depending on sizes and shapes) or until golden brown.

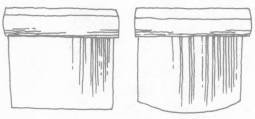

Dough cutters (*pâtes coups*)

METHOD: Direct.

SOURCE: Boulangerie-Pâtisserie le Feyeux, 56 rue de Clichy, Paris.

ELAPSED TIME: 2½ hours.

DOUGH TEMPERATURE: 76°F to 78°F.

TEMPÉRATURE DE BASE: 228°F to 234°F.

INGREDIENTS	MEASURES	
	METRIC	U.S.
bread flour	1 kg	2 lb, 3 oz
water	750 g	1 lb, 10 oz
yeast	35 g	1¼ oz
salt	25 g	¾–1 oz
sugar	25 g	¾–1 oz
powdered milk	25 g	¾–1 oz
butter	50 g	1¾ oz
potato starch	75 g	2½ oz
total	1,985 g	4 lb

MIXING: 10 to 15 minutes.

FIRST RISING: 30 to 40 minutes.

SCALING: Depending on the size of the Pullman pan, between 2 to 2½ pounds and 3½ pounds.

SHAPING: Shape into an oval loaf that will fit inside a greased Pullman pan; the dough should come at least half way up the pan.

FINAL RISING: Leave the lid of the pan sufficiently open to enable you to see inside. Rising time is around 1 hour or less. When the dough has risen to the top of the pan, it is ready to be baked.

BAKE-OFF: 450°F to 475°F; 40 to 50 minutes, depending on the size of the loaf.

PANE ALL'OLIO
OLIVE OIL BREAD

METHOD: Direct, with natural improvers.
SOURCE: Panificio, Bellagio (Lake Como), Italy.
ELAPSED TIME: 2 hours.
DOUGH TEMPERATURE: 78°F. *TEMPÉRATURE DE BASE:* 234°F.

This is one dough that can be used to make the dozens of types of *panini,* or small rolls, each distinctively named, that are to be found in Italian bakeries; see page 138 for a description of some of them. Directions for making *mano* (hand) and *banane* are given below.

INGREDIENTS	MEASURES	
	METRIC	U.S.
flour	10 kg	22 lb
water	5 ltr	10 lb
salt	300 g	7½ oz
yeast	500 g	12½ oz
malt extract	200 g	4 oz
vegetable shortening	I handful	6 oz
olive oil	200 g	4 oz
total	16 kg	33 lb

MIXING: 20 minutes.

FIRST RISING: 30 to 40 minutes.

SHAPING: For illustrations, see the home baker's recipe on page 139.

MANO: Scale the dough at 6 ounces for small rolls and 12 ounces for large. Roll out each scaled, 12-ounce piece of dough to make a long, oval shape about 12 or 14 inches long (6 or 8 inches for the smaller pieces). Roll up the dough, first from one end and then from the other, toward the middle. Use the other hand to stretch the dough out so that each end makes a tight roll with 5 or 6 layers. You will now have two 7- or 8-inch-long logs of dough side by side, connected in the middle by a flat piece of dough.

Twist the two rolled-up logs in toward the middle so they form Vs that point the same way to make the four fingers of a primitive hand. When the *mano* is turned over, the middle connecting piece of dough, lapped over all four fingers, will cover the base of the fingers and emulate a palm.

BANANE: These are small cylindrical rolls that are not easy to shape by hand.

Scale the dough at about 3 ounces. Send each piece through the molder once. The result will be a tight little roll about 4 inches long and, because the dough is so dense, the seams of the rolled-up dough will still be evident. For the second pass, hold the roll at a 45-degree angle to the feed rollers of the molder and push it in. The result will be a tight roll with a spiral overlap of the dough extending up its entire length. One end will be a little larger than the other.

FINAL RISING: Let the rolls rise just long enough (20 to 30 minutes) to allow the dough to relax, so that they will not burst irregularly in the oven.

BAKE-OFF: 12 to 18 minutes in a 400°F oven.

PANE TOSCANO
TUSCAN BREAD

METHOD: *Bouillie* (boiled mush).
SOURCE: Conversation with a baker from Il Fornaio.
ELAPSED TIME: 3½ hours.
DOUGH TEMPERATURE: 78°F. *TEMPÉRATURE DE BASE:* 234°F.

INGREDIENTS	MEASURES	
	METRIC	U.S.
bread flour	10 kg	22 lb
boiling water	6 ltr	13 lb
yeast	250 g	8¾ oz
old dough (12–15 hours old)	2 kg	4½ lb
enough bread flour to make a medium-wet dough		
total	18–20 kg	40–44 lb

BOUILLIE: Put the measured quantity of flour into a large ceramic or plastic bucket. Pour on the boiling water and let the ingredients sit for 5 minutes. Then mix to incorporate them. Let the *bouillie* rest, covered and out of drafts, for between 8 and 10 hours or overnight.

MIXING THE DOUGH: Put the *bouillie,* the yeast, and the old dough in the mixing bowl. After mixing to incorporate them, add enough flour to make a medium-wet dough. Mix for 20 minutes on second speed. (Because there is no water in the dough to cool down the dough temperature, and even if the mush is at room temperature, the *bouillie* may have to be put in the retarder a few hours before mixing to prevent the final dough from being mixed too hot.)

FIRST RISING: 2 to 3 hours.

SCALING: 2-pound, 6-ounce pieces.

FIRST SHAPING: Flatten each piece of dough and shape it into a loose round ball.

RISING: Let the loaves rise for between 1 and 1½ hours on the bench or on floured wooden boards.

FINAL SHAPING (*schiacciare*): With the flat part of the fingers, flatten the loaves slightly, and flip them over.

FINAL RISING: Let the loaves rise for 30 minutes.

BAKE-OFF: 425°F for 45 minutes; no steam. Leave the oven open at end of the bake to dry out the crust.

A SIMPLER TOSCANO
8 lb biga
6 lb all-purpose flour
4 lb water
¼ oz yeast

Mix into a medium-wet dough for 15 minutes, let rise for 2 hours, then proceed as above.

METHOD: *Biga.*
SOURCE: Signore Gianfranco, Leghorn (Livorno).
ELAPSED TIME: 5 to 7 hours for the *biga;* around 2 hours for the dough.
DOUGH TEMPERATURE: 76°F. *TEMPÉRATURE DE BASE:* 228°F.

INGREDIENTS	U.S. MEASURES
THE *BIGA*	
bread flour	4 lb
all-purpose flour	4 lb
yeast	I lb
water	4 lb
total	13 lb
THE DOUGH	
biga	13 lb
bread flour	4 lb
all-purpose flour	4 lb
water	17 lb
yeast	2 oz
salt	6 oz
malt extract	I oz
vegetable shortening	8 oz
total	39 lb

MIXING THE *BIGA*: Combine the ingredients to make a firm dough and let it rise for between 5 and 7 hours.

MIXING THE DOUGH: Mix all the ingredients except ½ cup of water, the malt extract, and the vegetable shortening, for 15 minutes on the first speed.

DIVIDING THE DOUGH: Leave two-thirds of the dough in the mixer bowl and add the 1 ounce malt extract dissolved in ½ cup warm water. Mix to incorporate, using extra flour if necessary. Remove the dough from the bowl; this is for *michette.*

Place the remaining one-third of the dough back into the mixer bowl, add the vegetable shortening, and mix to incorporate; this is for *schiacciata.*

Schiacciata

FIRST RISING: 1 hour.

SCALING: Divide the dough into 1-pound pieces, stretch them on oiled trays, flattening them with the hands into pieces measuring 8 by 10 inches, 2 to a tray. Cover with a little olive oil and salt.

FINAL RISING: 20 to 30 minutes; the pieces may be dimpled again with the fingertips.

BAKE-OFF: 15 to 20 minutes at 420°F to 425°F.

Stampa per michette

Michette

FIRST RISING: 30 minutes.

SCALING: Scale at the proper dough break weight for a bun press to yield 2½- to 3-ounce rolls. Pass each break through a dough break or sheeter 8 to 10 times to break down the gluten. Round the *pâtons* up tightly and coat them with oil.

SECOND RISING: 1 hour.

DIVIDING: Divide the dough in a bun press and arrange the buns on well-floured wooden peel. Let them rise for 20 minutes to relax, then stamp each roll with a *stampa per michette.* *

FINAL RISING: 30 minutes.

BAKE-OFF: Bake at 425°F to 450°F, right on the floor of the oven, with plenty of steam at the beginning and during the bake. Bake for 12 to 15 minutes or until very crisp.

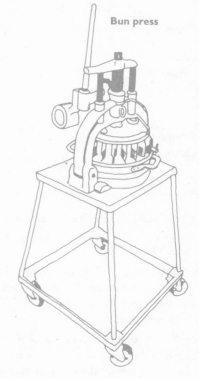

Bun press

Peels

Proofing cabinet (parisienne)

---

* They are available by mail from O. Zucchi, Via S. Antonio All'Esquilino (telephone: 7316.278) or Via Carlo Alberto (738907); 15 Rome, Italy.

METHOD: *Poolish* (sponge; called a *biga* in Italian).

SOURCE: Adapted from several recipes in *The Italian Baker,* by Carol Field.

ELAPSED TIME: 6 hours.

DOUGH TEMPERATURE: 76°F to 78°F.

TEMPÉRATURE DE BASE: 228°F to 234°F.

INGREDIENTS	U.S. MEASURES	
THE *BIGA*		
bread flour	10 lb	20 lb
water	5–6 lb	10–12 lb
yeast	1 oz	2 oz
total	15–16 lb	30–32 lb
THE DOUGH		
biga	15 lb	30 lb
bread flour	8 lb	16 lb
all-purpose flour	7 lb	14 lb
water	12 lb	24 lb
salt	8 oz	1 lb
total	42½ lb	85 lb

MIXING THE *BIGA*: Mix the ingredients for 8 to 10 minutes on second speed; the dough should be very firm. Let the sponge rise for between 12 and 15 hours.

MIXING THE DOUGH: Add all of the ingredients to the bowl except 2 quarts (4 pounds) of the water and the salt. Mix on the first speed to incorporate the ingredients, then add the salt and mix on the second speed. After about 15 minutes, slowly start adding the last 2 quarts of water to make a very wet dough. Total mixing time is 20 to 25 minutes.

FIRST RISING: 1½ to 2 hours.

SCALING: Scale at about 4 pounds, using plenty of flour on the bench.

SHAPING: Roll each loaf up roughly into a tight log, approximately 3 feet long. Let the logs rest on a well-floured bench or wooden boards for 30 minutes.

STRETCHING: Cut each log in half and stretch each piece to a length of 2½ to 3 feet. Let the loaves rise 20 to 30 minutes more.

BAKE-OFF: Bake in a 480°F oven without steam directly on the hearth for 25 to 30 minutes or until golden brown. Or set the oven at 500°F and turn it down to 400°F when the loaves go in.

Leave the bread in the oven with the door open and burners off for 10 minutes after baking to develop the crust and dry out the loaves.

METHOD: *Lievito naturale* (sourdough; the Italian version of *levain*).
SOURCE: Panificio Due Fratelli, Milan.
ELAPSED TIME: 24 hours.
DOUGH TEMPERATURE: 75°F. *TEMPÉRATURE DE BASE:* 225°F.

This is an entirely sourdough process I learned from the bakery Due Fratelli on the south side of Milan. It is the Italian version of *pain de campagne,* San Francisco sourdough, and Capitola sourdough. The sourdough starter is built in three refreshments, guaranteeing a bread of controlled acidity. The texture and the crust are only possible in a sourdough method that uses a lot of water in the final dough.

The *chef* may be pulled back from the previous night's dough and allowed to rise for eight hours or it may be a piece of *levain* ready to be used in a sourdough bread process (see the recipe for a basic sourdough starter on page 31).

INGREDIENTS	U.S. MEASURES
CHEF—8 HOURS	
	1 lb
FIRST REFRESHMENT—6 HOURS	
chef	1 lb
bread flour*	2 lb
water	1 lb
total	4 lb
SECOND REFRESHMENT—2 HOURS	
levain	4 lb
bread flour	4 lb
water	3 lb
total	11 lb
THIRD REFRESHMENT—2 HOURS	
levain	11 lb
bread flour	11 lb
water	8 lb
total	30 lb

Library Resource Center
Renton Technical College
Renton, WA 98056

INGREDIENTS	U.S. MEASURES
THE DOUGH	
levain	30 lb
all-purpose flour	30 lb
water	24 lb
salt (2.2%)	1 lb
total	**85 lb**

* High-gluten or whole wheat flour may be used in this step for variation.

MIXING: Mix the dough for a total of 15 to 18 minutes, the first 2 minutes on first speed to incorporate all the ingredients and then on second speed. Hold back the salt and about 4 pounds (2 quarts) of the water. Add the salt 5 minutes before the end of mixing, then add the rest of the water slowly to obtain a very, very wet dough (68 to 70 percent hydration).

FIRST RISING: 4 to 6 hours.

SCALING: 5 pounds.

SHAPING: Roll into large logs, each about 3 feet long.

SECOND RISING: 2 to 3 hours, on the bench or wooden boards dusted with plenty of flour.

STRETCHING AND FLATTENING (*stirato e schiacciare*): Cut each log in half and stretch each half to measure about 3 feet long.

FINAL RISING: 30 to 40 minutes.

BAKE-OFF: 30 to 40 minutes at 500°F with no steam. Evacuate the steam from the oven at the end of baking and turn the burners off to dry out the loaves.

Diviseuse (semiautomatic divider)

STIRATO
YEASTED ITALIAN-STYLE FRENCH BREAD

METHOD: Direct.
SOURCE: Panificio Danova, Via Cerva, Milan.
ELAPSED TIME: 6 hours.
DOUGH TEMPERATURE: 76°F. *TEMPÉRATURE DE BASE:* 228°F.

This is the bread Signore Danova's father invented. It is called *stirato* (or "stretched") because the dough is stretched in being made up. Danova uses sugar in the dough. That addition and a 70 percent water proportion are the only things that make this formula different from that of a straight-dough French bread.

If, after making a batch, you discover that the dough is too elastic in the stretching stage, you can accommodate the strength of flour simply by reducing the amount of yeast in the formula.

INGREDIENTS	U.S. MEASURES	
all-purpose flour	12½ lb	25 lb
bread flour	12½ lb	25 lb
water	18–19 lb	36–38 lb
malt extract	1½ oz	3 oz
yeast	4 oz	8 oz
salt	8 oz	1 lb
total	43 lb	85 lb

MIXING: Dilute the malt extract in a little warm water. Add the malt mixture, all of the flour, and all but 2 quarts of the water. Mix on the first speed to incorporate the ingredients, then add the salt and mix on the second speed. After about 15 minutes slowly start adding the last of the water to make a very wet dough. Total mixing time 20 to 25 minutes.

FIRST RISING: 4 hours.

SCALING: Scale at about 4 pounds, using plenty of flour on the bench.

SHAPING: Roll each loaf up roughly into tight logs, each approximately 3 feet long. Let them rest on a well-floured bench or wooden boards for 30 minutes.

STRETCHING: Cut each log in half and stretch each half to a length of 2½ to 3 feet. Let the loaves rise for 20 to 30 minutes more.

BAKE-OFF: Bake in a 480°F oven without steam and directly on the hearth for 30 minutes or until golden brown. Leave the bread in the oven with the door open and the burners off for 5 minutes after baking to develop the crust and dry out the loaves.

METHOD: *Lievito naturale* (Italian yeasted starter).
SOURCE: Panificio, Bellagio (Lake Como), Italy.
ELAPSED TIME: 15 hours for the starter; 2 hours for the dough.
DOUGH TEMPERATURE: 76°F to 78°F.
TEMPÉRATURE DE BASE: 228°F to 234°F.

This method is a modern variation, with a yeasted starter, that emulates sour-dough. It is actually a sponge method, using a very firm *biga* that is allowed to ferment overnight, for between fifteen and twenty hours. (The basic recipe for a *biga* is on page 35.)

INGREDIENTS	MEASURES		
	METRIC	U.S.	
lievito naturale	7 kg	7¾ lb	15½ lb
bread flour	5 kg	5½ lb	11 lb
water (100°F–110°F)	5 ltr	5½ lb	11 lb
salt	200 g	3½ oz	7 oz
yeast	150–200 g	3 oz	6 oz
powdered milk	200 g	3½ oz	7 oz
total	17.5 kg	19 lb	39 lb

MIXING: 25 minutes: 10 minutes on first speed; and 15 minutes on second speed. Add all of the ingredients to the bowl except 20 percent or so of the water. Add the remaining water during the last 6 to 8 minutes of mixing to achieve a moist and very wet dough.

SCALING: Strew a lot of flour on the bench, take the dough out of the mixer, and scale immediately: 12 ounces for small, and 1 pound, 8 ounces for large, loaves.

SHAPING: Shape flat in pieces about 4 inches by 8 inches for small loaves and 5 inches by 14 inches for large. Keep the loaves as rectangular as possible. If you have to add dough in the scaling, add it on top and keep the smooth side of the loaf down.

RISING: Let the loaves rise on the well-floured bench or wooden boards for 30 minutes.

FLATTENING *(schiacciare):* Flatten each loaf with the fingertips several times and flip the loaves over.

FINAL RISING: 30 to 45 minutes.

BAKE-OFF: Gently remove the loaves to a peel and slide them directly onto the oven floor. Bake at 400°F for 20 to 25 minutes until they are golden brown.

To make *maltagliatte,* "badly cut" flat rolls, cut 1 long loaf into 5 to 6 pieces with a dough cutter and bake them for 12 to 15 minutes. They should be golden, not pale or white, when done.

GRISSINI TORINESE
TURINESE BREADSTICKS

METHOD: *Pâte fermentée* (old-dough addition).
SOURCE: Panificio, Bellagio (Lake Como), Italy.
ELAPSED TIME: 2½ hours.
DOUGH TEMPERATURE: 76°F to 78°F.
TEMPÉRATURE DE BASE: 228°F to 234°F.

INGREDIENTS	U.S. MEASURES		
old *ciabatte* dough*	3¼ lb	6½ lb	13 lb
bread flour	1½ lb	3 lb	6 lb
water (warm)	½ lb	1 lb	2 lb
yeast	1 oz	2 oz	4 oz
salt	1 oz	2 oz	4 oz
olive oil	5½ oz	11 oz	22 oz
malt extract	½ oz	1 oz	2 oz
shortening	2 oz	4 oz	8 oz
total	6 lb	12 lb	24 lb

* The dough may be 2 to 3 hours old. It is usually best to use a dough that already has starter, *biga*, or sponge in it.

MIXING: 10 minutes on second speed. Mix all of the ingredients together at once, using very warm water, to a medium-soft dough.

SHAPING: Take the dough from the mixer and flatten it into a smooth rectangle about ¾ inch high. Cut this into strips about 4 inches wide. Coat the underneath and top of each strip of dough with additional virgin olive oil.

RISING: Let the strips rise for between 45 minutes and 1 hour.

STRETCHING: Using a metal dough scraper, cut each 4-inch-wide strip into narrower strips 4 inches long and ½ to ¾ of an inch wide. Stretch each piece to fit lengthwise onto an 18-inch-by-24-inch baking pan. (*Grissini* should be about ¼ inch in diameter after being stretched and no more than ½ inch in diameter after being baked.)

FINAL RISING: 30 to 50 minutes.

BAKE-OFF: Bake at 375°F for 14 minutes until golden brown and crispy. Bake just until the sticks become crisp. Test one breadstick before the others come out of the oven. When broken, it should snap without bending, and the interior structure should be very irregular.

METHOD: Sourdough.
SOURCE: Gayle's Bakery, Capitola, California.
ELAPSED TIME: Between 3 and 8 hours, depending on the amount of yeast.
DOUGH TEMPERATURE: 76°F. *TEMPÉRATURE DE BASE:* 228°F.

INGREDIENTS	U.S. MEASURES		
starter*	4 lb	4½ lb	5½ lb
bread flour	10½ lb	12 lb	14 lb, 10 oz
water	7 lb	7½ lb	9 lb
yeast	1 oz	1 oz	1¼ oz
salt	4 oz	4½ oz	5½ oz
malt extract	4 oz	4½ oz	5½ oz
olive oil	3 oz	3¼ oz	4 oz
total	22 lb	25 lb	30 lb

* A piece from yesterday's dough left, covered, in the retarder to ferment.

MIXING: 18 to 20 minutes on second speed. You may need extra water after the dough comes together. This is a very wet dough. Incorporate the olive oil during the last minute of mixing, on first speed.

FIRST RISING: 30 minutes. Then pull back a piece of dough for a starter for the next day or freeze the dough and pull it out of the freezer the day before it is needed.

SCALING: 2½ pounds for *pizza al metro;* 1¼ pounds for 15-inch round pizzas; 4 ounces for small individual pizzas; and 2½ ounces for miniature *calzone.*

SHAPING: Into *pizza al metro* (a long, rectangular pizza), round pizzas, or individual pizzas.

FINAL RISING: The quantities of yeast given in the ingredients table allow the dough to take a 3-hour final rising; less yeast will allow longer proofing times.

BAKE-OFF: Bake most pizzas at 600°F to 650°F.

FOCACCIA
GENOAN FLAT BREAD

Use the pizza recipe above for the dough.

After the first 30 minutes of rising, scale the dough at 4½ pounds for each *focaccia.* The dough will be wet and sticky. Use a little flour on the worktable and round it up into a tight ball. Place each piece of dough in a bowl that contains 1 cup of extra virgin olive oil, 1 teaspoon salt, 3 or 4 chopped cloves of garlic, and 12 whole leaves of fresh sage. Flip the dough over in the oil mixture and set it aside to rise for 3 to 4 hours.

Pull the dough out of the oil and spread it unto an 18- by 24-inch bun tray. Spread the dough out to the edges. Then pour the oil, the sage, and garlic that remain in the bowl over the top of the dough. Let it rise for 1 hour. Poke the dough with the fingertips several times. Bake in a 400°F oven for 15 to 17 minutes or until it is golden brown.

METHOD: Sour sponge.
SOURCE: König Bakery, Miesbach, Germany.
ELAPSED TIME: 24 hours—8-hour *levain*, 12-hour starter,
    4-hour dough.
DOUGH TEMPERATURE: 75°F. *TEMPÉRATURE DE BASE:* 225°F.

If it is inconvenient to use an eight-hour *levain*, one that has been refreshed and allowed to rise for between two and four hours will work. Even a piece of dough from a sourdough batch can be used, after the first one-hour rising. It is very important to control the sponge by using cool water and very cold water will be necessary if the sponge is to sit for up to twelve hours.

INGREDIENTS	U.S. MEASURES	
SEED MIXTURE		
sesame seeds	2 lb	4 lb
soy sauce *(tamari)*	½ cup	I cup
pumpkin seeds	4 lb	8 lb
total	6 lb	12 lb
STARTER		
whole wheat *levain* (8 hours old)	5 lb	10 lb
cool water	10 lb	20 lb
organic rye flour	3 lb	6 lb
organic unbleached white flour	3 lb	6 lb
total	21 lb	42 lb
DOUGH		
starter (at 65°F–70°F)	21 lb	42 lb
organic unbleached white flour	8 lb	16 lb
seed mixture	4½ lb	9 lb
sea salt	4½ oz	9 oz
total	34 lb	68 lb

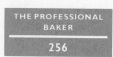

PREPARING THE SEED MIXTURE: Mix the sesame seeds and soy sauce together and toast for 20 to 25 minutes at 350°F. Toast the pumpkin seeds for 25 to 30 minutes, also at 350°F. When cool, take one-third of the sesame mixture and one-fourth of the pumpkin seeds and grind them in a food processor for 20 seconds, until the pumpkin seeds are in 1/16-inch chunks and the sesame seeds are pulverized. Add the ground mixture to the whole seeds.

PREPARING THE STARTER: Chop up the *levain* and dilute it with the cold water. Add the flours and mix with a wooden spoon into a soupy sponge. Let the starter rise for between 8 and 12 hours. When the dough is ready to be mixed, the starter may have to be cooled down in the refrigerator in order to achieve a 75°F dough temperature.

MIXING THE DOUGH: 5 to 8 minutes.

FIRST RISING: 1 hour.

SCALING: 2 pounds, 6 ounces for 2-pound loaves.

SHAPING: Oval loaves with slightly stubby ends.

FINAL RISING: Roll the loaves in seeds and let them rise in *couches* for 1 hour to 70 minutes, depending on the coolness of the dough.

CUTTING: Three diagonal cuts.

BAKE-OFF: 425°F with steam, for between 35 and 40 minutes.

VARIATION
RAISIN-NUT BREAD

Without the seed mixture, pumpkin seed bread would be a straightforward rye and wheat sourdough and so makes a good base for this raisin-nut bread.

INGREDIENTS	U.S. MEASURES
pumpkin-seed bread dough*	10 lb
organic raisins	4 lb
organic walnuts (in large pieces)	3 lb
total	17 lb

* Take the dough before the seed mixture has been added.

MIXING: Incorporate on the first speed until combined.

FIRST RISING: 1 hour.

SCALING: 2 pounds, 3 ounces.

SHAPING: Oval loaves.

FINAL RISING: Around 2 hours (may take longer than normal pumpkin seed dough, because of the raisins and nuts).

BAKE-OFF: 400°F, for between 45 and 50 minutes.

METHOD: Sour sponge.
SOURCE: Gayle's Bakery, Capitola, California.
ELAPSED TIME: 24 hours—8-hour *levain,* 12-hour starter,
    4-hour dough.
DOUGH TEMPERATURE: 75°F. *TEMPÉRATURE DE BASE:* 225°F.

If it is inconvenient to use an eight-hour *levain,* one that has been refreshed and allowed to rise for between two and four hours will work. Even a piece of dough from a sourdough batch can be used, after the first one-hour rising. It is very important to control the sponge by using cool water, and very cold water will be necessary if the sponge is to sit for up to twelve hours.

INGREDIENTS	U.S. MEASURES	
SOY MIXTURE		
soy beans	2 lb	4 lb
boiling water	5 cups	10 cups
total	4 lb	8 lb
STARTER		
whole wheat *levain*		
(8 hours old)	5 lb	10 lb
cool water	10 lb	20 lb
organic rye flour	4 lb	8 lb
organic unbleached		
white flour	2 lb	4 lb
total	21 lb	42 lb
DOUGH		
starter (65°F–70°F)	21 lb	42 lb
cool water	2 lb	4 lb
organic unbleached		
white flour	4 lb	8 lb
organic rye flour	2 lb	4 lb
soy mixture	2 lb	4 lb
sea salt	5 oz	10 oz
millet	1 lb, 14 oz	3¾ lb
flax seeds	14 oz	1¾ lb
ground caraway seeds	2 oz	4 oz
total	35 lb	70 lb

SOY MIXTURE: Soak the beans in the boiling water for 5 minutes; drain and allow to cool. Process the beans in a food processor until they are in 1/16-inch chunks. Dry the mixture in a 350°F oven for between 30 and 45 minutes until it is well dried out.

STARTER: Chop up the *levain* and dilute it with the water. Add the flours and mix with a wooden spoon into a soupy sponge. Let the sponge rise for between 8 and 12 hours. When the dough is ready to be mixed, the starter may have to be cooled down in the refrigerator in order to achieve a 75°F dough temperature.

MIXING THE DOUGH: 5 to 8 minutes; the dough is fairly wet because the millet and soy beans will eventually take on water.

FIRST RISING: 1 hour.

SCALING: 2 pounds, 6 ounces for 2-pound loaves.

SHAPING: Round loaves.

FINAL RISING: Let the loaves rise for between 1½ and 3 hours in *bannetons*.

CUTTING: Not necessary; brush off excess flour and glaze with egg wash.

BAKE-OFF: 425°F with steam, for between 35 and 40 minutes.

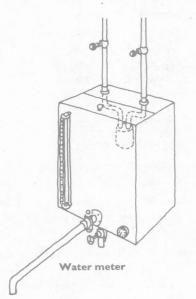

Water meter

Bench brush

Basket brush

METHOD: Sponge.

SOURCE: Gayle's Bakery, Capitola, California.

ELAPSED TIME: 3 hours.

DOUGH TEMPERATURE: 80°F. *TEMPÉRATURE DE BASE:* 240°F.

INGREDIENTS	U.S. MEASURES
THE SPONGE	
whole wheat flour	**5 lb**
water	**5 lb**
yeast	**I lb**
honey	**8 oz**
powdered milk	**4 oz**
soy or corn oil	**8 oz**
total	**12 lb**
THE DOUGH	
sponge	**12 lb**
white flour	**10 lb**
salt	**4½ oz**
water	**3 lb**
sautéed onions	**2 lb**
total	**27 lb**

MIXING THE SPONGE: Add all the sponge ingredients to the mixing bowl and mix for 2 or 3 minutes after they have been incorporated. Let the sponge rise in the bowl or in buckets for between 30 minutes and 1 hour.

SAUTÉING THE ONIONS: Slice 6 to 8 pounds of onions (they are reduced considerably in the cooking) and cook them in a steam kettle with 2 to 3 cups vegetable oil for 15 to 20 minutes until they are well browned. Reserve ½ pound of the mixture for topping the loaves before they go into the oven.

MIXING THE DOUGH: Add flour, water, and salt to the sponge and mix for 8 to 10 minutes on second speed. Add the onions and mix on first speed for 2 or 3 minutes to incorporate. Use a little extra white flour if necessary.

FIRST RISING: 30 to 40 minutes.

SECOND RISING: Knead briefly by hand and let the dough sit for another 10 minutes.

SCALING: Scale at 1 pound, 3 ounces for 1-pound loaves; at 4½ pounds for a 36-roll break.

SHAPING: Mold the loaves by hand or machine into torpedo shapes, then bend them to resemble horseshoes. Shape some of the rolls into torpedos and some into horseshoes.

GLAZING: Glaze immediately with water or egg wash and coat the tops of loaves and rolls with the remaining ½ pound of sautéed onion.

FINAL RISING: 30 to 45 minutes.

BAKE-OFF: 390°F to 400°F. The loaves will take between 35 and 40 minutes; the rolls between 10 and 12 minutes.

SAN FRANCISCO SOURDOUGH

METHOD: *Levain.*

SOURCE: Adapted from an article on Toscano Bakery
in *Bakery Magazine,* November 1980, page 100.

ELAPSED TIME: 24 hours.

DOUGH TEMPERATURE: 74°F to 75°F.

INGREDIENTS	U.S. MEASURES
SOURDOUGH STARTER	
PULL-BACK (PRÉLÈVEMENT)—8 HOURS	
dough from a previous batch or from an active sourdough starter	I lb
First Refreshment—6 hours	
prélève	I lb
high-gluten flour	2¼ lb
water (variable)	I lb
total	4¼ lb
Second Refreshment—6 hours	
sourdough	4¼ lb
high gluten flour	9½ lb
water (variable)	4¼ lb
total	18 lb
Third Refreshment—6 hours	
sourdough	18 lb
high gluten flour	40½ lb
water (variable)	18 lb
total	76½ lb
DOUGH	
sourdough	76½ lb
bread flour (12%–13% protein)	510 lb
water*	255 lb
salt	10¼ lb
total	851 lb

* A little more water may be added according to the baker's preference.

RIPENING THE *PRÉLÈVEMENT*: Set aside, covered in a warm place, for 8 hours.

REFRESHMENTS: To refresh the starter, mix the ingredients listed in the table for each refreshment to a very firm dough, at 74°F, and set it aside each time for 6 hours. After the third refreshment has fermented for its allotted 6 hours, it is ready to be used in the dough.

MIXING THE DOUGH: 8 to 10 minutes on second speed; a medium-firm to medium-wet dough. The dough temperature should be 78°F or below.

FIRST RISING: 45 minutes.

SCALING: Can be done with a pocket divider, rounder, and extended overhead proofer (to allow for a 20-minute intermediate proof).

SHAPING: Can be done on a molder with a curling chain and pressure-board extender.

FINAL PROOFING: In *couches* in covered cabinets. Proofing time, 5 hours. (Some bakers use a proof box at 90°F with 80 percent humidity.)

BAKE-OFF: 390°F for 45 minutes; use plenty of low-pressure, wet steam until the loaves reach their full expansion.

CAPITOLA SOURDOUGH

METHOD: *Levain.*

SOURCE: Glen Hess and Peter Conn at Gayle's Bakery, Capitola, California.

ELAPSED TIME: 24 hours.

DOUGH TEMPERATURE: 75°F. *TEMPÉRATURE DE BASE:* 225°F.

It is hard to figure the exact percentage of water in a *levain* bread because one ingredient—the *levain*—is already hydrated. In any formula in which the percentage of *levain* is mentioned, one can usually assume it to be a reference to the percentage of weight in the entire batch of dough. For this recipe, the *levain* constitutes 33 percent.

A refreshment schedule for this *levain* appears at the end of the recipe.

At Gayle's Bakery, we use the same *levain,* after the final refreshment, for both Capitola sourdough and Capitola sourdough sandwich breads (page 264).

INGREDIENTS	U.S. MEASURES	
levain	27 lb	54 lb
flour	31 lb	62 lb
water	22 lb	44 lb
salt	1 lb	2 lb
vitamin C	¼ tsp	½ tsp
total	80 lb	160 lb

MIXING: 10 to 12 minutes on second speed.

FIRST RISING: 1 hour in the mixer or covered on the bench.

SCALING: Hand scale at 2 pounds, 6 ounces for 2-pound round or long loaves; at 4 pounds, 12 ounces for 4-pound rounds.

SHAPING: 1 hour. Hand shaping is preferable, but many village bakers in France and America use a molder for large batches.

FINAL RISING: 10 to 12 hours in flour-dusted *bannetons* or in *couches,* uncovered but out of drafts. Loaves may have to be covered to avoid their crusting over.

BAKE-OFF: 375°F to 400°F, with low-pressure steam for the first few minutes. 1 hour for 2-pound rounds; 45 minutes for 2-pound long loaves; 1½ hours for 4-pound rounds.

Refreshment Schedule

Part of the finished refreshment is used for the Capitola Sourdough (page 262) and part is used for Capitola Sandwich (page 264). If you are making only one or the other, the quantities mixed can be adjusted.

INGREDIENTS	U.S. MEASURES	
FIRST REFRESHMENT—6 HOURS		
levain	2 lb	3 lb
flour	5¼ lb	7 lb
water	3 lb	4 lb
total	10¼ lb	14 lb
SECOND REFRESHMENT—6 HOURS		
levain	10¼ lb	14 lb
flour	6 lb	8 lb
water	3 lb	4 lb
total	19¼ lb	26 lb
THIRD REFRESHMENT—6 HOURS		
levain	19¼ lb	26 lb
flour	12 lb	18 lb
water	5 lb	7½ lb
total	36¼ lb	51½ lb

CAPITOLA SOURDOUGH SANDWICH BREAD

METHOD: *Levain-levure,* with enrichments.
SOURCE: Gayle's Bakery, Capitola, California.
ELAPSED TIME: 24 hours.
DOUGH TEMPERATURE: 75°F. *TEMPÉRATURE DE BASE:* 225°F.

INGREDIENTS	U.S. MEASURES		
levain	15 lb	22½ lb	30 lb
flour	19 lb	28½ lb	38 lb
water	12 lb	18 lb	24 lb
salt	8 oz	12 oz	1 lb
yeast	5 oz	7½ oz	10 oz
vitamin C	1 tsp	1½ tsp	2 tsp
powdered milk	8 oz	12 oz	1 lb
oil	1¼ lb	1 lb, 14 oz	2½ lb
total	48 lb	80 lb	96 lb

MIXING: 8 to 10 minutes on second speed. Add all the ingredients except the salt, which is added 5 minutes before the end of mixing. The dough will be firm or even stiff.

FIRST RISING: 45 minutes to 1 hour in the mixer or covered on the bench.

SCALING: Hand scale at 2 pounds, 6 ounces for 2-pound loaves in large pans. Scale at 1 pound, 14 ounces for small pan loaves.

SHAPING: 30 minutes. Hand shape and place seam-side down, in oiled loaf pans, mea-suring 9 inches by 7 inches by 2½ inches for large loaves and 9 inches by 5 inches by 2½ inches for small loaves.

FINAL RISING: 6 to 9 hours in a moist proof box. If you are not using a proof box, the loaves may have to be covered to avoid their crusting over.

BAKE-OFF: 375°F in rack or convection ovens, with low-pressure steam for the first few minutes; 40 to 50 minutes. In deck ovens bake at 400°F for 35 to 40 minutes.

METHOD: Sourdough.

SOURCE: Adapted from recipes used by the Cheeseboard and Acme Bread Company, both in Berkeley, California.

ELAPSED TIME: 24 hours.

DOUGH TEMPERATURE: Can be 80°F as the dough goes into the retarder after being mixed.

Some people believe that this starter, having been created in a shop that sells cheese, must have taken on characteristics of the cheese. The Acme Bread Company uses much the same method, showing that it can be done effectively in any carefully run bakery. The acidity of the soupy starter can only be guessed at so bakers must incorporate the starter into an ongoing process, using and feeding it day after day, in order to achieve predictable results.

INGREDIENTS		U.S. MEASURES	
THE STARTER			
levain (8 to 10 hours old)		1 lb	
flour		4 lb	
water		5 lb	
total		10 lb	
THE DOUGH			
starter	3 gallons	3 lb	24 lb
flour	100 lb	12½ lb	100 lb
water	5–7 gallons	7–8½ lb	56 lb
salt	3 cups	4 oz	2 lb
total	182 lb	23–24½ lb	182 lb

MIXING THE STARTER: Chop up the *levain* into small pieces. Combine the ingredients (the mixture will be soupy) and let the starter rise for 24 hours. If you need more than the 10 pounds, it can be built up over a matter of days.

Keep the starter in a 5-gallon plastic bucket. When some of the starter is used, leave a couple of inches in the bottom and refresh it with about 25 cups of flour and 2½ gallons of water, mixing carefully to the consistency of pancake batter. This must be done with a mixer or by hand, not with a spoon.

MIXING THE DOUGH: Originally done on a 140-quart, vertical mixer. Put in the flour, salt, starter, and half of the water. As the liquid is incorporated, more water is added carefully; pour it down the sides of the deep bowl so that it goes underneath the ball of dough. The amount is judged by feel and how the dough pulls away from the bowl. The dough is rather wet and sticky, much wetter than that of a

ACME SOURDOUGH

Refreshment

4 cups water

1 cup flour

Dough

4 gallons starter

27 pounds flour

13 ounces salt

Two-hour first rising; 8
hours in the retarder; 2
hours relaxing (letting the
dough warm up); make-up;
2-hour final rising in loaf
form; bake at 450°F with
steam.

normal *pain ordinaire*. When all the water has been added, the dough is mixed for 15 to 20 minutes on second speed.

FIRST RISING: Divide the dough into tubs or large plastic garbage cans coated with corn oil and set it to rise in a walk-in refrigerator for between 10 and 12 hours. Cover to avoid its crusting.

SECOND RISING: Set the dough aside, out of the retarder, for at least 1 hour.

SHAPING: The rustic method is to cut off a piece of dough that measures about 12 by 18 inches and, without punching it down, cut off strips of an appropriate thickness to make loaves that are then rolled out and put on trays to proof. The irregular sizes mean that the loaves must be weighed when they are sold.

The more modern method is to round pieces into *pâtons* (large pieces) of a given weight that will, after resting and warming up at room temperature, be put through a loaf divider to be scaled into *baguette* sizes. The loaves must then be allowed to rest for 20 to 30 minutes before being put through a molder. They may be shaped by hand.

FINAL PROOFING: 2½ to 3 hours, depending on the method used for shaping. Cover with cloths or plastic or proof in a covered proof box at ambient temperature to avoid crusting.

BAKE-OFF: 450°F in convection or rack ovens with an abundance of steam for 25 to 30 minutes.

WHOLE WHEAT BREAD

METHOD: Direct or sponge.
SOURCE: Gayle's Bakery, Capitola, California.
ELAPSED TIME: 3 hours.
DOUGH TEMPERATURE: 80°F. *TEMPÉRATURE DE BASE*: 240°F.

Direct Method

INGREDIENTS	U.S. MEASURES		
whole wheat flour	10 lb	15 lb	20 lb
water	6 lb	8 lb	12 lb
salt	3 oz	4¼ oz	6 oz
yeast	11 oz	16 oz	22 oz
honey	1 lb, 3 oz	1 lb, 14 oz	2 lb, 6 oz
powdered milk	2½ oz	4 oz	5 oz
soy or corn oil	8 oz	12 oz	16 oz
total	18¾ lb	27 lb	37½ lb

MIXING: Combine all the ingredients and mix for 10 minutes on second speed. The dough should be soft.

FIRST RISING: Let the dough rise for between 45 minutes and 1 hour.

KNOCK BACK: Punch the dough back briefly, round it again, and let it rise for another 15 minutes.

SCALING: Scale at 1 pound, 14 ounces for 1½-pound loaves. Scale at 4½ pounds for a 36-roll break.

INTERMEDIATE PROOF: Round up and let the dough rise for another 5 to 10 minutes.

SHAPING: Mold by hand or machine to fit rectangular loaf pans.

FINAL RISING: 30 to 45 minutes.

BAKE-OFF: Between 360°F and 390°F for 35 to 40 minutes.

Sponge Method

When this method is used, the bread is made without powdered milk and with smaller quantities of honey and oil.

INGREDIENTS	U.S. MEASURES		
whole wheat flour	10 lb	15 lb	20 lb
water	6 lb	8 lb	12 lb
salt	3 oz	4¼ oz	6 oz
yeast	11 oz	1 lb	1 lb, 6 oz
honey	1 lb	1½ lb	2 lb
soy or corn oil	6 oz	8 oz	12 oz
total	18¾ lb	27 lb	37½ lb

MIXING THE SPONGE: Add all ingredients to the mixing bowl except half of the flour and all of the salt. Be sure to use water cool enough so that the final dough will not go above 80°F. Mix to incorporate and then for 2 or 3 minutes longer. Let the sponge rise in the mixer bowl or in buckets for between 30 minutes and 1 hour.

MIXING THE DOUGH: Add the rest of the flour and all of the salt. Mix for 8 to 10 minutes on second speed.

FIRST RISING: 30 to 40 minutes.

SECOND RISING: Knead briefly by hand and let the dough sit for another 10 minutes.

Continue according to the recipe for the direct method, starting by scaling the dough. The final rising will be 5 or 10 minutes faster because of the activity of the sponge.

VARIATION
This is a method that makes it easier to control the dough temperature. For the 15-loaf batch make a sponge by mixing 5 pounds flour, 5 pounds water, and all of yeast, honey, and oil. Let this sponge rise for 1 hour.

For the dough, add 10 pounds flour, 3 pounds water, and 4¼ ounces salt. Proceed according to the recipe for the sponge method.

METHOD: Direct.
SOURCE: Gayle's Bakery, Capitola, California.
ELAPSED TIME: 3½ hours.
DOUGH TEMPERATURE: 80°F. *TEMPÉRATURE DE BASE:* 240°F.

INGREDIENTS	U.S. MEASURES	
cracked wheat	6 cups	9 cups
boiling water	8 cups	12 cups
whole wheat flour	8 lb	12 lb
rye meal	1 lb	1½ lb
medium rye flour	3 lb	4½ lb
wheat bran	2 lb	3 lb
water	4 lb	6 lb
yeast	1½ lb	2¼ lb
oil	12 oz	18 oz
molasses	12 oz	18 oz
honey	2 lb	3 lb
total	23 lb	34 lb

MIXING: Combine the cracked wheat and boiling water and set the mixture aside to soak for between 30 minutes and 2 hours. Then add it, with the rest of the ingredients to the bowl, but hold back between 2 and 4 cups of water. Mix for 10 minutes on the second speed; adding the reserved water at the end of the mixing. The dough should be fairly wet.

FIRST RISING: 45 minutes.

KNOCK BACK: Punch the dough back, knead it for a few minutes by hand, round it up again, and let it rise for another 30 minutes.

SCALING: Scale at 10 ounces for small 2-inch-by-5-inch-by-2-inch pans; 20 ounces for medium, 3½-inch-by-7-inch-by-2¼-inch pans; and 30 ounces for large, 3½-inch-by-7½-inch-by-2¾-inch pans.

INTERMEDIATE PROOFING: Round each loaf and let them all relax for 10 or 15 minutes.

SHAPING: Machine or hand shape the loaves to fit greased pans.

FINAL RISING: 45 minutes to 1 hour.

GLAZING: Glaze with egg wash and sprinkle the tops with bran flakes.

BAKE-OFF: 360°F to 375°F; 15 minutes for small, 17 to 20 minutes for medium, and 25 to 30 minutes for large loaves.

METHOD: Sour sponge.

SOURCE: Gayle's Bakery, Capitola, California; adapted from
The Gold Medal Rye Dictionary.

ELAPSED TIME: Sponge, 3 hours; dough, 2 hours.

DOUGH TEMPERATURE: 78°F to 80°F.

TEMPÉRATURE DE BASE: 234°F to 240°F.

INGREDIENTS		U.S. MEASURES	
MILK SOUR			
goat's milk or raw buttermilk		2 lb (1 quart)	
old rye dough		a walnut-sized piece	
water		2½ lb	
powdered milk		2 oz	
rye flour		1 lb, 9 oz	
clear flour (see glossary)		1 lb, 9 oz	
total		7½ lb	
RYE SPONGE			
milk sour	3¾ lb	5 lb, 10 oz	7½ lb
cream of rye flour	4 lb, 6 oz	6 lb, 9 oz	8¾ lb
yeast	5 oz	7 oz	10 oz
water	4½ lb	6¾ lb	9 lb
total	13 lb	19 lb	26 lb
THE DOUGH			
rye sponge	13 lb	19 lb	26 lb
water	7½ lb	11¼ lb	15 lb
clear flour	12½ lb	18¾ lb	25 lb
cream of rye flour	3¾ lb	5 lb, 10 oz	7½ lb
salt	5 oz	7½ oz	10 oz
malt extract	5 oz	7½ oz	10 oz
caraway seeds	1¼ lb	1 lb, 14 oz	2½ lb
total	40 lb	60 lb	80 lb

MIXING THE MILK SOUR: Let the goat's milk, preferably raw, sit out overnight with the piece of rye dough from a previous batch floating in it. The next morning prepare the milk sour by combining all of the rest of the ingredients in a large bucket. Cover and let the mixture sit overnight.

The following day some or all of this milk sour is used in the rye sponge. What is not used may be refreshed and used the day after or for successive batches. A refreshment schedule appears at the end of the recipe.

MIXING THE RYE SPONGE: Mix all of the ingredients in a 5-gallon plastic bucket. Do not allow the mixture to be any warmer than 80°F. Let the sponge sit covered, for 3 hours, until it has tripled in size and made a full drop.

MIXING THE DOUGH: After the sponge has risen and then started to fall, it is ready to be mixed into the dough. Mix all the ingredients, using 75°F to 80°F water. Mix on the first speed until incorporated, then mix on the second speed for 3 to 5 minutes; Do not overmix. The dough should be medium-wet and slightly sticky.

FIRST RISING: Pull the dough from the mixer and let it rest, on a floured bench and covered, for 45 to 60 minutes.

SCALING: 2 pounds, 6 oz for 2-pound loaves.

INTERMEDIATE PROOF: Round the loaves and let them rise on the bench 10 minutes.

SHAPING: Shape by hand into 4-inch-by-10-inch loaves with squared-off, not tapered, ends.

FINAL RISING: Place the loaves on wooden boards that have been sprinkled with cornmeal and let them rise in a covered rack for between 30 and 45 minutes. Do not overproof.

BAKE-OFF: Glaze the loaves with a mixture of whole eggs beaten with milk (3 parts egg to 1 part milk) and make sure loaves will slide easily off the boards into the oven after being glazed. With a curved razor blade, lightly cut the loaves across the width, starting at the bottom of one side, cut across the top and down to the bottom of the other side.

Slide the loaves onto the deck and bake at 410°F with lots of steam at the beginning, for between 40 and 45 minutes.

Milk Sour Refreshment

The quantities given in the refreshment formulas are applicable to the comparative quantities of the original milk sour, that is, for example, if the quantities are being tailored to the smallest batch, three and three-fourths pounds of milk sour will have been used to make the smallest batch of rye sponge, so there will be about four pounds (a depth of between five and eight inches in the bucket) of milk sour left. For the refreshment, use the smallest quantities of ingredients given in the chart below, to yield eight pounds of refreshed starter.

INGREDIENTS	U.S. MEASURES		
remaining milk sour	4 lb	6 lb	8 lb
clear flour	15 oz	1 lb, 6½ oz	1 lb, 14 oz
cream of rye flour	15 oz	1 lb, 6½ oz	1 lb, 14 oz
milk powder	2 oz	3 oz	4 oz
salt	¾ oz	1 oz	1½ oz
water	2 lb	3 lb	4 lb
total	8 lb	12 lb	16 lb

Add all of the refreshment ingredients to the remaining milk sour in the original bucket, mix them thoroughly with the hands, and let the sour sit overnight, a portion of which will be mixed into the next day's batch of 3-hour rye sponge.

If much larger quantities of bread are to be made, the formula for milk sour can be multiplied, but if it is to be effective, the sour should be refreshed at least once and set aside to mature for at least 8 hours before being used in a rye sponge.

RAISIN PUMPERNICKEL

METHOD: Sour sponge and *pâte fermentée* (old-dough addition).
SOURCE: Gayle's Bakery, Capitola, California.
ELAPSED TIME: 22 hours: 8 to 10 hours, from sponge to mixing; 2 to 5
hours in the retarder; 4- to 5-hour final rising; 2-hour bake-off.
DOUGH TEMPERATURE: 78°F to 80°F. *TEMPÉRATURE DE BASE:* 240°F.

This recipe is a complicated, two-day process that involves two separate
sponges, one raisin and one rye, and a piece of eight-hour *baguette* dough. If the
two sponges are mixed at about 10 A.M. of the first day, and the dough for the
old-dough addition pulled back at about noon, the dough itself can be mixed at
around 6 P.M. It is then retarded in the refrigerator, pulled out at midnight,
and allowed to rise until about 3 or 4 A.M. Then it is shaped and allowed to rise
for a few more hours before being baked.

INGREDIENTS	U.S. MEASURES	
RYE SPONGE		
yeast	1½ oz	3 oz
water	1½ lb	3 lb
rye meal	1½ lb	3 lb
total	3 lb	6 lb
RAISIN SPONGE		
rye meal	3 lb	6 lb
raisins*	6 lb	12 lb
water	2¼ lb	4½ lb
total	11¼ lb	22½ lb
OLD-DOUGH ADDITION		
baguette dough	1½ lb	3 lb
DOUGH		
rye sour	3 lb	6 lb
raisin sponge	11¼ lb	22½ lb
old dough	1½ lb	3 lb
high-gluten flour	3½ lb	7 lb
water	1¼ lb	2½ lb
salt	1¼ oz	2½ oz
sugar	1½ oz	3 oz
corn or vegetable oil	1½ oz	3 oz
caramel color	1½ oz	3 oz
total	20½ lb	41 lb

* The quantities of raisins used may be reduced by one-third.

MIXING THE RYE SPONGE: Combine all of the ingredients on the morning of the first day and let the sponge rise for between 8 and 10 hours.

MIXING THE RAISIN SPONGE: Combine the ingredients on the morning of the first day and let the sponge sit for between 8 and 10 hours.

OLD-DOUGH ADDITION: On the morning of the first day, around the same time that the other two sponges are mixed, pull the dough back from a batch that has been recently mixed and let it rise for between 6 and 8 hours.

MIXING THE PUMPERNICKEL DOUGH: Mix all of the ingredients, except the raisin sponge, on the first speed until they are completely incorporated. Then mix for 4 minutes on the second speed. The dough will be firm. Add the raisin sponge and mix on first speed until it is completely incorporated (1 to 2 minutes).

FIRST RISING: Put the dough into a plastic bucket or in large bowls, covered, in the retarder for between 2 and 6 hours.

SECOND RISING: Pull the dough out of the retarder and let it rise for 2 or 3 hours.

SHAPING: For the smaller batch of dough, shape the entire quantity into one 20-pound loaf: a large, flat oval loaf, measuring about 3 feet long by 1 foot wide by 6 inches high.

FINAL RISING: Liberally dust a wooden board or peel with cornmeal and place the loaf on top. Let it rise, covered if necessary to avoid crusting, for between 1½ and 2 hours.

BAGUETTE DOUGH DECORATION: About half an hour before bake-off, take a piece of fresh *baguette* dough weighing about 1 pound and flatten and roll it out so that it is about 3 feet long by 4 inches wide. Lay this piece lengthwise over the top of the large loaf and tuck it underneath neatly at each end.

BAKE-OFF: Make sure the loaf will slide easily off the board into the oven after being glazed. Glaze the pumpernickel section with a whole egg beaten with a little milk (3 parts egg to 1 part milk), and the *baguette* dough decoration with an egg white that has been whisked with 3 tablespoons cold water.

Slide the loaf onto the deck and bake it at 325°F with steam at the beginning of the bake, for around 2 hours.

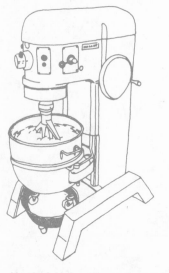

Vertical, Hobart-type mixer

METHOD: Direct.
SOURCE: Gayle's Bakery, Capitola, California.
ELAPSED TIME: 2½ hours.
DOUGH TEMPERATURE: 80°F. *TEMPÉRATURE DE BASE:* 240°F.

INGREDIENTS	U.S. MEASURES			
bread flour	10 lb	16 lb	24 lb	32 lb
water	5 lb	8 lb	12 lb	16 lb
salt	3 oz	4½ oz	6¾ oz	9 oz
yeast	6 oz	9 oz	13½ oz	18 oz
whole eggs*	16 oz	24 oz	36 oz	48 oz
sugar	8 oz	12 oz	18 oz	24 oz
soy or corn oil	8 oz	12 oz	18 oz	24 oz
total	17½ lb	27¾ lb	41¾ lb	55½ lb

* Or egg yolks only, to make a richer loaf.

MIXING: Add all the ingredients to the bowl and mix for 10 minutes on second speed. The dough should be soft and moist. A more voluptuous texture can be obtained by adding more water to the mix in the final few minutes.

FIRST RISING: Between 45 minutes and 1 hour.

SCALING: Scale at 1 pound, 3 ounces for 1-pound loaves. Scale at 3½ pounds for a 36-roll break.

INTERMEDIATE PROOFING: Round up the dough and let it rise for another 10 to 15 minutes.

SHAPING: Mold the loaves by hand or machine to fit rectangular loaf pans. (See page 206 for plaiting instructions and page 286 for an illustration.)

FINAL RISING: 30 to 45 minutes.

EGG GLAZING: Brush with a mixture of whole eggs whisked together with a little milk. Then sprinkle with poppy seeds or sesame seeds.

BAKE-OFF: 400°F for 20 to 25 minutes.

VARIATIONS

At the end of mixing, gently fold in one-third to one-half pound of raisins per pound of finished dough.

Use the dough, with or without raisins, to make Cinnamon Swirl. Roll out each 1-pound, 3-ounce, scaled loaf to an oval about 12 inches long. Glaze the surface (except for the last inch or two, where it will be sealed) with egg glaze and coat with a mixture of equal parts of cinnamon and sugar. Roll each loaf up 5 or 6 times and seal the middle and edges. Proof longer than normal and bake in loaf pans.

METHOD: Direct.
SOURCE: Gayle's Bakery, Capitola, California.
ELAPSED TIME: 2 hours.
DOUGH TEMPERATURE: 80°F.   *TEMPÉRATURE DE BASE:* 240°F.

INGREDIENTS	U.S. MEASURES
challah dough (page 273)	6 lb
Cheddar cheese, diced	1 lb
green onions, chopped	4 oz
fresh herbs, chopped	1 oz
total	7¼ lb

MIXING: After the dough has completed its first hour of rising, lay it out flat on the table. Combine the cheese, onions, and herbs and mix them in in much the same way as you would mix in the butter in a *croissant* dough: cover two-thirds of the dough with the cheese mixture and then press it gently into the dough. Fold the uncovered one-third of the dough over onto the middle and the remaining, covered third over that. Tuck in the ends, shape the folded dough into a round mass, and then continue to round it gently on the bench until the cheese and herbs are just visible under the surface of the dough.

FIRST RISING: Divide the dough in half, round the halves gently, and set them aside on the bench, covered, for 30 minutes.

SHAPING: Break each piece in a 36-roll divider, round each roll, and place them on papered trays.

SECOND RISING: 30 to 45 minutes.

BAKE-OFF: Glaze with egg; bake at 400°F for 12 to 15 minutes.

Every ingredient, technique, and method in bread baking can be adjusted. Most village bakers learn the basic methods and basic proportions and use them so many times that they begin to feel, firsthand, the rhythmic needs of a simple bread formulation. Variations in the basic method lead the way to the other methods and, at each stage, the possibilities multiply.

The following is just a bare outline of what has been discussed in detail throughout the rest of the book.

Water

In the formulas that French bakers use there is seldom more than 60 or 65 percent water. For some very dense breads, they use as little as 50 percent and the bread then has a tight grain and a dry texture. Many Italian bakers routinely use what the French would consider excessive quantities of water—between 70 and 75 percent. The additional water creates vapor in the crumb and gives a soft, voluptuous texture. Water in bread dough tries to escape through the crust during the bake-off and, if well baked, the bread will have a thick but chewable crust.

Yeast

In standard formulas for bread, yeast constitutes 1 percent of the dough. More than that will give yeastier flavors and create certain fermentation needs. Any quantity of yeast between none and 4 percent can be used by the baker to achieve different results. More yeast is needed, for example, in enriched bread, because it takes more push to raise a dough that is heavy with rich ingredients. More yeast can make a quicker bread; less yeast means that the bread will take longer to rise and it will taste more like the flour than the leavening agent.

Salt

Fermentation in bread without salt is faster than it is in salted bread. A lack of salt also makes the bread go stale quicker, but less likely to go moldy.

The health conscious baker may, with impunity, use less salt and still produce good bread. The less salt used, the quicker the bread will rise. Extra salt may be used for a sharp, sour flavor, a tight grain, and more control during the fermentation.

Flour

Not only can bakers use different strengths of flour, such as high-gluten, all-purpose, bread, or pastry flour, to alter the behavior of the fermentation and thus the texture of the bread, but also they can vary the types of flour, such as rye, corn, durum, oat, or barley. Special blends of rye, whole wheat, and durum flour together with white flour—all adding up to 100 percent in the recipe—can give bread a rustic quality, reminding us of a time when flours had more of their nutrients left intact. The observant baker will have to make some adjustments in the method—carefully monitoring the behavior of the dough and reacting to its fermentation needs—to create a superior loaf. A dense finished quality does not always have to be the result of darker, heavier grains.

To emulate an Italian bread, try using weaker flour; it makes the gluten break down faster, causing an uneven crumb. A strong flour will help the dough stand up to a long sourdough process. But do not use it at full strength; try cutting it with weaker flour to get the desired results.

Temperature

The temperature of the room and of the dough are usually intended to be fairly constant in bread baking. A cool fermentation (a 75°F dough temperature) gives the right development to the loaf, allowing it to do its greatest expansion in the oven. Bakers learn to accommodate varying climate changes by using dough retarders (refrigerators or coolers), adding cool water to the dough when necessary, and moving inactive loaves closer to the oven to speed them up. They can also use these techniques to vary their breads.

For example, in making *pain ordinaire* according to the recipes on pages 213–216, retarding the dough at the first rising stage is a way to achieve a heartier, more long-lasting crumb. In making *compagnon* (page 225), retarding the loaves in the refrigerator overnight can give a crumb that is very close to that of a true sourdough.

Some of the main textural differences in sourdough breads are the result of the relative warmth or coolness of the final proofing. A light, fluffy quality is developed in a warm make-up; a cool, long fermentation produces a moist and chewy texture.

Natural Improvers

American bakers, unlike the French, can use any number of ingredients that add a distinctive flavor or color to their bread or an extra boost to the fermentation. Their own combinations of such improvers can enable them to make what might be called "signature" breads.

See the recipe for fava bean improver on page 14.

The Sponge

Variations in the firmness and rising times of sponges can be used by advanced bakers to extend the shelf life of their breads and to alter fermentation timetables so that the baker can fit the development needs of the dough into his own schedule. The narrative on pages 23–24 explains how to manipulate sponges.

Some of the recipes that call for the direct method can, instead, be made with sponges. Among them are whole-grain bread, challah, *pain de mie, pain au lait,* and *brioche.*

The Fresh Rule

Most starters work best when the baker stays one step ahead of the dough's activity in the baking process (see the Fresh Rule, page 28). Keeping a bread dough young instead of old will generally make a superior bread, slightly acid and with a moist, voluptuous texture. Allowing the acidity to develop during the refreshments inhibits the rising power of the dough and creates a finished product of tangy sourness and large, usually undesirable air pockets. If this is, however, what the baker wants, it can be achieved. Any method may be changed to meet the requirements of the baker's personal taste or that of the customers.

Ancient brick oven

Building a Sourdough

The standard rules for building sourdough starters are:

- Mix the refreshment firm
- Keep a pre-established time pattern
- Either double or triple the *levain* each time

These rules ensure predictable results. To achieve a different outcome (and one that will itself be predictable once the method has been perfected), a baker can change the rules.

In comparing *pain de campagne* with San Francisco sourdough—two theoretically similar breads—we see differences in the types of flour and in the times (and firmness) of the refreshments. These variations create two distinct breads. The former has a coarse, irregular texture and a nutty flavor; the latter is more refined, often with a finer crust and a tangy taste.

A comparison of the two refreshment schedules shows the differences in the timing of the development of each type of bread. In fact, a baker can establish any pattern that seems appropriate to create a particular, personalized bread.

	PAIN DE CAMPAGNE	SAN FRANCISCO SOURDOUGH
pull-back	8 hours	6 hours
1st refreshment	8 hours	6 hours
2d refreshment	2 hours	6 hours
3d refreshment	2 hours	6 hours
dough	8 hours	6 hours
total	28 hours	30 hours

Home Refrigerator Sours

Home refrigerator sours usually do not work well in professional baking because it is hard to predict the level of acidity in them. But controlled sour sponges made from firm *levains* can help the baker create interesting textures; *Korni* and pumpkin seed bread are examples.

A soupy sour can be kept active and liquid to promote acidity and then be made into a firm *levain,* which is easier to control and gives more predictable results.

Dédoublé
Doubling a levain *to create successive batches*

For any baker the size of the largest batch is limited by the size of the oven. One good way to create multiple batches in a sourdough process is to produce a large final refreshment of the starter. Two-thirds of this final starter (*le levain de tout point*) goes into mixing the first batch of bread and one-third sits on the bench for a few hours to gain more acidity before it is mixed into the second batch of bread.

This technique is no more than one of a series of variations. The baker must calculate the amounts of salt, flour, and water needed for each batch (because the amount of starter is different in each batch). More important, each successive batch, because the quality of ferments differs, yields a different result. For an example, see *pain de campagne*.

Enrichments

Nothing other than flour, water, salt, and yeast can be added to any bread in France that bears the name of "French bread." But milk, butter, eggs, and sugar have become an important part of the village baker's craft throughout the world because so many customers have come to love these deluxe ingredients. In Germany grains, whole or cracked seeds, fruit, and legumes are also used to create different varieties of breads.

These enrichment ingredients can provide scores of variations on simple recipes. The village baker must understand that enriched breads cannot be considered French bread. He can use such ingredients with integrity as long as the customers know what goes into the final loaf.

Appendixes

- **Bread Sculpture (*Pain Fantaisie*)**
- **Glossary of Shapes and Decorations**
- **Glossary of Baking Terms**

MANY VILLAGE BAKERS SPECIALIZE in bread sculpture and can justify charging a higher price for their creations. Because the dough is shaped by hand, this is something that the amateur baker can do quite easily at home. *Pain fantaisie* may merely be ordinary French bread dough made into primitive, decorative, or animal shapes, in which case the baker must take into account any rising the dough will do.

To describe every move, turn of the hand, and fabricated mold (many of which are made of tinfoil or everyday objects such as bottles, cups, knife handles, and so on) that a baker could use to fabricate a sculpture out of dough could fill an entire volume and has—see Bilheux et al., listed in the bibliography. But, rather than ignore this fascinating subject, I have decided to provide two recipes and some brief comments and allow home bakers themselves to provide the creative energy to make their own *pain fantaisie.*

The glossary of shapes and decorations beginning on page 284 is a visual workbook of end products. Most of the breads in this book are made into *baguettes* or *boules;* very often a specific regional bread will be made only in a specific shape. I am suggesting that *almost* any dough can be made into *almost* any shape. Use your imagination as did, centuries ago, the village bakers who first created these shapes.

The "decorations" part of the visual glossary shows shapes that can be made from the sculpture dough that follows (or, with care, from a bread dough such as *pain ordinaire* or challah): roses, scrolls, grapes, leaves, and any number of decorated loaves.

The following recipes are for doughs that contain no yeast and will not, therefore, rise. This makes them easier than *pain ordinaire* dough is to work with, as the sculpted shapes will still be much the same size when baked.

BREAD SCULPTURE DOUGH I

MAKES 8½ POUNDS DOUGH

    2⅛ pounds (1 kg) salt

    4¼ pounds (14 cups) (2 kg) white flour

    4⅛ cups (4 kg) water

Mix the salt and flour together in a large bowl. Slowly add the water while mixing the dry ingredients, until you obtain a firm dough. Mix just long enough to eliminate the dry spots. This dough may be kept, covered with plastic wrap, for several days in or out of the refrigerator.

Bake at 350°F for between 25 and 40 minutes (depending on the thickness of the sculptured piece) until the bread is golden brown.

BREAD SCULPTURE DOUGH II

Adapted from *Le compagnon boulanger* by J.-M. V____d, page 301.

    6 to 7 cups (1 kg) bread flour

    2 cups (400 dl) water

    2 ounces (2 tablespoons) (50 g) salt

    ½ cup (200 g) melted margarine or sho____

Mix the ingredients and use accordin___ ___ ___ directions given in the previous recipe, having taken the following p_____s:

- Mix the dough several hours before using so that it has the chance to relax.

- Always keep it covered with plastic wrap as it tends to crust easily.

- Use within 3 or 4 days because it tends to discolor.

ALTHOUGH THE NOTION may offend a regional village baker who feels that, in order to preserve its authentic, regional quality, a certain dough can only be made into a given shape of bread, virtually any dough in this book can be made up into any of the following shapes.

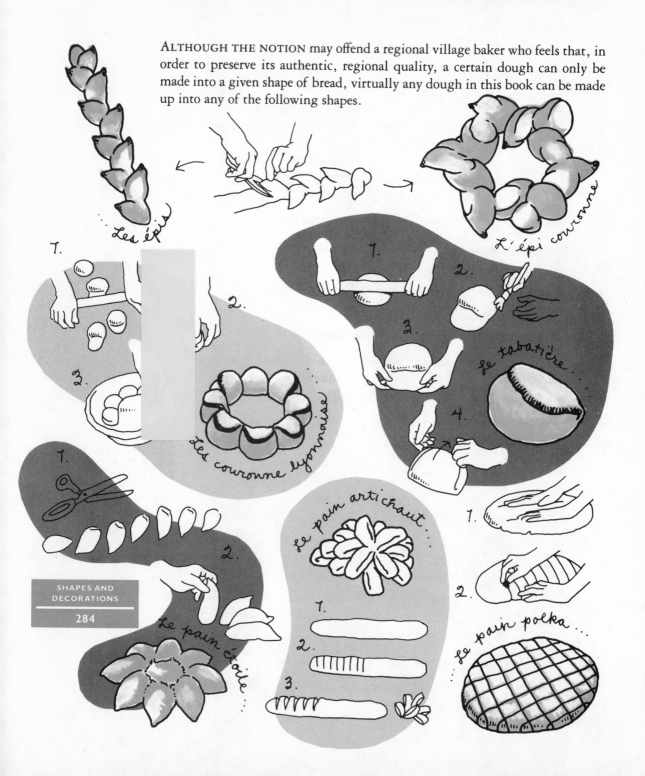

... Les épis

L'épi couronne

Les couronne lyonnaise

Le tabatière...

Le pain artichaut...

Le pain étoile...

Le pain polka...

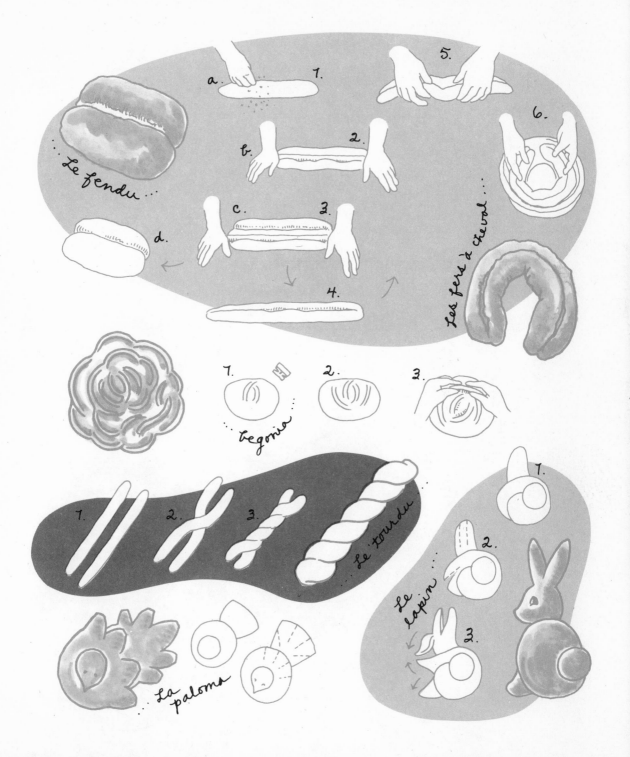

... Le fendu ...

a. 1.
b. 2.
c. 3.
d. 4.
5.
6.

... Les fers à cheval ...

1. 2. 3.
... begonia ...

1. 2. 3.
... Le tourdu ...

1. 2. 3.
... Le lapin ...

... La paloma ...

1.

2.

3.

... Le tourtu ...

1.   2.   3.

4.

... La tresse ...

1.   2.   3.

... L'auvergnat ...

Le crocodile

... La fougasse ...

La couronne ....

1.

2.   3.

... La tortue ...

Les Pains Décorés

1. 2. 3. 4.

wheat stalks...

...roses...

personalized scrolls...

PaPa

1.
2.
3.

PaPa

1.
2.
3.
...grapes...

different kinds of leaves

AMYLASE: A natural enzyme that helps change starch into sugar; used in some French bakeries in a product called *levit* as a yeast food.

L'APPRÊT: In American baker's terms, this means make-up or floor time. It signals the time between the shaping of the loaves and their placement in the oven.

ASCORBIC ACID: *See* Vitamin C.

ASH CONTENT: The mineral content of any flour, usually around .5 to .6 percent. The higher the ash content, the grayer the crumb.

AU LITRE D'EAU: French bakers signify the other quantities in a bread recipe according to the quantity of water. Therefore you might hear them say, "Thirty-five grams of salt per liter of water." (When they talk about ingredients in percentages of a batch, they mean, as American bakers do, the percentage in relation to the flour, which is 100 percent.)

AUTOLYSE: A process used by some French bakers whereby all or some of the ingredients in a batch of dough are mixed to incorporate them, then the dough is allowed to rest for 5 or 10 minutes, right in the mixing bowl. After this rest period, the *autolyse,* which allows the flour to be fully hydrated and the gluten to relax, the dough is then mixed to full development.

BAKE-OFF: The process of cooking the loaves in the oven.

BAKER'S YEAST: *See* Yeast.

BAKING STONE: A flat stone or tile, which may be square, rectangular, or round, that is placed in a domestic oven to emulate old-fashioned brick-oven baking. The loaf is slid right onto the stone to bake. The baking stone should be placed on a wire shelf before the oven is heated. A loaf to be baked on a stone is usually given its final proofing in a *banneton.*

BANNETON: A basket lined with Belgian linen and used to hold a loaf while it is undergoing its final rising. At home bakers can use a wicker basket, lined with a plain dishtowel and sprinkled with flour.

BASSINER: To moisten a dry dough by pouring in more water and incorporating it. It is easier to obtain a very wet dough (or to correct the consistency of a dough) by adding water later, than by starting out with too much.

BÂTARD: Literally, "bastard," this is a medium-long oval loaf that is neither a *baguette* nor a *boule.* In America it is often called a French loaf. See also *Pâte batarde.*

BENOÎTONS: Raisin-nut rolls made with rye bread dough.

BIEN CUIT: Well baked; used to describe a loaf that has been baked for the proper amount of time and at the right temperature. The crust is "set" and the crumb is perfect, neither dried out nor soggy.

BIGA: The Italian name for a yeasted starter that is mixed very firm and set to rise overnight. It helps give Italian breads their characteristic earthy flavor and uneven crumb.

BLÉ: Generally means wheat, but it can mean corn or kernel or grain.

BLOOM: The rich color and attractive physical appearance of a loaf that was put into the oven at the right time and was well baked.

BOUILLIE: Porridge, mush, or gruel. It also describes a method of bread baking, which predates sourdough, in which a fermented mixture of grain, cereal, or flour is used as a starter. The technique produces moist, rustic textures and strong, earthy flavors.

BOULAGER: To shape into a *boule* or round loaf. This is the word from which the name *boulanger* was derived.

BOULE: Ball of dough or round loaf.

BREWER'S YEAST: See Yeast.

BUÉE: Steam, which is usually introduced into the oven during the first few minutes of baking, to produce an expanded loaf and crisp crust. Also called *la vapeur.*

CAKE FLOUR: See Flour.

CARAWAY POWDER: A flavoring agent similar to that used by German bakers to add distinctive tastes to different breads.

CHEF (CHEF LEVAIN): Original or chief leavening agent. It is usually a natural starter that is given the first of many refreshments; thereafter it is known as the *levain.*

CONTRE-FRASER: To add more flour to a wet dough.

COUCHES: Sheets of Belgian linen used to hold and separate loaves while they are rising. Cotton duck or a plain kitchen towel can be used at home.

COUP DE LAME: Literally, the blow of the blade, that is, the slashing of the top of a loaf with a razor-sharp blade to help it burst in a pleasing pattern. It also helps the loaf to develop properly in the oven and can have a beneficial effect on the interior texture of the loaf.

COURONNE: A crown-shaped loaf.

CREUSER: The hollow spot left in the middle of a sponge or *poolish* that signals maturity. American bakers say "when the sponge falls" or "after a full drop."

LA CUISSON: Baking the loaf. The first moments in the oven often give the dough an accelerated push in volume that continues until the yeast is destroyed by the heat.

DÉDOUBLÉ, DÉDOUBLER: A process of doubling a *levain* or starter so that two successive batches of dough may be made instead of just one.

DÉTENTE: Literally, the relaxing of tension. It refers to the intermediate proofing time when pieces of dough are set aside to rest after being scaled (or scaled and rounded) so that any tightness that has developed can relax before the pieces are made into loaves.

DEVELOPMENT: A property, achieved in mixing a dough, that gives optimum strength to the gluten. When used to describe a loaf, it refers to the final rising or the expansion in the oven, where, in most breads, a good, rich bloom is desirable.

DIVISEUSE: A mechanical, *preferably hydraulic,* divider that produces loaves of a uniform size and weight. *See also* Pocket divider.

DOCK: To puncture a dough full of holes, instead of slashing it with a razor, so that it will not explode irregularly when exposed to the heat of the oven.

DONNER UN TOUR: (also *ROMPRE* or *RABBATRE*) To knock back or punch down a risen dough before either setting it aside to rise again or shaping it into loaves. The action dispels the gas and gives the dough an extra push or starts the rising again.

DURUM: *See* Flour.

ÉLASTICITÉ: The favorable quality, attained in the mixing stage, that allows a bread dough to stretch.

EXTENSIBILITY: The elastic quality provided by wheat flour, allowing the dough to expand in the manner of a blown-up balloon and providing the proper tension to entrap gases created by the yeast.

FAÇONNAGE: The shaping of the dough into loaves.

FARINA DOPPIO ZERO: A very fine milling of wheat flour used in Italy. Frequently it is *calibrata* or calibrated so that each tiny grain of flour is of a similar size, making it exceptional for pasta.

FARINE:
bise: A second milling similar to American whole wheat flour.
de fève: Fava bean flour added in French mills as an improver.
gruau: The finest French wheat flour.
méteil: Flour made of half wheat and half rye grains.

FERMENTATION: A word used to describe the activity of the dough. Bacteria, in consuming the sugars in the flour, create carbonic gas, which in turn causes the dough to rise.

FLOOR TIME: *See* Makeup.

FLOUR: (See also *Farine*)
all-purpose: A soft flour having between 8 and 10 percent gluten.
bread: Usually made of hard winter wheat and in America it contains enough gluten—between 11 and 12 percent—to give most breads good volume and a homogeneous crumb.
cake and pastry: A soft-wheat flour, finely milled, that is used for cakes, tart doughs, and delicate pastries.
clear: Also called "patent flour," it is extremely pure and high in gluten.

durum: A hard winter wheat used to make flour for pasta and some breads.
high-gluten: A very strong flour that contains between 13 percent and 15 percent gluten and is used for pizza, bagels, and the building of sourdough refreshments.
rye: Made from rye grain, it has no gluten.
type 55: a standard type of bread flour used in France.
weak: Refers to a flour containing a low percentage of gluten, such as cake flour or all-purpose flour. It can also refer to a flour that has lost some of its punch because it has been too long in storage or in transport.
whole wheat: a dark wheat flour that is more nutritious because it has not had all of the wheat germ and bran milled or sifted out.

FOCACCIA: An Italian flat bread.

LE FONTAINE: A method of mixing bread by hand that was derived from the days when dough was made in wooden troughs. A well is made in the center of the flour and the liquid and yeast mixture are placed inside. The surrounding flour is gradually incorporated into the liquid.

LA FORCE: A visible and metaphysical quality of the dough; it is denoted by strength and gives an active and favorable push to the fermentation. Too much force leads to the undesirable quality of excess elasticity.

FOUR BANAL: Communal oven.

FOURNIL: The bakehouse or bake room of a bread shop.

FULL DROP: A term used by American bakers to describe the stage a sponge or *poolish* reaches when it increases to three times its original size and then collapses. This indicates that the gluten has ripened, the acidity fully developed, and the sponge is ready for use.

GALETTE: A dense cake that in ancient times predated bread. Today it is a flat bread enriched with butter, eggs, and sugar.

GLUTEN: The constituent of flour that gives a dough its plastic qualities and allows it to entrap carbonic gas.

GRIGNE: The network of fibers that develops where the loaf has been cut by the *lame* (the blade) and thus where it bursts to reveal the inside of the loaf. The *grigne* shows the aspiring baker that bread can be aesthetic as well as nourishing.

HAND SCALED: *See* scaling.

HAND SQUARED: The dough is first flattened with both hands to dispel all the air, then the sides are folded in toward the middle to create a neat, square package ready for another rising. The air is pushed out of the dough to prevent overrising.

HYDRATION: A term that may be used to describe the moisture level of a particular dough, the percentage of moisture in the flour, or the quantity of water a given flour is capable of taking on.

IMPROVER: Additional ingredients included in bread and not considered harmful to the human body. In France, legally allowed improvers in any bread called "French bread" are fava bean flour, vitamin C, small quantities of rye flour, and a yeast food called *levit*.

KNOCK BACK: See *donner un tour*.

LACTOBACILLUS: A particular bacteria that has been identified as the strain of natural yeast in San Francisco sourdough.

LAME: A curved wire blade with a sharp edge that is used by French bakers to slash loaves before they go into the oven.

LEVAIN: A natural starter, sourdough, or mother dough (the latter is the name given by American bakers to the dough from which all new life is taken).

LEVAIN DE TOUT POINT: A *levain* that has been refreshed for the final time, has undergone its appropriate rising time, and is ready to be mixed into a bread dough.

LEVAIN-LEVURE: A starter made with commercial yeast and *levain*.

LEVIT: A type of yeast food invented by French millers and containing wheat flour, salt, dry yeast, ascorbic acid, and amylase. Added at the mill, it improves the strength and rising ability of weak flours.

LEVURE SAUVAGE: Wild yeast.

LIEVITO NATURALE: The Italian term for natural yeast; it may also mean a starter made of commercial yeast.

MAKE-UP: Used by American bakers to denote the procedure of shaping the dough into loaves. More properly, and in French baking terms, it denotes the time of rising between the shaping of the loaves and their being placed into the oven.

MALT EXTRACT: A syrup made of roasted grains; it is more concentrated than sugar and has a distinctive and appealing flavor.

METHOD, STRAIGHT-DOUGH: The method by which all the ingredients, including commercial yeast, are mixed at the same time; also known as the direct method.

MÉTHODE:

au levain: the sourdough method, the oldest and most organic method of mixing bread dough.

classique: See *Pétrissage classique*.

directe: The straight-dough method of mixing bread, using commercial yeast and no starter or sponge.

poolish: The sponge method; portions of the ingredients are mixed together several hours before the actual dough is mixed.

MIXING: Combining the ingredients and kneading them together into a well-developed bread dough.

MOU, MOLLE: Used to describe a soft or wet bread dough.

OLD-DOUGH ADDITION: See *Vieille pâte*.

OVERFERMENTATION: An overly active, unwanted acidity in a bread dough, starter, or sponge.

OVERRISING: The point at which a loaf or mass of dough goes beyond its proper fermentation state in being ready to go onto the next stage. It can also be called "old" instead of "young."

PÂTE BATARDE: An easily handled dough used for most breads; not too wet and not too firm.

PÂTE COUP: A hand tool used for cutting dough or scraping off the worktable.

PÂTE DOUCE: A moist or "soft" dough.

PÂTE FERME: A firm dough used only for specialty breads or breads in which the baker is striving for a tight grain.

PÂTE FERMENTÉE: The method of using a piece of fermented or old dough as a starter to give extra flavor to a newly mixed bread dough and to improve its texture.

PÂTON: A small mass of bread dough, rounded and allowed to rise, that is then scaled by hand or run through a mechanical divider.

PESAGE: The weighing or scaling of each piece of dough to achieve loaves of a consistent size. It can be done by hand or by machine.

PÉTRIN: A mechanical mixer with a wishbone-shaped arm used mostly in France.

PÉTRISSAGE: The process of mixing the ingredients for bread and kneading them into a dough.

accentué: Modern, accentuated mixing technique calling for a wetter dough mixed at twice the speed for a longer time. It creates a very fluffy texture and crisp crust.

amélioré: Ameliorated or improved mixing; the dough is mixed initially for three minutes on low speed, then for ten or twelve minutes on a higher speed. Often the best method for strong American flours.

classique: An old method rarely used today. The ingredients are mixed together by hand or with a mechanical mixer on low speed. This delicate mixing leads to a slow, natural fermentation, which necessitates prolonged rising times.

PILLOW LOAVES: Sandwich loaves baked in a bread pan that is a few inches wider than normal bread pans.

PLASTICITÉ: A characteristic of dough that allows it to be molded without losing its shape.

POCKET DIVIDER: A machine used in some large village bakeries in which a mass of dough is fed through a hopper that, in turn, feeds it into a chamber where it is divided by a piston. Some bakers feel that this action unduly punishes most bread doughs. See also *Diviseuse*.

POINTAGE: The first rising of the dough.

POOLISH: A liquid starter made with commercial yeast and some of the flour and water of a bread recipe. *See also* Sponge.

POUSSE: The push or rising of the dough.

PRÉLÈVE, PRÉLEVER, LE PRÉLÈVEMENT DU CHEF: The piece of dough, the pull-back, that has been taken off a previously made batch to act as the mother dough or *chef* to feed future batches.

PRESSURE-BOARD EXTENDER: A plate that fits onto an Acme-type sheeter for molding bread.

PROOF BOX: A warm, moist box or chamber in which dough is set to rise.

PUNCH DOWN: See *Donner un tour*.

RABAT, LE: See *Donner un tour*.

RABBATRE: See *Donner un tour*.

RACCOMMODER: To accommodate, control, or repair; it refers to the guarding and caring for the activity of a *levain* or sourdough starter.

REFRESHMENT: The act of mixing a *levain* or sourdough starter with more flour and water so it has something fresh to feed on and continue growing.

REPOS: A moment, or several minutes of relaxation, usually provided so that a dough can be relieved of tension and be more easily shaped.

RETARDER: A refrigerator or coolbox designed specifically for arresting the activity of yeast in a bread dough.

RISEAU DE GLUTEN: A network of gluten fibers engendered by the elastic qualities developed during mixing that allows the dough to capture pockets of gas.

ROMPRE: See *Donner un tour.*

ROULEAU À PIQUÉ: A small rolling pin with sharp nails protruding from it, used to dock or puncture a bread (or puff pastry) to prevent its rising excessively.

ROUND UP: To shape into a ball or *boule.* See also *Boulager.*

SAUERTEIG: German for sourdough.

SCALING: Weighing pieces of dough by hand on a balance scale in order to achieve loaves of equal size and weight.

SELF-LEAVENING: Strong flours that are newly milled have the ability, independent of the effects of the yeast, to supply a good kick to the rising process.

SEMOLINA: A winter wheat flour usually used to make pasta and sometimes bread in southern Italy.

SOURDOUGH: Natural yeast captured in bread dough that has been allowed to ferment and pick up bacteria from the air. The bacteria create the gas that makes the dough rise.

SPONGE: A process in mixing bread in which portions of the flour, water, and some other ingredients—including yeast but not salt—are mixed together and allowed to ferment for several hours before the final dough is mixed.

STARTER: Any natural, sourdough, sponge, or yeasted piece of dough that adds extra fermentation activity to a newly mixed bread dough.

TAUX DE CENDRE: The percentage of ash in the flour.

TAUX D'EXTRACTION: The percentage of whole grain left in flour after milling.

TEMPÉRATURE DE BASE: The term used by French bakers to describe the average of the combined totals of the temperatures of the room, water, and flour. The number is used to calculate the temperature of water needed to attain a desired dough temperature.

TENACITÉ: An excessively plastic quality provoked in the dough by too much force and making it undesirably tight and unworkable.

TOLÉRANCE: The extent to which a dough can support fault during fermentation. (A slight under- or overdevelopment of the dough or scheduling that results in loaves being ready to bake a few minutes before the oven is ready to be loaded are faults.) Because it has a longer fermentation, a sourdough has more tolerance than a dough made with commercial yeast.

TRECHE: A braided loaf.

UNDERDEVELOPMENT: Used to describe a dough in which the gluten has not been sufficiently activated. It looks lifeless and has no visible force or response when it is touched.

VIEILLE PÂTE: A piece of dough that is left over from a previous batch and used in the *pâte fermentée* method. Added to a newly mixed batch it gives some of the flavor and texture of a sourdough bread.

VITAMIN C: Powdered ascorbic acid, added in minute quantities by French bakers to give their dough *tolérance* and provide the strength to permit the full development of the loaf.

YEAST:

active dry: Readily available packaged yeast that, properly stored, will keep for months.

baker's: Compressed yeast usually packaged in one-pound blocks.

brewer's: Yeast used for making beer.

commercial: Distinguished from natural yeast because it is made in factories.

natural: A primitive, spontaneous ingredient that grows out of a mixture of flour and water. It is more difficult and time consuming to use than is commercial yeast, but it produces a more complex, longer-lasting loaf.

Bilheux, Roland, Alain Escoffier, Daniel Herve, and Jean-Marie Pouradier. *Special and Decorative Breads.* Written under the direction of Jean Chazalon and Pierre Michalet. New York: Van Nostrand Reinhold, 1989.

The most complete treatise on decorative breads, with no detail left unexplained. Many recipes and instructive color photographs.

Boriani, Guido, and Fabrizio Ostani. *Il pane.* Milan: Ottaviano, 1986.

History, recipes, and lots of good photographs. In Italian.

Calvel, Raymond. *Le gout du pain.* Éditions Jérôme Villette, 1990.

A slick, modern book on every aspect of French bread making; well illustrated with color photographs. In French.

———. *Le pain et la panification.* Paris: Presses Universitaires de France, 1979.

A small paperback that is a condensation of *La boulangerie moderne.* Part of the publisher's series, *Que sais-je?* In French.

———. *La boulangerie moderne.* Paris: Éditions Eyrolles, 1978.

The most complete textbook on French baking by the premier authority in France.

Clayton, Bernard, Jr. *The Breads of France.* Indianapolis and New York: Bobbs-Merrill, 1978.

The book that encouraged a lot of people to make French bread at home—and in American village bakeries.

Dubois, Urbaine. *Boulangerie d'aujourd'hui.* 3d ed. Paris: Éditions Joinville, 1962.

A complete look at professional bread baking. In French.

Dupaigne, Bernard. *Il pane.* Milan: Edizioni Studio Editoriale, n.d.

A full-color, coffee-table book on bread, including history, evolution, and ancient and modern production. In Italian.

Field, Carol. *The Italian Baker.* New York: Harper and Row, 1985.

The book that brought Italian baking to Americans. A wonderful and well-researched resource.

General Mills, Inc. *The Gold Medal Rye Dictionary.* Minneapolis: General Mills, 1948.

An out-of-print, spiral-bound pocket book put out by the flour company and showing bakers how to use Gold Medal flour.

Greene, Bert. *The Grains Cookbook.* New York: Workman, 1988.

A healthful approach to cooking with grains.

Guinard, J. Y., and P. Lesjean. *Le pain retrouvé.* Éditions Jacques Lanore, 1982.
  An exceptional book with color photographs, recipes, and instructions for braided loaves and *pain fantaisie.* In French.

Mathiot, Ginette, and Lionel Poilâne. *Pain: cuisine et gourmandises.* Paris: Albin Michel, 1985.
  One hundred fifty easy recipes that are amusing, light, and savory for using bread with food. Ancient and modern recipes for toast, sandwiches, soups, and puddings. In French.

Montandon, Jacques. *Le bon pain des provinces de France.* Édita Lausanne, 1979.
  Full color. Includes the history of bread, cereals, milling, today's modern bakery, and recipes of how to use bread with food. In French.

Parazzoli, Vittorio. *Sapore di pane.* Milan: Idealibri, 1984.
  History, folklore, and color drawings of Italian bread. In Italian.

Parmentier, [A.-A.] *Le Parfait Boulanger, ou Traité Complet Sur la Fabrication & le Commerce du Pain.* Paris: 1778.
  An elegantly written treatise on and for the Perfect Breadmaker, discussing everything from flour and water to *la manière des raccommoder les levains,* "on the manner of repairing sourdough starters." In French.

Poilâne, Lionel. *Faire son pain,* Paris: Dessain et Tolra, 1979.
  A well-written and accessible book for the home baker, showing many regional breads that use sourdough starters. In French.

————. *Guide de l'amateur de pain.* Paris: Éditions Robert Laffont, 1981.
  A warm, chatty look at the younger Poilâne's life as a baker. Contains his list and color photographs of the eighty regional breads of France and an interesting set of plans for constructing a small brick oven. In French.

Reiter, Susanne. *Vollkornbrot.* Falken-Verlag, 1988.
  A concise and colorful presentation of whole-grain German breads. In German.

Root, Waverley. *The Cooking of Italy.* New York: Time-Life Books, 1968.
  A great read, mostly on the regional foods of Italy. Contains some bread and pizza recipes.

Schafer, Werner. *Fare il pane.* Milan: Ottaviano, 1980.
  Originally published as *Brot Backen* in German. A very concise but thorough book with history and some recipes. In Italian.

Viard, Jean-Marie. *Le compagnon boulanger.* Éditions Jerome Villette, n.d.
  A synthesis of the technology and practice of modern bread baking. In French.

Viard's book and two of Calvel's can often be found at the food and kitchenware store called M.O.R.A. (in the First Arrondissement) at 13 rue Montmartre in Paris; the abridgement of *La boulangerie moderne* can be found in many bookstores in Paris.

Recipes are indicated by page numbers in boldface type, illustrations by page numbers in italics, and margin references and notes by page numbers followed by n.

flax seeds, 173, 175
flour (see also *farina; farine*), 8-11, 274-75
  adding extra (*la contrefrasage*), 124, 211
  all-purpose, 9
  barley, 103
  for *biga*, 146
  bread, 213*n*.
  cake and pastry. *See* flour, pastry
  durum, 4, 10
  fava bean, 13, 14
  pastry, 9
  rye, 10, 112
    as an improver, 13-14
    to use, 110-11
  strong American, 44, 214, 216, 218
  unrefined, 78
  whole wheat, 161, 178
  whole-grain, 98
flûte gana, 80
focaccia (Genoan Flat Bread), 165, 255
fontaine. See fountain method
food processor, *58*
  to make *brioche* in, 128
  for mixing wet doughs, 56, 149
  pain ordinaire in, 71-72
  pizza dough in, 163, 164
  stirato in, 149
force (*la force*), in fermentation, 18, 45
fougasse, 122-24, **239**
  starter for, 35
  use of *le bassinage* in, 56
fountain method of mixing (*la fontaine*),
    39-40, 41
four banal, 2
Fran Gage Pâtisserie Française (San Francisco),
    188
France:
  bread in, 56-69
  recipes from, 69-135, 213-38, 240-44
  use of improvers in, 13-15
freezing:
  brioche dough, 242
  ciabatte dough, 152-53
  a starter, 147*n*.
French Bread:
  Classic Yeasted (*pain ordinaire*), 69-74,
    213-16
  Country-Style (*pain de campagne*), 82-85,
    219-24
  Italian-Style. *See pane francese*
  see also France, bread in; *pain*

G

galette, 184
Ganachaud Bakery (Paris), 80
garlic, 165

Gayle's Bakery (Capitola, California), 161, *189*,
    192, 194, 197, 198
  recipes from, 219, 231, 239, 255, 258-60,
    262-64, 266-74
Gayle's Herb and Cheese Rolls, 207, 274
General Mills Company, 200
Genoan Flat Bread (*focaccia*), 165, 255
Germany:
  bread in, 166-69
  recipes from, 170-71, 173-83, 256
glaze, for rolls, 132, **229**
gluten, 9, 10, 214
  to develop, 55
Gold Medal Rye Dictionary, The (General Mills),
    200, 269
Gourmet magazine, 65, 66, 188
grain:
  Mixture, 11
  use of, in bread, 97-98
  whole, in German bread, 166, 168-69
grigne, described, 51-52
grissini torinese (Turinese Breadsticks), 152,
    156-57, 254
  starter for, 36
Guerra, Gratienne, 186, 188
gueulard, 88, *215*
Guide de l'amateur de pain (Poilâne), 4
Guinard, J. Y., 240
Guisto's, 9

H

Haettel, Jean, 74, 78-79
handwork, described, 38-42
herbs, green, 207
Hess, Glen, 262
honey starter, 33, 238
hydration, of dough, 20

I

ice cubes, 19, 149
ice water, to use, 19, 71, 72
improvers, 13-16, 275
  permissible, in France, 13-15
  use of, in America, 15-16
ingredients, 4, 8-16
  in enriched breads, 121, 279
  in German bread, 166-67
  in Italian bread, 137
International Bread Tasting, 188, 189
Italian Baker, The (Field), 138, 249
Italy:
  bread in, 136-37
  recipes from, 137-65, 245-47, 250-54

rolls *(continued)*
    Piedmontese *(michette)*, 247-48
    Raisin Rye *(benoîtons)*, 238
        with walnuts, 120-21
    to shape, *49, 139*
    whole wheat, 197-98, 266-67
room, temperature, 19-20
rosemary, 142, 159
rouleau à pique, 108
rounding, method of *(la tourne en boule)*,
    47-48, *49*
Rule, Fresh, for sourdough, 28, 29, 277
rye:
    bread *(see also pain de seigle; seigle)*, 107-11
        German, 170-77, 256-59
        Jewish-Style, 200-201, 269-70
        M. Costa's *(pain de seigle de Costa)*, 118-20,
          237-38
        with Old-Dough Addition *(pain de seigle—
          pâte fermentée)*, 113-14, 233
        Porridge *(pain bouillie)*, 105-107, 232
        Raisin-Nut, 99, 257
        Sponge-Method, *(pain de seigle sur poolish)*,
          114-15, 120, 234
        Thiézac *(pain de seigle de Thiézac)*, 109,
          116-17, 235-36
        Wheat and *(pain méteil)*, 60, 111, 112-13
    cereal, 176
    flour. *See* flour, rye
    grain (berries; seeds), 11, 106, 160, 176
    meal, 176, 198, 231
    rolled, 185
    sour (starter), 170, 172

S

sage, 121, 165, 239, 255
Saint-Flour (France), 108, 109, 111
salt, 12, 98, 180, 275
    fermentation and, 20, 61, 237
    lack of, in Italian bread, 12, 141
    in sourdough, 29, 219
    in the sponge method, 24
    for topping *grissini*, 156
San Francisco, sourdough bread in, 186-87
San Francisco Sourdough Bread, 190-91,
    261-62
    basic sourdough starter for, 32
Sandwich Bread *(pain de mie)*, 134-35, 244
Sanitary Bakery of A. Zito (New York), 188
Sauerteig, 3, 166
scaling *(le pesage)*, 45-46
schiacciare, technique for, 153, 246, 255
schiacciata (Tuscan Flat Bread), 142, 247
Seed Mixture, 170, 172
seigle (see also *pain de seigle)*:
    French regulations on, 110

sources of, in France, 111
    types of, 110
Semifreddi's bakery (Kensington, Calif.), 188
semolina, 4
sesame seeds, 158, 167, 170, 184, 185, 205
shaping *(le façonnage)*, 49-50
    baguettes, 50, 70
    breadsticks, *157*
    by stretching *(schiacciare), 142*, 149-50, 153
    loaves, *50, 102, 106-107, 123, 132, 284-86*
    pizza, *164*
    pretzels, *181*
    rolls, *49, 129, 131, 133, 138, 139*, 182
Sheer, Mme., 97, 108
slashing *(le coup de lame)*, 51-52
Snails:
    Cream-Cheese, 130-32
    Raisin-Cinnamon, 130-31, 132-33
Sonoma French Bakery (Sonoma, Calif.), 188
Sourdough Bread: 29 *(list)*
    Acme, 266*n.*
    Apple *(pain aux pommes)*, 124-27, 240-41
    Berkeley, 195-96, 265-66
    Capitola, 192-93, 262-63
    Capitola Sandwich, 194-95, 264
    Country-Style *(pain de campagne—trois levains)*,
      82-85, 219-21
    Italian-Style French *(pane francese naturale)*,
      146-48, 250-51
    Korni, 175, 258-59
    Pumpkin Seed, 172
    San Francisco, 32, 190-91, 261-62
    White *(pain blanc au levain)*, 95-96, 227-28
    Whole-Grain *(pain de régime au levain)*,
      104-105, 268
sourdough method *(la méthode au levain)*, 21,
    27-30, 67, 68-69. *See also* old-dough
    method
sourdough *(see also levain; yeast, natural)*:
    to build, 278
    to control, 28
    Crêpes, 37
    culture, 27-28
    distinguished from *lievito naturale*, 146
    in Germany, 3, 166
    home refrigerator, 278
    ingredients for, 28
    in Italy, 136
    list of breads made from, 29
    old, 29
    pancakes, 34, 37
    strong, 29
    Waffles, 37
    young, 29
Soy Bean Mixture, 173, 175
soy beans, 173, 258